EXPLORATIONS IN SOCIOLOGY
British Sociological Association conference volume series

* *from the same publishers*

Practising Identities

Power and Resistance

Edited by

Sasha Roseneil
University Principal Research Fellow in Sociology and
Director of the Centre for Interdisciplinary Gender Studies
University of Leeds

and

Julie Seymour
Lecturer in Social Research
School of Comparative and Applied Social Sciences
University of Hull

First published in Great Britain 1999 by
MACMILLAN PRESS LTD
Houndmills, Basingstoke, Hampshire RG21 6XS and London
Companies and representatives throughout the world

A catalogue record for this book is available from the British Library.

ISBN 0–333–74758–5 hardcover
ISBN 0–333–74759–3 paperback

First published in the United States of America 1999 by
ST. MARTIN'S PRESS, INC.,
Scholarly and Reference Division,
175 Fifth Avenue, New York, N.Y. 10010

ISBN 0–312–22227–0

Library of Congress Cataloging-in-Publication Data
Practising identities : power and resistance / edited by Sasha
Roseneil and Julie Seymour.
p.   cm. — (Explorations in sociology)
Includes bibliographical references and index.
ISBN 0–312–22227–0 (cloth)
1. Group identity.   2. Identity (Psychology)   I. Roseneil, Sasha,
1966–   .   II. Seymour, Julie.   III. Series.
HM131.P677   1999
305.3—dc21   99–18649
                                                        CIP

This book is printed on paper suitable for recycling and made from fully managed and
sustained forest sources.

10   9   8   7   6   5   4   3   2   1
08   07   06   05   04   03   02   01   00   99

Printed and bound in Great Britain by Antony Rowe Ltd, Chippenham, Wiltshire

Contents

List of Plates

Acknowledgements

Practising Identities: Power and Resistance comprises revised versions of papers originally presented at the British Sociological Association (BSA) Annual Conference, which was held at the University of York, 7–10 April 1997, on the theme 'Power/ Resistance'. It is one of four volumes, all published by Macmillan Press, produced from the papers given at the conference. The companion volumes are: *Consuming Cultures: Power and Resistance*, edited by Jeff Hearn and Sasha Roseneil; *Relating Intimacies: Power and Resistance*, edited by Julie Seymour and Paul Bagguley; and *Transforming Politics: Power and Resistance*, edited by Paul Bagguley and Jeff Hearn.

The conference was one of the largest ever held by the BSA. Over 330 papers were presented, which made the task of selecting papers for publication particularly difficult. We would like to thank all the conference participants for their patience whilst we read the papers; inevitably there were many papers that we would have liked to have included but were unable to, in trying to make this and the other volumes into coherent collections. The contributors to this volume are thanked for revising their papers so swiftly and efficiently in response to editorial comments and suggestions.

The theme of the conference – 'Power/Resistance' – is both a long-established theme within the discipline of sociology and one that has seen increased interest and re-evaluation in recent years. This sense of continuity and change was present throughout the conference. The four volumes bring together papers on major sub-themes that *emerged from* the conference, and as such it is probably fair to say that they give an indication and taste of some of the major preoccupations of sociology, particularly British sociology, in the late 1990s.

We are extremely grateful to the wonderfully good-humoured and patient staff at the BSA office both in Durham and at the conference itself – Nicky Gibson, Judith Mudd, Jean Punton (until November 1996), and especially Nicola Boyne. We also thank the Conference Office and the Department of Sociology at the University of York for their advice and hospitality, and the student helpers at the conference for their invaluable assistance. Special thanks are due to Sarah Irwin, who was a member of the conference organizing committee in its early stages, prior to the demands of motherhood. Our thanks are also offered to our colleagues at the Universities of Leeds and Hull for their support and encouragement for the 'Yorkshire BSA Conference'. Finally, the other two members of the organizing committee, Paul Bagguley and Jeff Hearn, were a pleasure to work with, and the overall shape of the four volumes and the selection of the papers was decided collectively by all four of us.

Notes on the Contributors

Nadia Joanne Britton is a Research Assistant in the Department of Sociology at the University of Manchester, where she is carrying out collaborative research funded as part of the ESRC 'Cities' programme. She completed an ESRC-sponsored PhD in the Department of Sociological Studies at the University of Sheffield. She has been awarded a Special Research Fellowship by the Leverhulme Trust to begin in 1999. Her research interests are race and criminal justice, racialized identity and equal opportunities.

Malcolm D. Brown is in the final stages of writing a PhD thesis in the Department of Sociology at the University of Glasgow, on the subject of Muslim identities in the United Kingdom and France. His research interests include the sociology of racism and migration, the sociology of religion, the study of nationalism, and the sociology of contemporary France.

Ben Carrington is a Lecturer in Sociology at the University of Brighton. He has written widely on aspects of popular culture and identity, particularly in relation to sport. He is currently co-editing a book on racism, sport and British society.

Emma Clarence is employed as a Research Assistant in the Department of Public Policy at the University of Central England. Her chapter in this book is part of ongoing research towards a PhD entitled 'Constructing National Identity: Britain and Australia Compared', for which she is registered at Staffordshire University.

Ian Cook is a Lecturer in Human Geography and Cultural Studies at the University of Wales, Lampeter.

Philip Crang is a Lecturer in Human Geography at University College London.

Lorraine Culley is a Principal Lecturer and Head of the Health Studies Section of the Department of Health, De Montfort University, Leicester. Her current research interests include ethnicity and health, the experiences of minority ethnic health workers, equal opportunities, and infertility and health policy.

Simon Dyson is a Principal Lecturer in Health Studies at De Montfort University, Leicester. He is author of *Mental Handicap: Dilemmas of Parent–Professional Relations*. His current research interests include the social aspects of sickle-cell anaemia and thalassaemia.

Silvia Ham-Ying is a Principal Lecturer in Nursing and Head of the Section of Continuing Professional Studies at De Montfort University, Leicester. She was born in Antigua and emigrated to England as a teenager in 1962. She worked within the NHS from 1964 to 1995 in a variety of capacities. She has been involved in the education of nurses and other health and social-care professionals since 1975. Her current research interests include holistic health care, transcultural nursing and continuing professional development.

Joseph Maguire is a Reader in Sociology of Sport in the Department of Physical Education, Sport Science and Recreation Management at Loughborough University. He has published widely on a variety of themes and issues in the sociology of sport, and his current research interests include national identity, labour migration and globalization, and body culture.

Louise Mansfield is a Senior Lecturer in the Sport Science Department at Canterbury Christ Church College. Her current research interests include the sociology of the body, sport and gender. Her doctoral work at Loughborough University concerns women and the sports experience.

Sasha Roseneil is a University Research Fellow in Sociology and Director of the Centre for Interdisciplinary Gender Studies at the University of Leeds. She is the author of *Disarming Patriarchy: Feminism and Political Action at Greenham* (Open University Press, 1995) and *Common Women, Uncommon Lives: The Queer Feminisms of Greenham* (1999), and co-editor of *Stirring It: Challenges for Feminism* (1994), and (with Jeff Hearn) *Consuming Cultures: Power and Resistance* (Macmillan, 1999). She is one of the editors of the new journal *Feminist Theory* (to be launched in 2000).

Julie Seymour is a Lecturer in Social Research in the School of Comparative and Applied Social Sciences at the University of Hull. Her current research interests are the distribution of resources in households and the associated negotiations between household members with a particular emphasis on gender; disability and social exclusion; and research methodology. She is co-editor (with Paul Bagguley) of *Relating Intimacies: Power and Resistance* (Macmillan, 1999). Recent publications include contributions to *Men, Gender Divisions and Welfare* (1998) and *Gender, Power and the Household* (forthcoming).

Paul Sweetman is a Lecturer in Sociology at the University of Durham. Previously based at the University of Southampton, his research interests centre around issues of the body, identity, fashion and consumption.

Shirley Tate is a Senior Lecturer in Sociology at Leeds Metropolitan University. She is currently a PhD student in the Department of Sociology at Lancaster University where she is looking at how hybridity can be illuminated through looking at how Black women and men perform identifications in contrastive story-telling sequences.

Mark Thorpe was the Research Associate on the ESRC-funded 'Eating Places' project at University College London.

Stephen Whitehead is a Lecturer in Postcompulsory Education in the Department of Education at Keele University. His research interests and publications concern the critical study of men and masculinities; gender and education management; poststructuralism; and subjectivities, epistemologies and identities in organizations. He is co-editor of *Transforming Managers: Engendering Change in the Public Sector* (1998).

Wendy Young was formerly a Research Assistant in the Department of Health and Continuing Professional Studies at De Montfort University, Leicester. Previously, she worked for twenty years as a care assistant alongside Caribbean-born health workers who were not qualified as first-level nurses.

1 Practising Identities: Power and Resistance
SASHA ROSENEIL and JULIE SEYMOUR

Who am I?
Who do I want to be?
Who can I be?
How do I want to be me?
Who are we?
Who do we want to be?
Who can we be?
How do we want to be us?

Questions of identity, individual and collective, confront us at every turn at the end of the twentieth century. We are interpellated and interrogated by a multiplicity of voices to consider and reconsider our identities. How we think of ourselves and how we perform ourselves in terms of gender, nationality, ethnicity, race, sexuality and embodiment is up for grabs, open to negotiation, subject to choice to an unprecedented extent. Or so the story goes. In the powerful discourses of consumer culture, in advertising, magazines, self-help manuals, pop songs, we are told that we can seize control of our 'selves' to 'be who we want to be'. Contemporary culture offers up a 'smorgasbord' (Cook, Crang and Thorpe, this volume, Chapter 11) of identity options, encouraging us to explore and harness difference in the construction of our identities. We can model our femininity on Baby Spice or Posh Spice, Sporty or Scary, kd lang or Cindy Crawford, Ellen de Generes or Naomi Campbell; we can be 'new lads' or 'new men', 'family men' or 'career men'; we can be gay or straight, dyke or queen, queer, bisexual, transsexual, transgender; we can be English, British, European, Welsh, Scottish, Irish, Loyalist, Republican, black, Black British, Asian, Muslim, Jewish. The options and combinations of possible identities seem to be infinite.

1

Yet we are not entirely free to choose our identities, like shades of paint from a colour chart. The range of identity options available to any individual is limited, the act of choosing circumscribed by a wide range of social constraints. Our economic situation, our spatial location, our physical capabilities and bodily appearance, our relational responsibilities, our age, our family histories, amongst many other factors, impact upon our identity choices. It is easier to be a Spice Girl rather than a riot grrrl in school, a new lad rather than a new man in most workplaces, straight rather than queer, British rather than Black British in rural England. All identities are not equally available to all of us, and all identities are not equally culturally valued. Identities are fundamentally enmeshed in relations of power.

But whilst we cannot regard identities as existing within the realm of unfettered individual free choice, nor should we too hastily subscribe to the view that identities are merely imposed upon us, constructing us without our active involvement. For as much as we may be channelled into particular identities, our identities may be a means of enacting resistance and rebellion. Our identities may be a weight around our neck, or a source of pride and joy.

THEORIZING IDENTITY

In recent years social and cultural theorists have rediscovered identity.[1] This relatively new interest in identity, and intricately linked to it, in difference, has to be seen in its social and historical context. It has occurred in the wake of the wave of social movements which have placed issues of gender, race and sexuality firmly on the political and intellectual agenda.[2] These movements, and the scholarship they spawned – feminist, black, postcolonial, lesbian and gay, queer – pushed from the margins to demand attention to the identities of those who were outside the normative framework of white, European, heterosexual masculinity within which academic disciplines tacitly operated.[3] As marxism and concern with class interests and class consciousness lost their centrality within social theory, and their purchase in the real world of politics, a focus on seeking to understand and theorize the politics of identity and the demand for recognition of difference has developed.[4]

There are two main strands within this recent theorizing of identity:[5] a social theory strand, and a poststructuralist cultural theory strand.[6] These two strands of theory offer different ways of thinking about identity, both of which provide the theoretical backdrop to this book. The social theories offer an historicized narrative of the development of identity, which is conceptualized as *self*-identity, the individual's conscious sense of self. From this work a particular understanding of the importance of identity in the contemporary social formation emerges, which underlines the significance of studies of identity to a sociology of the late modern world. The cultural theories, in contrast, are interested in the problematic of identity and cultural difference, and in the theoretical deconstruction of identity categories. This work highlights the importance of attention to power in the construction of identity through difference. Both strands of identity theory reject the Enlightenment philosophical tradition which conceives of identity as essential, unitary, fixed and unchanging. In so doing they offer a challenge to common-sense notions that identity can be 'reclaimed' or 'uncovered', notions which still have much purchase, particularly amongst marginalized and oppressed groups who are seeking to create a politicized collective identity.[7]

The social theory strand of work on identity, implicitly drawing on the agency-oriented tradition of symbolic interactionism, explores the relationship between identity, modernity and late modernity (Giddens, 1991; Beck, 1992; Kellner, 1992; Beck *et al.*, 1994; Calhoun, 1995; Bauman, 1996).[8] Although, as Calhoun (1995) points out, all cultures have paid attention to distinctions between self and other, and us and them, identity takes on a new and particular importance in modernity, an importance which shifts again in late modernity. The discourse of self – of the rational, thinking individual with an identity – is distinctively modern, the product of the Enlightenment, and o social processes of commodification and urbanization.[9]

According to these social theorists of identity, identity really start to matter as uncertainty increases, as tradition loses its hold, as 'al encompassing identity schemes' (Calhoun, 1995: 195) are destabilize In other words, identity becomes a problem as modernity unfolds, an particularly as we enter 'late modernity' (Giddens, 1991), or 'ris society' (Beck, 1992). In the contemporary era, globalization an rapid social change disturb the temporal and spatial certainties whic had continued to be offered through modernity by community ar place, stable employment and class structures, and the nuclear fami The variety of life choices facing us increases, and our knowled about these choices explodes in a media-saturated world.[10] Less a less seems to be determined by tradition and social structure, a establishing our identity becomes both more important and mo difficult, as our identities are subject to ever more frequent and complex challenges. Attempting to anchor our sense of self in this maelstrom of social life, to create ontological security in a world of rapid social change, we each as individuals face the task of construct- ing for ourselves our biographical narratives. In Giddens's terms, the self becomes a reflexive project: 'We are, not what we were, but what we make of ourselves' (Giddens, 1991: 75). Thus, 'reflexive modern- ization' (Beck, 1992; Beck *et al.*, 1994) is understood as linked to processes of de-traditionalization and individualization.

Developing in parallel with (but largely seemingly in ignorance of) the social theories of identity and the sociological heritage on which they draw, there is a body of cultural theory on identity which takes this constructivist position in deconstructionist directions. With its roots in Althusserian structuralism, and drawing on the work of, vari- ously, Derrida, Foucault and Lacan, a poststructuralist paradigm has emerged, particularly strong within cultural studies, feminist theory and postcolonial theory, which radically challenges the humanist con- ception of the unified, essential subject (e.g., Weedon, 1987; Butler, 1990, 1992, 1993; Hall, 1990, 1996; Scott, 1992, 1993). Poststructuralist theories emphasize the instability, fluidity, fragmentary and proces- sual character of identities, to a greater extent perhaps than the social theorists of identity. Moreover, they reject the idea that there exists some 'ontologically intact reflexivity to the subject' which pre-exists the subject's placing in a cultural context (Butler, 1992: 12), and instead regard the subject as constituted through discourse. Following Foucault, what is developed is 'not a theory of the knowing subject, but rather a theory of discursive practice' (quoted in Hall, 1996: 2). Identities are, according to Hall (1996) 'points of temporary attach- ment to the subject positions which discursive practices construct for us' (Hall, 1996: 6).

The question of power is central to poststructuralist theories of identity. Identities are seen as constituted through discursive exclu- sion, in terms of binary oppositions, and in relation to their Other, their 'constitutive outside' (Derrida, 1981; Fuss, 1991; Butler, 1993): the identity of 'woman' against that of 'man', 'black' against 'white', 'homosexual' against 'heterosexual', and so on. Yet, it can appear that the power operates all one way. Although the agency of the subject emerges for discussion (e.g., Butler, 1992; Benhabib *et al.*, 1995; Hall, 1996), ultimately poststructuralist theories of identity tend to empha- size processes of subjectivization in which human beings have little agency against the power of discourse, to resist or transform dominant discourses and therefore to produce new identities.[11] Butler's theory of 'performativity' explicitly rejects notions of choice and intentionality, such as are fundamental to the social theorists of identity, and sees the production of the (gendered) subject as 'not as a singular or deliberate "act", but, rather, as the reiterative and citational practice by which discourse produces the effects that it names' (Butler, 1993: 2). This approach is in sharp contrast to the emphasis on reflexivity of the social theorists of identity, whose work highlights the active, creative, conscious practices of identity construction.

PRACTISING IDENTITIES

The contributors to this book make use of this substantial body of social and cultural theorizing about identity in a variety of ways, but are not restrained by it. As a whole the book straightforwardly follows neither the social theory approach nor the poststructuralist approach; rather it is characterized by a theoretical pluralism and pragmatism. Some of the papers orient themselves towards notions of identity as a reflexive project (e.g., Sweetman), others are more concerned with thinking about cultural identity as difference (e.g., Brown; Cook, Crang and Thorpe). But the book is not primarily a work of theory. Rather it is a collection of papers mainly grounded in empirical research, which seek to develop sociological understandings of identities in the contemporary world. Amidst the recent explosion of writing about identity surprisingly little has taken this form, and the book therefore offers a distinctive and much-needed sociological intervention in current debates. Many of the contributions gain a richness of texture to their insights into the formation and experience of identity from the local and/or intensive, qualitative character of the research on which they draw. Over half of the contributions are by young/new academics whose research on identity was begun as part of their doctoral theses, a point which suggests that this book is likely to be an early marker of a growing literature of original empirical research on identity.

In general, the authors are united by a sociological orientation to the subject-matter of identity, which sees identities as actively constructed, chosen, created and performed by people in their daily lives. Through their empirical studies of identity practices they offer a range of grounded analyses of identities as they are actually lived, and which recognize that identities are open, processual and complex, often fractured and fragmented. In keeping with the original conference theme of 'power/resistance', the question of power and the possibilities of creating identities of resistance are to the forefront throughout the book. The chapters explore the processes through which people establish their identities and the arenas and means by which this 'identity work' is done. The means and sites of identity creation covered include: sport and exercise (Carrington; Tate; Mansfield and Maguire); bodily inscriptions and personal appearance (Tate; Sweetman; Mansfield and Maguire); involvement in voluntary organizations (Carrington; Britton); paid work, and particularly, professional careers (Whitehead; Culley, Dyson, Ham-Ying and Young); the construction of narratives about self and others (Culley, Dyson, Ham-Ying and Young); state policy (Clarence); and practices of eating (Cook, Crang and Thorpe).

A number of different identities, individual and collective, are explored in the book, with many of the chapters focusing on the complex interplay of identities, and the tensions within particular identities, experienced by individuals. Some authors are primarily concerned with self-identity, with how invididuals consciously think of themselves (e.g., Tate; Whitehead), and the stories they tell about their lives (Culley, Dyson, Ham-Ying and Young), others with collective cultural identities, as they are constructed by individuals in specific social contexts (e.g., Carrington; Britton). A third focus is on the discursive possibilities of identity at a more macro-cultural level (e.g., Clarence; Cook, Crang and Thorpe).

Carrington; Britton; Culley, Dyson, Ham-Ying and Young discuss racialized identities, and in particular, black identities in Britain. Ben Carrington's ethnographic study of the Caribbean Cricket Club (CCC) in Chapeltown, Leeds, examines the place of cricket and of this 'black space' in the lives and identities of its members, both black and white, British and Caribbean-born. Nadia Joanne Britton's study of a black voluntary organization – an explicitly political organization – directly addresses the question of the complex meanings of the term 'black' and thus the possibility of a politicized black identity amongst its volunteers. Lorraine Culley, Simon Dyson, Silvia Ham-Ying and Wendy Young's chapter discusses the biographical life narratives and the moral positionings of self which have been developed by Caribbean-born nurses who migrated to Britain to make sense of their experiences as workers in the racist environs of the National Health Service.

Ethnic identities and religious identities, and their intersection with national identities, are another prominent theme in the book. Drawing on the work of Edward Said (1995), Malcolm Brown argues that the treatment of Muslims in Western Europe is an example of 'internal Orientalism', and he goes on to detail the options for resistance through the ways in which they practise their identity which are open to Muslims in the West. Emma Clarence's chapter on the history and contemporary problems associated with the development of an inclusive, multicultural conception of citizenship in Australia highlights the politically contested nature of national identity. And Ian Cook, Philip Crang and Mark Thorpe examine the recent surge in popularity of 'ethnic' cuisine in Britain, and its meanings in terms of British identity and multiculturalism.

The other main focus in the book is on gender identities. Ben Carrington's chapter is explicit about the role of sport in the construction of black masculinity, and highlights the complexities of gender identity practices within the male world of the CCC. Shirley Tate's research with women weight-trainers discusses the identity projects of women who inscribe their bodies with markers of 'the masculine', thereby constructing transgressive femininities. Paul Sweetman's work on the recent revival of interest in tattooing and body piercing continues the theme of identity construction through embodied performance, asking a broad question about the oppositional potential of these practices, and homing in particularly on their meaning in terms of gender identities. A further chapter by Louise Mansfield and Joseph Maguire on the significance of sport and exercise in the creation of identities is concerned with women's experiences of aerobics and the power relations which exist in the exercise class where feminine identities and bodies are forged. Finally, moving away from the embodiment of gender identities, Stephen Whitehead's research on the changing organizational culture of further education suggests that masculine identities are contingent, plural and open to moments of disruption.

Practising Identities does not promise to answer the identity questions with which this chapter began because identity questions are, by their very nature, open-ended and ultimately unanswerable. They are questions we have to live with, uncertainties that constitute the meaning of life in the late modern world. Practising identities, unlike practising the piano, the tango, or one's backhand, can never make perfect. But therein, perhaps, lies their fascination and our compulsion.

NOTES

1. We say '*re*discovered' because it should not be forgotten that there is a significant history of interest in identity formation and construction within sociology and social psychology, particularly within the tradition of symbolic interactionism, most notably including the work of Mead (1934) and Goffman (1959).

2. These movements are often referred to as 'new social movements', and are contrasted with the *old* social movement, the labour movement, for their concern with identity. Roseneil has argued elsewhere (1995) that movements concerned with identity (e.g., the women's movement) are hardly 'new', and Calhoun (1995) points out that the labour movement was itself concerned with the identity and consciousness of the worker.

3. For a discussion of the impact of the social movements of the 1960s and 1970s on 'new social knowledges' see Seidman (1994).

4. See Calhoun (1995) and Fraser (1997).

5. There is also an important psychoanalytical tradition of identity theory which is not addressed in this chapter because it is not drawn upon in the work collected in this volume. See for example Rose (1986).

6. This distinction between social theory and cultural theory is not unproblematic, but it is used here as a heuristic device in order to draw attention to the explicitly sociological orientation of the former, and the focus on cultural difference of the latter. There are points of contact between these two strands of theorizing, particularly in the cultural studies work of Hall (1996), who accepts the proposition that in late modern times identities are increasingly fragmented and fractured, and locates his work within an understanding of the processes of social change discussed by the social theorists of identity. Bauman's (1996) work on difference and otherness in modernity and postmodernity similarly crosses this social theory/cultural theory distinction.

7. For a discussion of this in relation to women's identities, lesbian and gay identities and feminism, see Fuss (1989) and Roseneil (1995: Chapter 8), and in relation to black identities see Hall (1990).

8. There are differences in emphasis and terminology between these writers (e.g., Kellner (1992) and Bauman (1996) speak of 'postmodernity', rather than the 'late modernity'/'reflexive modernity' favoured by others), but the main themes in their work are similar enough for them to be grouped together in this way.

9. For a critique of what he calls this 'sociological "just so story" of how the human being got its individuality' see Rose (1996). Rose rejects a singular linear narrative and argues instead that we should spatialize

our understandings of self in order to see the multiplicity of practices of self which exist at any historical moment.

10. The work of social psychologist Gergen (1991) on technologies and processes of 'social saturation' suggests that as a result of our exposure to a wide range of high-intensity social relations in postmodernity we develop a capacity to readily adopt new identities. Subject to 'today's increasing cacophony of competing voices' we become 'multiphrenic'. Thanks to Beth Longstaff for this reference.

11. The debate within feminism about identity and agency is played out in Benhabib *et al.* (1995).

REFERENCES

Bauman, Z. (1996) 'From Pilgrim to Tourist – or a Short History of Identity', in S. Hall and P. du Gay (eds), *Questions of Cultural Identity* (London: Sage).

Beck, U. (1992) *Risk Society: Towards a New Modernity* (London: Sage).

Beck, U., Giddens, A. and Lash, S. (1994) *Reflexive Modernization: Politics, Tradition and Aesthetics in the Modern Social Order* (Cambridge: Polity).

Benhabib, S., Butler, J., Cornell, D. and Fraser, N. (1995) *Feminist Contentions: A Philosophical Exchange* (New York: Routledge).

Butler, J. (1990) *Gender Trouble: Feminism and the Subversion of Identity* (New York: Routledge).

Butler, J. (1992) 'Contingent Foundations: Feminism and the Question of "Postmodernism"', in J. Butler and J. W. Scott (eds), *Feminists Theorize the Political* (New York: Routledge).

Butler, J. (1993) *Bodies that Matter: On the Discursive Limits of Sex* (New York: Routledge).

Calhoun, C. (1995) *Critical Social Theory* (Cambridge, MA: Blackwell).

Derrida, J. (1981) *Positions* (Chicago, IL: University of Chicago Press).

Fraser, N. (1997) *Justice Interruptus: Critical Reflections on the 'Postsocialist' Condition* (New York: Routledge).

Fuss, D. (1989) *Essentially Speaking: Feminism, Nature and Difference* (New York: Routledge).

Fuss, D. (1991) *Inside/Out: Lesbian Theories, Gay Theories* (New York: Routledge).

Gergen, K. J. (1991) *The Saturated Self: Dilemmas of Identity in Contemporary Life* (New York: Basic Books).

Giddens, A. (1991) *Modernity and Self-Identity: Self and Society in the Late Modern Age* (Cambridge: Polity).

Goffman, E. (1959) *The Presentation of Self in Everyday Life* (London: Allen Lane).

Hall, S. (1990) 'Cultural Identity and Diaspora', in J. Rutherford (ed.), *Identity: Community, Culture, Difference* (London: Lawrence & Wishart).

Hall, S. (1996) 'Introduction: Who Needs "Identity"?', in S. Hall and P. du Gay (eds), *Questions of Cultural Identity* (London: Sage).

Kellner, D. (1992) 'Popular Culture and the Construction of Postmodern Identities', in S. Lash and J. Friedman (eds), *Modernity and Identity* (Oxford: Blackwell).

Mead, G. (1934) *Mind, Self and Society* (Chicago, IL: University of Chicago Press).

Rose, J. (1986) *Sexuality in the Field of Vision* (London: Verso).

Rose, N. (1996) 'Identity, Genealogy, History', in S. Hall and P. du Gay (eds), *Questions of Cultural Identity* (London: Sage).

Roseneil, S. (1995) *Disarming Patriarchy: Feminism and Political Action at Greenham* (Buckingham: Open University Press).

Said, E. (1995) *Orientalism: Western Conceptions of the Orient* (London: Penguin).

Scott, J. W. (1992) '"Experience"', in J. Butler and J. W. Scott (eds), *Feminists Theorize the Political* (New York: Routledge).

Scott, J. W. (1993) 'Women's History', in L. S. Kauffman (ed.), *American Feminist Thought at Century's End* (Cambridge, MA: Blackwell).

Seidman, S. (1994) *Contested Knowledge: Social Theory in the Postmodern Era* (Cambridge, MA: Blackwell).

Weedon, C. (1987) *Feminist Practice and Poststructuralist Theory* (Oxford: Blackwell).

2 Cricket, Culture and Identity: an Ethnographic Analysis of the Significance of Sport within Black Communities

BEN CARRINGTON

INTRODUCTION

As a number of commentators have noted (for example see Hargreaves, 1986; Williams, 1994) little is known about the social significance and meanings associated with sport within black communities in Britain, and sport's role in the construction of black identities. The critical study of aspects of sport and 'race' has been neglected as the subject-matter has fallen between a number of disciplines; the sociology of sport has yet to develop a critical theorization of 'race'; mainstream sociology, and even cultural studies, have tended to overlook sport as a cultural practice; and black cultural studies, whilst significantly advancing our understandings of many aspects of black popular culture, have also suffered from a form of cultural amnesia when it has come to the question of sport.[1] Similarly, the recent 'explosion' (Hall, 1996a) of studies and research on aspects of cultural identity, and the related concerns with questions of hybridity, 'difference' and multiculturalism, within sociology and particularly within cultural studies, has tended to remain at a frustratingly theoretical and abstract level with too few grounded empirical studies. This chapter attempts, therefore, to redress some of these concerns by providing an account, based on ethnographic research, of a how a black men's cricket club in the north of England is used as a symbolic marker in the construction of cultural identities. The chapter also explores some of the complexities and shifts within black British male identity, as well as the complex positioning of white people within black community spaces, and the limits to the 'black community discourse' found within black sports clubs.[2]

CARIBBEAN CRICKET CLUB AND COMMUNITY

Caribbean Cricket Club (CCC) was first established in the late 1940s by 'demobbed' servicemen from Jamaica who had settled in the city of Leeds, and is one of the oldest black sporting institutions in Britain. With few social amenities available, the early migrants formed the cricket club as an informal social club and arranged local friendlies with other teams in the area. The club, over the following decades, became progressively more successful, as larger waves of Caribbean migration arrived in the city and increased the team's strength, resulting in the club's current position of having its own pitch and pavilion (the result of local government money in the mid-1980s), running three senior men's teams as well as junior boys' sides, and playing in one of the strongest leagues in Yorkshire. The club's ground, 'The Scott Hall Oval', lies just outside Chapeltown, where the majority of the city's Asian and black residents live, and where most of CCC's players and members come from. As with many black sports clubs, CCC has over the years battled against racism, from apparently racially motivated arson attacks on the pavilion, to biased umpiring, problems with league officials and even occasional racial abuse from opposition players and spectators. For many of the members the club has come to symbolize Chapeltown's black community's own historical development in the city; thus the club is often used, in discussions, interchangeably with 'the black community' and Chapeltown itself. CCC can therefore be seen as a symbolic marker of the local black community, allowing its members to construct their own cultural identities through their identifications with the club. It is not that CCC itself expresses a given, fixed meaning, but rather that it allows its members the capacity to make their own meaning; CCC acts as a referent for their own individual identity construction (cf. Cohen, 1985). Given the historical role of the club within an environment where the black community of Leeds has faced various forms of racial persecution (see Farrar, 1996, 1997), the club can be seen as having a wider social role within a hostile white environment. It operates as a discursively constructed black cultural space; a space removed, albeit not entirely, from the discourses and practices of white racism.[3] In this sense the club becomes a site of cultural resistance within the local black community, exemplifying black pride and achievement, and constituting a form of local community politics.

CRICKET AND BLACK MASCULINITY

As C. L. R. James (cf. 1994) noted, cricket – due to its position both as, perhaps, *the* cultural embodiment of the values and mores of 'Englishness', and its 'missionary' role within British imperialism and colonialism – occupied a central site in many of the anticolonial struggles both within the Caribbean and elsewhere within the Empire. The game itself not only assumed heightened political significance in narrating the unequal power relations between the British and West Indians but it also, concomitantly, played a central role in the cultural identities of many West Indian men, in articulating a unified and an empowered sense of self, whether they were living in the Caribbean or elsewhere within the black diaspora.

A constant feature from the interviews and discussions undertaken with the older black players was an awareness of the importance of cricket in producing and reproducing a 'West Indian identity'. Cricket was often seen as being a 'binding force' for those in the Caribbean diaspora, connecting those from the different parts of the Caribbean within a single, wider identity. The chance to play cricket for a *black* club was therefore a powerful factor for the newly arrived migrants to Leeds in helping to maintain some sort of connection with 'home'. For instance one of the older players, Freddie, on reflecting on his reasons for joining CCC felt that the club provided a reminder of his previous life in Barbados. When asked what it was like when he first joined CCC, he replied, 'Ah, it started to bring back memories, man, it was like being back home for the time being.' This nostalgic idea of a 'home from home' was therefore important for the older black players at the club in providing a black space 'free' from racism and allowing for black expressive behaviour. When asked why he had joined CCC rather than another club, Ron, the Chair and manager of CCC, said:

RON: Because there were people like myself. It was a black team ... I felt more at home if I played with Caribbeans.

B.C.: So were you aware that, for you, Caribbeans was a black club?

RON: Oh yeah, it wasn't just any other cricket club, it was a *black* club.

The current club secretary, Terence, was one of the longest-serving members of the club, having played for CCC since 1969 after he arrived from Barbados in 1967, aged 15. He saw cricket as having a wider significance for 'West Indians' to the extent that cricket and his cultural identity were almost one and the same:

> It's the one area where we have that cultural identity in the West Indies, and it's cricket. If you look at other nations many of them have the religion to bind them together. You've got the Asians, so on and so forth, the Jews, the Irish and so on and we don't, as a people, seem to have anything to hold us together other than cricket.

Such views, in seeing cricket as a 'binding force' in trying to reconcile the inherent differences within Caribbean identity, was a common feature of the discussions, and therefore gave cricket itself, as a cultural practice, a greater significance in their lives. As Ron said, 'cricket is the only thing, to some extent, that *binds* black people together, as one force. So in a sense it's *more* than cricket.'

The importance of CCC as a 'black space' went beyond providing a cultural space for the local black population; it also functioned as an important cultural and social resource for black cricketers in the county of Yorkshire as a whole, especially those 'overseas players' from the Caribbean who often found themselves isolated playing for predominantly white teams in rural parts of the county. Many of the black overseas cricketers playing throughout Yorkshire would play friendly games for CCC and were grateful for the existence of the club to make their time in England more endurable. As CCC's overseas player, Harold, remarked:

> To me, in the north of England, in Leeds, they carry probably one of the most populated black areas and in that sense when someone is in the north playing cricket from any Caribbean island they would assume to relate to that club where it brings them back to their culture... . It should be projected to the overseas players who come here from Barbados, Trinidad, Guyana, Jamaica, that here is a home for anyone out there, 'Come here because it's home.'

The club, Caribbean culture and notions of 'home' thus become intertwined within the black community discourse which operated to discursively construct the club as a black space, and by their involvement and investment with the club. It provided many of the black men with a sense of ontological security.

'HOME' AND NATIONAL IDENTIFICATION

Given the significance of the Caribbean as a central aspect of their identities, for many of the older black players their present location in England was often problematic. Although many had been born in the Caribbean and had spent their early years there, shaping in part their outlook and sense of self, most had spent the vast majority of their lives living and working in England. However, to be called 'English' at the club was a form of mild abuse, as the term suggested that such people had lost their 'Caribbean identity', thus questioning their blackness. These attempts to reconcile such difficulties in relation to national identification can be seen in Ron's comments:

> RON: I was born in St Kitts, so I'm not an Englishman, even though when I was born there, the actual island was a colony of Great Britain, the United Kingdom.
>
> B.C.:   How do you see yourself now because you said you don't see yourself as an Englishman?
>
> RON: Well, I suppose a crucial question, or how I would answer that, is what does English society see me as, init? I listen to the news and I hear a 'West Indian born in London', so what am I? And those are the questions that I need re-dressing before I can really answer whether or not I consider myself an Englishman. I suppose ideally, and if you are looking at it in any logic, because of the length of time I've been here, I suppose you would call me a naturalized Englishman as they call it, or whatever. But I must say quite categorically, and without reservation, 'No I'm not an Englishman.' Because English society, whilst I've grown up in it, has never been accessible to black people as such ... so to some extent for me to say I'm an Englishman is really difficult.

Ron acknowledges that, due to the length of time he has been in England, he should, in a technical sense, be able to call himself English. Yet it is the degree to which the black presence in England is always seen as being 'foreign' that is the more important issue, i.e. not whether he considers himself to be English, but rather on what grounds is his Englishness questioned in the first place. These aspects came to the fore most clearly when the players returned to the Caribbean, as it was here that the tensions between their racial and national identities were, paradoxically, reversed, i.e. in not being accepted as English by the dominant culture in England, yet being regarded as English when they went back 'home'. Asked how he was perceived when he went back to St Kitts, Ron replied:

RON: I've never been back. And I'm always skitted in the club, they call me, 'Ronnie from Leeds'.

B.C.:   How does that make you feel?

RON: Well, it makes me feel a little pissed off to tell you the truth, Ben. But ... I've always desired to go back and see what it's like.... Yes, of course, I long to go back, and eventually I will go back, one way or the other, either in a box or whilst I'm breathing, but yes, I'd like to go back.

The fact that Ron had never returned to St Kitts is instructive as it marked him out from most of the older players, many of whom often returned whenever they could, thus retaining some sort of connection with the Caribbean, which perhaps reflects Ron's more relaxed attitude to the possibility that he could be considered 'English', and why he was teased at the club as being 'from Leeds' (as opposed to 'from St Kitts'). In contrast to Ron's more ambivalent and reflective sense of national identification, most of the other players were more adamant that they were 'West Indians' and had no time for the suggestion that the Caribbean was anything other than home, and a place where they would definitely return, and hopefully sooner rather than later. The club was often, therefore, viewed as a cultural resource, making the time spent in England more tolerable, before the return 'home'.

SOME KIND OF BLACK

Ossie Stuart (1996: 125) has suggested that, for black men, 'cricket represented social status, social mobility, it meant modernisation and it meant West Indian success'. This is no longer automatically the case for many black British youth who, whilst being aware of the symbolic and social significance of cricket, and particularly in relation to the West Indies cricket side, do not have the same emotional attachment to the game as do previous generations. Pete's comment, which typified the older players' view of the game and its meanings, that CCC was important to Chapeltown because 'it's the only sporting club, cricket club, that black people have got in the area, and when I say black I mean West Indian', reflected a black identity that is based around a black *Caribbean* identity. For black British youth the Caribbean, though not irrelevant, is no longer the cultural dominant it was 20, or even 10 years ago, thus the relevance of cricket, tied as it is to a Caribbean-based black identity, is similarly diminished. Thus the negotiations of their black identity, for the younger players, meant that they were marked out, to some extent, from the culturally hegemonic notion of blackness at the club articulated as a black Caribbean presence – so the youngsters were more likely to listen to jungle or swing than to soca music, more likely to talk with a Yorkshire inflection than to use a strong Caribbean patois. They were, in Diran Adebayo's (1996) telling phrase, 'some kind of black'; in, but not fully of, this particular black cultural space.

Nicholas, who was 17 years old when I first met him, was born in Leeds and considered himself to be both English and West Indian. He enjoyed playing for the juniors because it was 'more fun, less serious' than the senior team, and he felt that some of the older players took their cricket 'too seriously'. In contrast to the older players, and in line with most of the younger players, Nicholas was more receptive to the idea of being described as English. Asked how he saw himself in terms of national identity, he said:

NICHOLAS: I see myself as being, like, both. Like I'm an English person just 'cause I were born in England but I'm also West Indian because of background and parents.

B.C.:   You consider yourself to be English and West Indian. What about when it comes to cricket Tests, who do you support?

NICHOLAS: I support the West Indies.

B.C.:   Why is that?

NICHOLAS: Because they're all black and, well … also they're all better than the English team anyway and I don't agree, you know, when people say like 'If you're born in England you have to support England', I don't agree with that, because it's like, your choice you can support whoever you like… . The only way I'll support England is if they're playing Australia 'cause I don't really like Australians much.

B.C.:   What about the black players that play for England?

NICHOLAS: Well, I still want them to do well and I always support them. I don't really support the English team, but if they, like, play Australia and, like, if Chris Lewis take 5 wickets or make 200 runs, I'd be happy with that, even if the English team lose.

Nicholas was, through his sporting identifications, in a complex way, trying to establish a 'new' social identity for himself in line with many black British youth (cf. Back, 1996). He was able to situate himself as both 'West Indian' and 'English', although he did not subscribe to the ethnic absolutist logic of the 'Tebbit test' in arguing that all people living in England had, by default, to support the England team.[4] He could remain English whilst supporting the West Indies, thus challenging the terms on which Englishness itself was based. What Nicholas tries to do is to locate himself within a definition of Englishness that does not necessarily entail a notion of whiteness, in effect attempting to rework dominant notions of 'Englishness' and 'whiteness' in relation to cultural racism. He adopts an anti-racist position, which allows him to make identifications with individual black English players whilst distancing himself from identifying with the England team (and its symbolic resonances) as a whole. The only acceptable situation in which England could be supported would be against the Australians, who were viewed at the club as the most abusive and racist of cricketing nations; hence England could be supported against Australia, almost by proxy.

Significantly, many of the younger players were distanced from the older generation of black players in how they saw cricket and the importance of the game to their lives. Far from cricket being one of the central facets of his life and cultural identity, Nicholas saw cricket as just 'a weekend sport really. I do something different on the weekdays, it's just an outdoor interest.' Nicholas's cultural identity was one which was more grounded in a black British experience which distanced him from the dominant notion of blackness at CCC. He referred disparagingly to some of the CCC players as 'just a bunch of old men'. He was more critical and dubious of the claims made about the club's representative community role, and even questioned the long-term future of CCC. When asked how he saw the club and the club's relationship to 'the community' he said:

NICHOLAS: Well really, most of the older people here, seeing that they are from the West Indies, they all like cricket and that, but most of the youngsters, now, like basketball and that, so that's like taking over …

B.C.:   So you think there are generational differences?

NICHOLAS: Yeah, I mean, maybe when the old people are gone, in say ten, fifteen years time, Caribbean Club might not be here anymore because quite a lot of other people want to play other sports which they see on the TV and see as more exciting. Because I went down to the Prince Philip Centre [a local community centre] and there's quite a lot of youngsters down there and they play basketball there and then you ask them to come and play cricket and they say, 'It's boring. We don't want to. We don't want to stand there and nothing's going on, you know, when you're fielding.' So it seems like cricket's really going down-hill.

A WHITE MAN IN A BLACK MAN'S TEAM

Given the club's environment, and the way in which CCC was perceived as a 'black club' by both the players and opposition sides, the position of the white players was particularly interesting. When I first arrived at CCC there were three white players who played regularly. Steve, the youngest of the players in his late teens, had been at the club the longest, since 1991 when he joined as an 11-year-old. Tom was 19 when I first met him; he kept wicket for the second team and was very quiet, sometimes being the butt of jokes for his apparent reluctance to speak up. He helped out with the juniors but stayed very much on the sidelines. Like Steve, Tom lived on the nearby, predominantly white, working-class estate that separated the club from Chapeltown. Finally there was Shaun, who was 30 years old when I first met him. On my first training night I had been paired to bat with Shaun who told me he was a teacher 'in the community'. Later in the season Shaun played his first game and told me that he could have played for another side but did not fancy 'a typical, traditional and boring cricket club'. He seemed to feel quite comfortable at the club, with his white wife and children often spending some time at the games and his parents, particularly his father, often coming to watch.

For the youngest player, Steve, the fact that the club was seen by many as a 'black club' was not an issue, and certainly not one that had attracted him to play for the club. He first started playing for CCC after going over one day when everyone else was practising and after a while joined in himself. He joined CCC, 'Probably, just because it were close. If it hadn't been there I probably wouldn't have played cricket, but 'cause it were there I just went up and started playing.' Steve seemed to have little awareness of his own 'whiteness' and it was hard, during the interview with him, to broach such questions. It seemed to be something he had never really considered. His own lack of awareness of the club's racial signification may have been due to his young age when he first went to the club. Asked if he was aware that he was the only white player at the club when he first joined, Steve said:

> No, not really [*laughs*]. 'Cause I weren't like, I didn't exactly not like black people or owt. Just went up there and saw them for who they were, not from what people say that they're bad and that, 'cause they're alright ... when you get to know them they're the same as everyone else.

For Steve, CCC was simply his local club where he played cricket. The racial composition of the club, or the arrival of other white players, was, he said, of no significance to him. Although Steve did not admit to being aware that the CCC's 'blackness' was a factor, it seemed that Steve did like the idea of being associated with this black cultural space, which his cricketing ability gave him access to, and that this was a part of the attraction of playing for CCC. The degree to which Steve identified with aspects of black culture could be seen in the way he would sometimes use black vernacular in his speech, although no-one ever commented on this. Thus it appeared that part of the attraction for Steve was his ability to be accepted into, and be around, a black cultural space like CCC.

Tom had joined CCC in 1993, after being introduced to the club by one of the senior players whom he had known before. Similarly to Steve, Tom decided to join CCC because it was close to where he lived. However, unlike Steve, and maybe because he joined when he was a lot older, Tom was more aware of his whiteness:

> B.C.:   What was it like when you first came to Caribbean?
>
> TOM: I felt a bit funny at first because I think there is only a couple of white guys there and I didn't really blend in. I kept myself to myself but then after a couple of weeks I started to talk to people, it was alright, people made me feel welcome.

In a similar way to Steve, although perhaps more self-consciously, Tom was part of a white working-class culture that was less overtly racist in its orientation and perhaps even progressive in its occasional strongly anti-racist posture; a form of a new 'mixed' ethnicity that Back describes as being born out of negotiation between white and black working-class youth: 'a new ethnicity that contains a high degree of egalitarianism and anti-racism' (1996: 123). For Tom the racial identity of those he played with was largely irrelevant:

> TOM: It doesn't matter to me whether they are black, Asian or anything. As long as I go out there and enjoy my cricket I don't

want to get involved in any racist remarks. I just go out there play cricket and that's it. I don't want to get involved with anything stupid.

B.C.:   Is that because of the way you've been brought up?

TOM: Yeah, yeah, it's the way I've been brought up. Because even at school most of our friends at school and even now are mostly black, Pakistanis, and Indians. I have a few white friends but mostly Indians and blacks ... I live on the outskirts of Chapeltown and you hear about all this stuff about blacks and this, that and the other but the whites are just as bad. It's not only blacks that are doing it [crime] but it's all over the place, whites are doing it, Indians are doing it, so it's not just the black people that are bad. It's the way I've been brought up ...

It was Tom's lived experience that provided a basis for a form of 'common sense anti-racism' that was generated out of his close contacts with Asians and blacks as friends, thus he saw no contradiction in being a white player within a 'black club', indeed playing for CCC actually reinforced his own sense of cultural identity.

Shaun was a local school teacher and had started playing for Caribbean in the 1993 season after one of the coaches from Action-Sport (a community sports project in Chapeltown), who played for CCC, had asked him to come down to the club. His background was significantly different from that of both Steve and Tom, who were locally born working-class inhabitants. Shaun had been born in Bangladesh and had lived there until he was seven, when his parents, who were both missionaries, moved to Leeds. This background clearly had an important effect on Shaun's 'world-view'. The interview with Shaun was more involved than with Steve and Tom – perhaps because we were both similar in terms of our education and I could approach certain questions more abstractly, and perhaps because, being in his 30s and given his occupation, Shaun appeared more comfortable talking about himself and 'race issues'. Apart from a shared racial identity, Shaun's commitment and involvement with CCC were markedly different from those of Tom and Steve. Indeed his decision to live close to Chapeltown and work in the area reflected a personal choice more than a need to do so, thus his choice to play for Caribbean was in part linked to these other decisions. Asked how he first perceived CCC, Shaun replied:

I didn't know what to think of it. Because I had grown up in Leeds I had watched the Caribbeans play on Beckett Park and the only time

I had ever seen it was when I was out with my mates and it was dusky and it was the end of an innings and these big black lads were bowling some wicked fast balls at these poor fellas at the other end! And it was a dodgy wicket anyway, and I remember walking past thinking, 'That's seriously fast bowling and I'm glad I'm not there', and that was my only experience. So when I heard that Caribbean were playing up at Scott Hall I had a mental image already in my head of what it would be like, and I imagined the scene I had seen in Beckett Park. ... So I went there kind of nervous and also just pleased to have a chance to play some cricket and to see what it was like and when I got there I was really pleasantly surprised by how warm it was.

It is interesting that Shaun's early perceptions about CCC and black cricketers was one of fear (and respect) as big black bowlers, under the cover of falling night, terrified white batsman at the other end. Yet this same image was what attracted Shaun, in part, to joining the club as well. There also appears to be a slightly voyeuristic, if genuinely held, fascination with black culture that gives Shaun the status of 'outsider', which he would not have had had he joined a 'typical, traditional and boring cricket club', i.e. a white team.

Although Shaun felt he had become 'accepted', he acknowledged that not all of CCC's members accepted him and the other white players. Part of this is reflected more generally in his position as a white person within a black setting where the discourse of 'the white man' was often used in referring to racism. This clearly made Shaun's position within the club difficult, but because he had an understanding of what was being articulated he was able to distance himself from such discussions. When asked whether there had ever been times when he had felt uncomfortable, Shaun said:

SHAUN: There is this thing about 'the white man' that's passed which I don't take as an insult. Partly because, I think it was Brett, or it might have been Richie, or somebody early on said, 'When we're talking about the white man we're not talking you'! [*both laugh*]

B.C.:   They actually said that?

SHAUN: Yeah, it was before I went to one of the first meetings we were going to go to ... somebody addressed this, one of the senior guys, said, 'When we're talking about the "white man", and I was like, 'Yeah?', 'We're not talking about you', and I understood what he was saying, and I said, 'OK!'

Shaun's self-awareness about his place as a white male in a black club meant he was aware of certain situations where his presence might become problematic.

> Occasionally I'll walk into a situation that I know is not my situation and I'll walk out again. So if there's banter going on, sometimes after a game there is a lot of humour, especially if we've won, there's a lot of drinking and a lot of laughing and a lot of Caribbean stuff going on that I just do not understand, I can't understand the language, a lot of it, and although it is very amusing to be around, I feel like I'm not in the right place and occasionally I'll step away from that. Less and less, but when I was there early on I would step away from it because I didn't want to interfere or inhibit other people because they knew I was a by-stander, a spectator rather than a participant.

Shaun's position here is very reflexive as he is aware that his presence in certain circumstances may be construed almost as voyeuristic if he is not partaking in any discussions, yet the fact that he felt 'accepted in the club' meant he was able to leave such situations without feeling that his right to still be a part of the club was therefore undermined. In a similar way to Tom, although perhaps more self-consciously, Shaun's involvement with a black club actually confirmed, rather than questioned, his own cultural identity, demonstrating how a white presence within a black space need not, necessarily, be viewed as incongruous.

'BLACK', WHICH 'BLACK'?

There are clearly tensions that CCC is currently facing around the way in which the club has traditionally signified a 'black' identity. The meanings invested in and derived from the club have changed over the past 50 years: from being primarily a social space for black men to enjoy cricket, it has become a more competitive club which, whilst still invoking the notion of a black identity, now has a wider membership and therefore a more varied purpose. The expansion of the club to three senior teams, and the relatively recent introduction of junior teams, has meant that the club has become, racially, more mixed. Thus the automatic association of CCC as a 'black club' is less easy to maintain. Whilst many of the members, especially the older ones, still see CCC as being essentially a black club, others have become aware of the more polysemic nature of the club. Given the club's financial problems and the difficulties in recruiting young black players the future of CCC was a constant topic of discussion during the fieldwork. Many of the older players saw the younger players as lacking the same relationship to cricket which they had, and therefore their commitment to CCC was also questioned. For example, when I asked Freddie if there were generational differences in how cricket was perceived he replied:

> Yeah, it is. I think the older ones, like my generation, sees cricket as – cricket to me, like, was an everyday ting in the West Indies, that's the way I was brought up. But over here it's like *football*. Over here you only get made-up cricketers. ... There's not a West Indian I know who don't know about cricket, the older generation, they *know* their cricket. So somewhere along the line, you know what I mean, it's inbredded [*sic*] in some of them that's born over here. It's just getting it out them, init? It's just getting to them to get it out of them.

Cricket, here, is seen as not only something that blacks from the Caribbean should play, but as a part of the biological make-up of any 'true West Indian'. Thus the perceived movement away from cricket by younger blacks becomes, almost, a metaphor for the ontological insecurity of a certain generation of Caribbean migrants about their own identity. There were also problems for the older players in reconciling the club's historical black identity and its 'community' aspirations with both Chapeltown's contemporary diversity and, more recently with the advent of the racially diverse junior teams, the club's diversity. Asked how he felt about the club's growing racial diversity, Richie said:

> RICHIE: I don't think it's a bad thing. We reflect the community that we live in within the cricket team but I do feel that the management must be African–Caribbean led.
>
> B.C.: Why is that important?
>
> RICHIE: That is important so you don't lose the history and the heritage, the purpose of, or the reason why, the cricket club came into being in the first place. You can't lose that history ...
>
> B.C.: Do you see the inclusion of more Asians and whites as a worry?
>
> RICHIE: I don't see that as a worry really. The club reflects who is playing cricket at the time. And if it's Asian and white people then so be it, but I strongly believe the club's management

committee need to remain in the hands of African–Caribbean. It's similar to the West Indian Centre, even though you have lots of mixtures of people going to the West Indian Centre, it still should remain in the hands of African–Caribbean. I wouldn't expect to run the Sikh Centre, for that would be out of order, and I wouldn't expect a Sikh person to run the Caribbean Cricket Club either, I think it should be African–Caribbean. And that is not being racist, it's just a fact.

Most of the older black players seemed to have accepted the inclusion of white and Asian players, though not without some reservations. Brett, however, in contrast to Richie who equated the club with a specifically black identity, argued that the club could embrace greater racial diversity and still remain 'Caribbean':

B.C.:   How do you feel about Asian and white players playing for Caribbean?

BRETT: It don't bother me, not in the least. ... As far as I'm concerned if you're in the same team as me and you say you're Caribbean then let's go. ... Because it's not every West Indian who is black, and it's not every Caribbean person who is black. ... I've always had a degree of acceptance and tolerance of the fact that, I mean, though it's called Caribbean, it's called Caribbean based on the fact that the guys who were the original founders and starters of the club were predominantly Caribbean people but it was never solely a domain of the black. If you were white, or whatever you came, you played for Caribbean, you played under the banner of Caribbean. But it was not Caribbean as in you must be from the Caribbean only, because a lot of the guys who play now, or who have played from the seventies were born here. And a lot of the players' children who have played were born up here so it's not necessarily solely the domain of black, in inverted commas, only.

What is apparent here is that some of the members, like Brett, perceived CCC as a sign that could encapsulate diversity, and which did not, therefore, need to be racially homogeneous in order for it to still signify the club as being 'Caribbean'. This tension in trying to reconcile the 'blackness' of the club with its current reality was expressed by Terence, when he was asked whether he saw CCC as a black club:

Well, we try and get away from the black issue, although it has to be there; I'm afraid it has to remain because the community is predominantly black. I know it's a very diverse community with some 40 odd different nationalities within Chapeltown alone ... I think until, certainly the last two or three years, when we didn't have junior teams, yes, it was very much black. But with the arrival of the juniors you can see how diverse the club's becoming, and it's only last night I was having a conversation with a fellow member and we were pointing out, you know, we've got the Chinese, we've got the Asians, and we've got several other cultures within the club now and we hope to keep that going.

This not only acknowledges that the club itself has now become more ethnically mixed, but that the local community is itself diverse, yet at the same time it illustrates the wish (perhaps need) to maintain the notion that the club is still, in some way, a black club, even if this is couched in somewhat apologetic terms. Yet Terence's final comment that 'we've got several other cultures within the club now and we hope to keep that going', indicates not only an acceptance, but a positive acknowledgement, that the way forward for the club is to embrace the cultural diversity of both Chapeltown and the Caribbean Cricket Club.

'COMMUNITY', WHOSE COMMUNITY?

It is important to acknowledge some of the discontinuities and tensions that inevitably arise from a 'black community sports club' such as CCC. First, as has been clear from the beginning, is that the 'black community discourse', as Back (1996) terms it, is highly gendered; that is to say, it is largely a discourse generated and sustained by men. In a similar way to Stuart's (1996) study of the African Caribbean Cricket Club in Oxford, CCC does not actually represent, in a literal way, the community of Chapeltown, nor even the black community of Chapeltown, but rather represents a group of very committed, mainly older, black men. This seemingly contradictory view of the club, oscillating between truly reflecting the community of Chapeltown and representing the interests of a very small number of men, is illustrated by Ron's comments:

I think, in a sense, Caribbean Cricket Club, in its essence and its spirit, is in the black community in Chapeltown ... but in reality it's in a core membership of about 35 to 40 people who come every cricket season and play cricket, but then there is a small minority that during the winter months maintain the club to ensure that it is there in the summer.

The position of women within the club is, in many ways, marginal. The senior teams and junior teams are all men's/boy's teams, and although there is talk of developing a women's team, this has not materialized. Also the women who are involved in the club appear, at first glance, to occupy the marginal and subordinated positions that have been characteristic of many male-dominated sports institutions (Dempsey, 1990; Thompson, 1990).

There is a danger, however, in simply ascribing a fixed role to the participants without acknowledging the full complexity of the gender relations within the club. For example, during the first summer season when the research was conducted, the 'teas' were done by two women, which has conventionally been read as an example of the marginal and exploitative use of female labour and presence within cricket clubs. However, the money collected from the teas went to the women themselves, and it was thus a financial exercise, in which the women were using the club as an outlet for their business activities, although the club also benefited. Also, the second team's scorer is the daughter of one of the players, and she too is paid for her time. Thus the women who are directly involved with the club certainly have a degree of autonomous control over their relationships with both CCC and the men there. In line with the club's desire to be 'part of the community', CCC is also used as a place where other social events such as christening parties are held, for which women have taken over and run the club. Thus although the actual playing (and to some extent spectatorship, though not exclusively) of cricket tends to be male dominated, the wider running and social use of the club is more open.

The extent to which traditionally prescribed gender roles within sporting contexts reinforce wider sexist notions of appropriate 'feminine' and 'masculine' behaviour is also problematized within this context. This can be shown by the way two areas in which gender roles have traditionally been constructed and maintained – cooking and child-caring – are often reversed within CCC. For example, during the first summer's research, the meals, as mentioned earlier, were provided by two women. However, following the replacement of the Chair at the end of the season, these women left too. Thus in the second season the provision of teas and drinks was taken over, seemingly without any fuss, by some of the male members. On one occasion, when the rice for one of the meals was deemed not to have been properly cooked, there was an 'argument' between one of the players from St Kitts and the cook who was accused of not being a proper (black) man as he was unable to cook chicken and rice properly and was criticized as being 'a typical Nevis man'. Apart from the inter-island rivalry behind the comments, what was most interesting was that being able to cook properly, and thus to be able to look after yourself, was seen as being an affirmation of someone's black masculinity and not undermining it, and certainly not an activity which should (necessarily) be 'left to the women'.

Also, during the hot summer months, and especially when teams were playing at home, a few of the players would bring their young children along, who would play in and around the pavilion. When the particular player was batting, or fielding, the rest of the players and spectators would keep an eye on the children; the club acted as an informal 'crèche' for the children. This was never seen as infringing on the club's functioning (except on the few occasions when the children would run behind the 'bowler's arm'!), and the club's bounded space was not closed to 'men only', as has been explored in some studies of male-dominated cricket clubs (for example, see Imray and Middleton, 1983). These examples are used to suggest that a more negotiable and flexible approach to gender roles is available within this sporting context than has traditionally been documented within much of the academic literature on sports clubs.

In many ways the changing and contradictory gender roles of the black men, and the place of cricket as a site of black cultural resistance to racism at CCC, were similar to those analysed by Westwood (1990: 71) in her study of a black men's football team in Leicester:

> There is a collective mobilization through football that calls up black masculinities as part of the resistances that black men gener-ate against the racisms of British society and by which they validate each other. It is a male space; women are not involved but the world of family and home is often present on warm days when the men bring babies and toddlers to the matches, caring for them while they watch the game and demonstrating as they do that even within the male world of football men too can call up very different black mas-culinities from those associated with the machismo world of the football pitch. The juxtaposition is an important visual reminder of the varieties of black masculinities and our understanding of them as shifting terrain.

In a sense, then, the undoubtedly marginal position of women within CCC should not be seen as denying the 'positive' function that the club also holds out for many of the black men involved with the club, illustrated above, in resisting the effects of racism and in providing a social space for the construction of collective black identities. An important prospect, though as yet not fully realized at CCC, is its potential to act as a more open space for genuine dialogue between black men and women, and others, particularly in relation to gender roles, within the context of a black community setting.

CONCLUSION

This chapter has argued that sport, and in particular cricket, has often been central to the construction of cultural identities for Caribbean-descendant black men in Britain. It has shown some of the complexities and shifts, and the changing significance of cricket itself, within contemporary black British identities. The chapter has also shown how white players, within black sports clubs, can often negotiate a different positioning within such spaces as a way of affirming their own sense of self, which for many means constructing a more open form of cultural and racial identity.

These issues can be seen in relation to the Caribbean Cricket Club itself. That the club will have to change and evolve is almost inevitable given not only the demographics of the area but also the extent to which cricket no longer functions in the same way for British-born blacks as it did for blacks from the Caribbean from the 1940s onwards. As argued earlier, the suggestion that for black men cricket represents social status and mobility is no longer the case for many black British youth who, whilst acknowledging the wider social significance of cricket, do not have the same emotional attachment and investment to the game, and therefore to CCC, as did previous generations. For black British youth the Caribbean, though not irrelevant, is no longer the cultural dominant it was previously, thus the relevance of cricket, tied as it is to a Caribbean-based black identity, is similarly diminished. We might see, then, the club itself as mapping some of the shifts within black identity in Britain over the past 50 years, moving away from a direct connection with the Caribbean, towards the maturing of a more coherent and credible black British identity, that is influenced by, but no longer reducible to, the Caribbean.

It is clear that the only way for the club to survive is for it to attract youngsters from different backgrounds to the club, like the junior teams were currently doing. This may mean that the club, ironically, becomes more 'Caribbean' than it currently is. Though perceived as such within the popular imagination, the Caribbean is not a single entity and is in many parts racially as well as ethnically very diverse. In discussing the diasporic dimensions to Caribbean identity, Stuart Hall has observed:

> The diaspora experience...is defined, not by essence or purity, but by the recognition of a necessary heterogeneity, diversity; by a conception of 'identity' which lives with and through, not despite, difference; by hybridity. Diaspora identities are those which are constantly producing and reproducing themselves anew, through transformation and difference. One can only think here of what is uniquely – 'essentially' – Caribbean: precisely the mixes of color, pigmentation, physiognomic type; the 'blends' of tastes that is Caribbean cuisine; the aesthetics of the 'crossovers', of 'cut-and-mix' (Hall, 1996b: 220)

There is, perhaps, no need to see the involvement of a wider range of racial and ethnic groups at the club as a loss of an essential identity, as some in the club fear. Indeed, it may be that the future Caribbean Cricket Club will be able to live up to its name more fully than it has done in the past and embrace a more 'hybrid', non-essentialist, black identity, using the club's history as a resource in its future development, without being restricted by it.

ACKNOWLEDGEMENTS

The author thanks the participants of the 1997 BSA Annual Conference in York for providing critical feedback on an earlier draft of this chapter. I also acknowledge the help and encouragement throughout the research process of Pete Bramham and Sheila Scraton. Finally, Sasha Roseneil and Alan Tomlinson provided helpful comments on reworking this chapter. None of the above should bear any responsibility for what remains.

NOTES

1.   See, for example, Birrell (1989), who has clearly shown the paucity of critical studies of 'race' and sport within the sociology of sport and leisure studies; see Blake (1996) for a critique of the absence of sport within cultural studies; the reader *Black British Cultural Studies* (Baker *et al.*, 1996) is instructive in showing how every aspect of black culture, from film to photography, music and fine art, has received critical engagement from black British cultural theorists, yet sport does not even feature in the index, let alone as a subject, in and of itself, for study. These silences are all the more astonishing given the central, though not always acknowledged, position of C. L. R. James to the development of these fields of study, and his own belief that sport was central to any understanding of cultural politics within contemporary societies.

2.   This chapter is based on my doctoral study. In-depth semi-structured interviews conducted between 1995 and 1997, and participant observation during the summer cricket seasons of 1995, 1996 and 1997, have been used to collect the data. Pseudonyms for the players and club members are used throughout. My use of the nomenclatures 'black' and 'Asian' refers to those groups which, due to the process of racialization, are visibly marked as belonging to different 'races'. Within this context those referred to as 'black' are those people of sub-Saharan African descent, and those referred to as 'Asian' of south Asian descent.

3.   The concept of 'black space' used here is not meant simply as reference to a geographically bounded area, although clearly this is a dimension of any use of the term, but rather refers to the social production of space, i.e. the complex ways in which socioeconomic, cultural and political discourses construct spatial relations *and* the ways in which individuals themselves negotiate, and reconstruct, these discourses. As Farrar notes (1997: 108): 'In everyday speech, many residents of an urban area of black settlement would readily comprehend a phrase such as "black space" … in terms of their effort to forge discourses and practical activities in a particular part of town which are, to some extent, "free" from the discourses and practices which they associate with a coercive white power structure. Establishing nearly autonomous territory is the conscious aim of all sorts of actors in the black inner city – in churches, mosques, temples, community centres, clubs, pubs, and in certain "open" spaces.'

4.   In 1990 the (then) Conservative MP Norman Tebbit argued that Asians and blacks who continued to support the cricket nations from where they had migrated, instead of England, were disloyal British subjects, and proposed that a test of their citizenship should be whether they supported England in Test matches – see Marqusee (1994) for a critique of the 'Tebbit test' and cultural racism in cricket.

REFERENCES

Adebayo, D. (1996) *Some Kind of Black* (London: Virago).

Back, L. (1996) *New Ethnicities and Urban Culture: Racisms and Multiculture in Young Lives* (London: UCL Press).

Baker, H., Diawara, M. and Lindeborg, R. (eds) (1996) *Black British Cultural Studies: A Reader* (Chicago, IL: University of Chicago Press).

Birrell, S. (1989) 'Racial Relations Theories and Sport: Suggestions for a More Critical Analysis', *Sociology of Sport Journal*, 6, pp. 212–27.

Blake, A. (1996) *The Body Language: The Meaning of Modern Sport* (London: Lawrence Wishart).

Cohen, A. (1985) *The Symbolic Construction of Community* (London: Routledge).

Dempsey, K. (1990) 'Women's Life and Leisure in an Australian Rural Community', *Leisure Studies*, 9(1), pp. 35–44.

Farrar, M. (1996) 'Black Communities and Processes of Exclusion', in G. Haughton, and C. Williams (eds), *Corporate City? Partnership, Participation and Partition in Urban Development in Leeds* (Aldershot: Avebury).

Farrar, M. (1997) 'Migrant Spaces and Settlers' Time: Forming and De-forming an Inner City', in S. Westwood and J. Williams (eds), *Imaging Cities: Scripts, Signs, Memory* (London: Routledge).

Hall, S. (1996a) 'Who Needs "Identity"?', in S. Hall and P. du Gay (eds), *Questions of Cultural Identity* (London: Sage).

Hall, S. (1996b) 'Cultural Identity and Cinematic Representation', in H. Baker, M. Diawara and R. Lindeborg (eds), *Black British Cultural Studies: A Reader* (Chicago, IL: University of Chicago Press).

Hargreaves, J. (1986) *Sport, Power and Culture* (Cambridge: Polity).

Imray, L. and Middleton, A. (1983) 'Public and Private: Marking the Boundaries', in E. Gamarnikow, D. Morgan, J. Purvis and D. Taylorson (eds), *The Public and the Private* (London: Heinemann).

James, C. L. R. (1994) *Beyond a Boundary* (London: Serpent's Tail).

Marqusee, M. (1994) *Anyone but England: Cricket and the National Malaise* (London: Verso).

Stuart, O. (1996) 'Back in the Pavilion: Cricket and the Image of African Caribbeans in Oxford', in T. Ranger, Y. Samad and O. Stuart (eds), *Culture, Identity and Politics: Ethnic Minorities in Britain* (Aldershot: Avebury).

Thompson, S. (1990) '"Thanks for the Plates": the Incorporation of Women into Sport', *Leisure Studies*, 9(2), pp. 135–43.

Westwood, S. (1990) 'Racism, Black Masculinity and the Politics of Space', in J. Hearn, and D. Morgan (eds), *Men, Masculinities and Social Theory* (London: Unwin Hyman).

Williams, J. (1994) '"Rangers is a Black Club": "Race", Identity and Local Football, in England', in R. Giulianotti and J. Williams (eds) *Game without Frontiers* (Aldershot: Arena).

3 Making your Body your Signature: Weight-Training and Transgressive Femininities

SHIRLEY TATE

INTRODUCTION

In a consumer culture obsessed with appearance, the status of the body has been transformed from a fixed natural given to a malleable cultural product.

(Tseelon, 1995: 4).

The body is capable of being fashioned to become a representation of the self, a signifier of personal identity. The specific body which is of interest here is that which has been inscribed by women with 'the masculine' through the rigorous diet and exercise regime of weight-training for muscular gain. Using Black and white women's narratives as data, I look at the power of the women I researched to redefine 'the feminine' and 'the erotic'. I focus on how women construct transgressive femininities by subverting stigma (Goffman, 1984), redefining physical capital (Bourdieu, 1978) and negating the beauty model (Tseelon, 1995), through building their bodies to their own design. This design is based on a 'latent' inner image which allows the women to become their own significant others, to challenge the gaze of others and to 'be for themselves'. Their bodies, therefore, become sites of empowerment.

In choosing to be embodied in ways which contradict male definitions of 'the feminine' inherent in the tyranny of slenderness (Chernin, 1983) and its dominant feminine aesthetic (Lloyd, 1996), I argue that women enter the masculine domain of power over nature. Further, I suggest that in challenging the phallus directly through the creation of bodies which incorporate and eroticize 'the masculine', women go some way towards transforming the beauty model. I also show that through the 'power over their bodies' and 'power within their bodies' which they create, women weight-trainers transgress the accepted boundaries of femininity whilst still being located within the discursive spaces of compulsory heterosexuality.

THE RESEARCH

This chapter draws on research which focused on women who trained alongside men in 'men's spaces' but were not interested in competitive body-building.[1] I interviewed 15 women – both Black and white – in different gyms in a town in the north of England. These women were all in employment, working in different environments in the public and private sectors, for example graphic design, nursing, accounting, city planning and the academy. I was specifically interested in why they trained, how people reacted to their bodies and how they saw themselves as women. I started with women whom I knew myself initially, and then was given names and contacts for other women. I was aware that when women go to the gym they do not tend to have time to talk, so my questions had to be succinct and allow women a variety of ways to reply. For example, I asked women to write down responses when they had time, or to audio-record conversations with their friends in answer to the research questions outside of the space of the gym. Inside the gym I recorded women's responses in writing before or after their training sessions.

WOMEN, EMBODIMENT, IDENTIFICATIONS

As early as 1899, Dr Arabella Kenealy warned of the sex transformation which may take place through participating in 'mannish' activities (Pugh, 1993: 79). Women had been lifting barbells in private for years by the time Tillie Tinmouth and Ivy Russell competed against each other in a weightlifting contest in England in 1932. In 1907 Kate Sandwina, a British woman described as having massive proportions, appeared on stage and performed various feats of strength, including a two-handed clean and jerk of 250 pounds (Henry, 1996). Weight-training as a serious women's activity is, therefore, not a recent phenomenon. Nor is it just the preserve of middle- and upper-class women with the money and the leisure to go to the gym and invest in a personal trainer, in order to create the desired physical capital (cf. Bourdieu, 1984). The culture of going to the gym, being fit, being toned, being thin, being muscled, runs deep within a wide cross-section of women, irrespective of class, 'race', sexuality or location (Hargreaves, 1994). Since the end of the 1970s the 'worked-on' female body has become not only permissible, but presented as desirable (Hargreaves, 1994).

Contemporary gym culture contains a rather interesting paradox. This is shown in the differing desires of those women who want to be 'super-model thin' and those women who want to gain muscle. These desires then lead to differing inscriptions on the body, and to different ways of being 'embodied'. Women who 'wanna-be-waifs' seem to desire to be 'debodied'. Women who 'wanna-be-muscular' desire to be 'bodied'.

Is it as straightforward as this, though? How much agency do we have to create our bodies? Perhaps the answer lies in Bordo's claim that:

> The body is not only a *text* of culture. It is also ... a *practical*, direct locus of social control ... through the organization and regulation of the time, space and movements of our daily lives, our bodies are trained, shaped and impressed with the stamp of prevailing histori-cal forms of selfhood.
>
> (1995: 165–6)

In Krais's (1993) view the division of labour between women and men becomes embodied in terms of male and female bodily shapes. It guides perception of one's own body and others' bodies and, there-fore, determines identity in a very fundamental 'bodily' sense. 'The body cannot be thought of if not as "male" or "female" '(Krais, 1993: 161). The male/female dichotomy is rooted in social practice (Krais, 1993: 165). It is through the socialization process that women acquire a 'gendered habitus'.[2] It is within this gendered habitus that the opera-tion of ambiguities is operationalised along the antagonistic concept of male and female. The space of the possible is thus prescribed within the binary oppositions in which the 'other' as a possibility is sup-pressed. Acquiring gender identity, then, is a process of narrowing, of cutting off, of suppressing ambiguities (Krais, 1993).

The symbolic violence of the 'tyranny of slenderness' (Chernin, 1983) faces women in the West. Today, the current body of fashion is taut, small-breasted, narrow-hipped and so slim as to border on emaciation (Bartky, 1990: 66). The ideal is of a body that is tight, contained, firm, signifying that its internal processes are under control (Bordo, 1995: 189). Women then should desire to be 'debodied', to be super-model thin like Kate Moss and Jody Kidd, and in so doing should take up as little space as possible. Bordo (1995: 191) sees the necessity within our culture to *not* have soft, loose flesh as forming a bridge between compulsive dieting and body-building. Both of these bodily practices are panoptic technologies producing self-monitoring, docile bodies (Mansfield and McGinn, 1993: 53). Contemporary images of female attractiveness then can vary between 'a spare "minimalist" look and a solid, muscular, athletic look' (Bordo, 1995: 191). Bordo goes on to say that it is when the female body 'is developed to extremes' that the 'old association of muscles with brute, unconscious materiality surfaces' (1995: 191). So, given that slimness is a culturally defined ideal, the only muscles that are admired and valued on women are those which are 'toned' as they do not significantly add bulk (White *et al.*, 1995; Lloyd, 1996).

Given the symbolic violence of the tyranny of slenderness and the nature of the gendered habitus, why do women choose to become muscular through weight-training? In looking at this question I argue in what follows that women who weight train for muscular gains are engaged in a body project which is about using a bodily practice to construct identifications in the social world. Weight-training, and the muscles which arise from this, come to be a way in which women embody their identities as incorporating 'the masculine' into their physical beings. I will argue that, whilst they are constrained by the category 'feminine woman', they are also actively transforming and expanding that category through the purposive production of their bodies, risking social disapprobation as their transgression of the 'natural' order of gender becomes obvious.

WEIGHT-TRAINING, MUSCLES AND EMBODYING CONTROL

Muscles can be seen to be transgressive of contemporary conceptions of 'the feminine body', which in line with the tyranny of slenderness, means that:

> women are forbidden to become large or massive; they must take up as little space as possible. The very contours a woman's body takes on as she matures ... have become distasteful. The body by

which a woman feels herself judged and which by rigorous discipline she must try to assume is ... a body lacking flesh or substance, a body in whose very contours the image of immaturity has been inscribed.

(Bartky, 1990: 73)

The disciplinary practices of femininity produce an inferiorized body, and a woman has to conform to the stereotype as the shape and size of her body is the most important thing about her as a woman. The concept of stigma is relevant here, as the size and shape of a woman's body can be an attribute which is deeply discrediting (Goffman, 1984) and, there-fore, also the basis of negative physical capital (Bourdieu, 1978).

Transgressions will be noticed and stigmatized because of the power of the stereotypes of femininity and masculinity and their ideal physi-cal forms. Indeed, even the world of female body-building is subject to patriarchal control, as is evidenced by contests based on physique being phased out by the men who run them in favour of the figure competitions (*3D*, 20 June 1996). Women who enter physique contests in Britain are now judged to be 'too muscular' in comparison with women in figure competitions, who are judged to be muscular and toned but not 'excessively' muscular. 'Real women', then, do not want to have defined muscles and very low levels of body fat, and should not want to display such obvious control over their bodies.

Yet it is defined muscles and lower body fat which women who weight-train desire. Indeed control and being in control of their bodies, nature, appetites, femininities and lives, figure very centrally in the women's accounts of why they trained:

I feel like I'm in control of my body and in a way if I am in control of my body I'm in control of my *life*, cos as I say, that's the only thing you can control. Yourself, isn't it? Nothing else.

(Sheila)

And that is the nice thing about having control over how you look, how you train, what you eat, which part of your body you want to change if you're not happy with it. You just *feel* in control and the only thing you can control is yourself.

(Carol)

Embodying control through the development of a muscular body was also spoken about by women in terms of the physical pain of 'the burn' which this involves. For something which is enjoyable, and which has as its outcome the building of an aesthetically pleasing body, to give oneself pain seems misplaced, illogical. What then does pain signify to the women? It is a signifier of 'working to the max'. Of being in control of one's outer body and inner emotions, of being in control of one's body project. Being able to feel and overcome the physical and psychological pressure of the burn, of the after-training aches, signifies a woman with body discipline. It shows a woman prepared to push herself through the pain barrier to get her desired self:

> Yeah it's like the *dips*. I do, I love them. Oh I used to *hate* them. I used to hate them because of the pain. They just killed my triceps and my pecs. But oh, it's *beautiful*, absolutely *beautiful*.
>
> (Carol)

Pain becomes beautiful and pleasurable. The women spoke of the pleasure of having control over their bodies and of the pleasure they feel when they have challenged themselves, worked through the pain and beaten it. The women knew that the pain of the burn signifies that their muscles are being transformed in order to produce an-other body, so they see it as part of the process of the body project:

> What's the pain of the burn when you have experienced childbirth? When you feel it you just concentrate on something else in your head and work through it. The pleasure of the burn is being in control of your body and mind and the pleasure you get from looking at the product of the burn, your body.   (Carol)

Embodying control through practising the motto 'no pain, no gain' enables women to expand the space of the possible as they attempt control over nature, the ultimate male preserve. In accomplishing their body projects, and in routinely maintaining that body, a public space is established within the masculinized space of the gym, where the female body is reconstructed and the boundaries of femininity redefined by the women involved in the process.

LATENT IMAGES, MANIFEST INSCRIPTIONS

The women become involved in training for different reasons. At the level of the individual, dissatisfaction with the body is, in some cases, a prime motivating factor in becoming involved in training initially:

> I first started out when I was about sixteen. I think then I was very shy and wanted to meet people. So why didn't I take up flower

arranging? I have always been a very self conscious person, forever worrying about being too fat, about my legs being too big, my chest too small, my bum looking like the back end of a bus!

(Sasha)

There is a tendency, then, for the body to be seen as a project to be worked on in order 'to become' (Shilling, 1994). This is a reflexive process in which the owner of the body reconstructs it in line with her own design specifications. Individuals, thus, are actively concerned with the design, development, routine maintenance and appearance of their bodies. The control metaphor is again applicable here:

What I like about training is, right, is you can *choose* the bit of you that you're gonna do. You can control your development.

(Sonia)

It's like a body blitz. You just mould yourself. You work on one bit and you think hmm okay then my shoulder's lookin good. Now I can lessen the reps on that and develop like my back or whatever.

(Celia)

Investing time and effort in their body provides the women with a means of self-expression and a way of potentially feeling good about themselves, while at the same time increasing the control they have over their body shape:

What I really like about it you know, right, is I decide I want my shoulders to look this way. So I go and see Albert or some other instructor or do it in my own head. You plan which exercise you're gonna do, you know the specific muscle it's workin. You know whatever the contour is gonna be. So in a way you are making your body from your brain.

(Sheila)

And the other nice thing about it is like it's my wedding in September and I can say exactly how I am gonna look. I can say I wanna wear something off the shoulder and deep in the back. So I'll work on my back and shoulders, especially in July so they'll be firm and tight.

(Celia)

Confidence then comes from the reactions of people to their bodies and the strength which they know they have and are capable of developing in their muscles. The affirmation of women and men in terms of the respect shown when one's body is visible is an important motivator, as it reflects back that someone appreciates the years of dedication, hard work and denial that have been entered into in order to make these inscriptions on the body:

> Women respect us for all the hard work we put into our bodies. Men body-builders respect us because they know all of the work that has gone into the way we look.
>
> (Brenda)
>
> Other people see me and you can see the surprise on their faces if they've never seen me before. I feel I get a lot of respect at the gym, from the men I train with especially because they know the dedication it takes to build like this naturally.
>
> (Sasha)

The women's views about their existing bodies and ideas about the bodies they want to have lead to a preferred 'latent' image. This inner schematic becomes evident through its inscription on their bodies by exercise and diet. Through this image, and its concomitant body project, women experience their bodies as being controllable. This image is a re-working of the dominant aesthetic into the desire to be bodied in a specific, personally aesthetically pleasing way, according to the women's own design:

> I have always wanted one of those 'perfect bodies'. In my mind's eye, I see that perfect shape and I will strive for that forever.
>
> (Sasha)
>
> I look better defined, rather than round and flabby. I have an image of myself which I want to achieve and maintain, as muscular, but still feminine. Not over the top because I had enough of being stared at and pointed at when I was a competitive body-builder. So now I train for strength and stamina.
>
> (Alma)
>
> What I want is a firm bottom, thin, defined legs, bigger shoulders.
>
> (Janine)
>
> Toned, defined, athletic, muscular. Like FloJo before she started taking all those steroids. I am aiming for zero body fat, a firm bottom, developed shoulders, muscular/defined legs, but not over the top muscular.
>
> (Yvette)

I was talking to Sue about like the image I have in my head about how I'd like to be you know. Like I was saying to you before *wide* shoulders, narrow hips, *strong* legs, not too like *built* because I'd look too chunky then, you know? But *slim*, slim body with muscles.

(Sheila)

Definitions of what is acceptable muscularity and what is 'over the top' vary between the women, as each has her own aesthetic of the body. This aesthetic is based on an interaction between what women see as being 'butch' or 'feminine' and what they can live with 'as a body'. This shows the inner dialogue between the discourses of the 'social' and the 'personal' which women enter into in order to construct the latent image and its manifest inscriptions on the body. The extracts which follow also show the tightrope which the women tread between 'masculinity' and 'femininity' within the disciplinary discourses of heterosexuality as they work to create 'a suitable surface presentation of individual identity' (Lloyd, 1996: 90):

I haven't really had many views from other people, as most people don't know how hard I work out. A couple of times I have been asked if I'm a lesbian. I was never quite sure how serious they were! But that makes me panic into thinking – 'God, do I look butch?' Because I don't see any change in my body shape. It makes me aware that other people do.

(Sasha)

I don't want too much muscle because I don't want to look butch. Men don't like too much muscle.

(Janine)

EMBODYING POWER AND CHALLENGING THE GENDERED HABITUS

By choosing inscriptions of 'zero body fat and hard' or 'slightly more body fat and hard', the women are offering challenges to the binary oppositions of the identities prescribed by the 'gendered habitus' (Krais, 1993). Such challenges revolve around their construction of a version of 'the feminine' which co-opts 'the masculine' within their inscriptions. Inscribing 'the masculine' on a feminine body is about inscribing power and is thereby transgressive as, in contrast to men, women tend to be restricted in embodying power in their physical selves (Shilling, 1994). Women weight-trainers, therefore, are marked, and have marked themselves, as similar to the broad category of 'woman' but as different from this category because of the bodies they have chosen to create. They represent themselves as women capable of co-opting 'the masculine', thereby exerting a self-defined transgressive femininity, while being aware of the ambiguity that their bodies can produce. They feel strength, they believe that they embody strength, they can take on men in their world:

> That's what I say, you have *confidence*, yeah? And I go out on site and I see some *big, burly builders.* And you know what their mouth is like. So abusive. There's another woman planning officer and she sometimes goes out on site and comes back crying. I go out on site, say my piece, if you don't like it, *tough.* Do something about me, right? But you better be strong or you better be a fast bloody runner.
>
> (Carol)

> And I tell you what, having a muscular body makes me less afraid of men like that, you see. Because I know I can push him. Because I know if they hit me I know I can get up and hit them back. I know I can take the punch because of my muscles. So, I'm not bothered at all about aggressive men.
>
> (Alice)

THE TYRANNY OF THE LATENT IMAGE

In the process of identification with the latent images of their body projects, the women negotiate a fine line between 'the masculine' and 'the feminine', whilst always seeking to maintain the identity of 'woman'. This is obvious, for example, when they express concern not to be 'butch' or 'over the top muscular', and yet continue to train even when their heterosexuality is being questioned. The image is a powerful source of identity, which offers strength in this process of negotiating a path between masculinity and femininity. However, it can also be seen as exercising a certain tyranny in terms of the control it exerts over them. The image rules women's lives – how they perceive themselves, their diets, training routines, leisure time, relationships at the gym, fear of what they would become if they didn't train. It is about both asceticism and aestheticism:

> After going to work at 8.30, finish 4.30, starting in the gym at 5.00, getting home between 8.30 to 9.00p.m., I am shattered. Five nights a

week. I come in, make my dinner for the next day, repack my gym bag then go to bed. No, I don't have a social life in the week, I admit it. I don't know whether that is a good or bad thing.

(Sasha)

When I get to the image of myself of firm bottom, thin legs, bigger shoulders, I'll have achieved something.

(Janine)

I train five days a week. I have to. If I don't, I feel really as if something important has been left out of my life. Besides, if I don't, I can't eat what I like and as much as I like without getting fat.

(Alma)

Yeah, I am happy as I am, chocolate-less and slim and muscular. It's like, ah mean, Andre had this joke about me, right? At the top of every card he's ever written for me, under client requirements he puts *lean* and *mean*. So, we have this joke, lean and mean Sheila, yuh know, that's what I wanna be.

(Sheila)

The image becomes tyrannical to the extent that it dictates that if they eat a burger or some other fat-laden food, they then know that they have to spend a larger proportion of their gym time that week on some form of cardiovascular exercise, in order to burn the fat. Their relationship with food becomes one in which food does not necessarily need to be enjoyable. It is merely the raw material which they need to produce the body they want, with the consumption of food which is anti-the personal body project, becoming anathema because of the feelings it engenders:

When I was thinking of competing, I tended to look at food not as food to enjoy and to be tasty, but more in the context of proteins, carbohydrates and fats. Food became a solid fuel to serve a purpose and nothing else. I wasn't meant to enjoy it, it only served to help me train and gain muscle and energy. All fats and sugars didn't even come into it and had to be avoided at all costs. Now, I have a passion for chocolate, and believe me, that was hard to give up. Eventually I got bored of it and I didn't seem to look any better for eating so strict. So I now eat what I like most of the time. I won't go overboard, but a piece of chocolate every day does me good. Fats I do avoid.

(Sasha)

Because I know what I put in my body isn't what I should put in my body and I would feel ... I wouldn't feel guilty, it's not guilt. It's just thinkin', *well* why did I do that because now I've to go to the gym and work that off. And it's gonna take me how many hours of being on the stepper to work that off. I just see *food* in this way. Is it going to *enhance* my training or detract from it? And that's how I look at food these days. Rather than I must pile everything in my mouth that's going.

(Sheila)

It's the control thing for me as well though. Because to me I could go out with everybody else and eat all the MacDonalds, all the pizza, all of the Kentucky Fried Chicken. But how would I feel afterwards?

(Carol)

The image rules the women's lives because, unless they decide to change this image, training and a low-fat, high-carbohydrate/protein diet will have to be part of their lives for life. The women then are making lifestyle choices based on the image, in which the self-discipline of body regimes become central to self-identity because they connect habits with aspects of the visible appearance of the body (Giddens, 1991). To cease to train is to become fat, flabby, or thin without a defined shape, descriptions which women involved in weight-training would not want to incorporate within their latent images. So, life is training and training is life:

When I think of how weedy I used to look before I began training. I was this seven stone woman with flabby legs and no biceps and a stomach with loose skin because of having the kids. I don't want to go back to that.

(Claudia)

Out of all the hours in the week, work comes first and for most people home comes second, but for me the gym comes second place and home third. It has got to a point where nothing will stop me going training, unless it's life or death I will go to the gym and maybe do whatever else afterwards. But I will try and put everything off until the wekend.

(Sasha)

For years my legs have been the *horror* of my life. But all of a sudden all of my muscles have popped up. I know that it is because I've lost most of my body fat because of being on a low-fat diet for years, yeah? But it's also because I've been *training* them for about *seven* years to finally get something.

(Sheila)

And then you know, when you see a part of your body is good you make sure you keep it, you maintain it and improve it all the time and get the rest to match it.

(Celia)

TRANSGRESSIVE FEMININITIES AND THE BEAUTY MODEL

Tseelon asserts:

Femininity is ... a disarming disguise: it is donned like a masquerade to disguise the female's desire of the phallus (of power). Afraid to challenge the male who possesses the phallus directly, the woman deflects attention from her desire for power through its opposite: constructing a very feminine, non-threatening image of herself.

(1995: 37–8)

This makes sense in terms of sartorial and other forms of artifice. However, when a woman has a body which she has designed and created, which contradicts the norms of the beauty system, new desires are being made manifest. What is being made known is a challenge to the gaze of the other, because 'a being which is for-others cannot be authentically for-itself' (Tseelon, 1995: 38). 'Being for others' has to be rejected by the women because of the pejoratives attached to women who weight-train, which range from speculation about their sexuality, to being thought of as being too butch or addicted to exercise:

A lot of people don't see it as you controlling your body. A lot of people can't see that. They say she's addicted, she's addicted. They just see obsession. They see us as being fanatic women.

(Sheila)

We're fanatic because we want to *control* ourselves. Control the way you look, the way you feel because the way you look is important to you.

(Celia)

If a woman is for-herself, she has a power to control nature, to define herself, within her own personally defined boundaries. Through the body she has chosen to develop 'she risks censure for so deliberately transgressing the normative ideal for a natural female body' (St Martin and Gavey, 1996: 55) and subverts male power's definition of who she is or who she is capable of becoming. She rejects the phallus and actively challenges the gaze of the male other:

> When men see us they see threat and competition. They always want to arm-wrestle us when we go out socially. In fact we have even heard men say, 'there are those women I was telling you about', even when we don't know them. So we are obviously talked about. In the gym men seem to be amazed that we can and do lift so much, do so many chins and press ups, yet have stamina as well.
>
> (Brenda)

The ability of women weight-trainers to defy the beauty system and stand outside the male gaze, also must in itself mean the development of a particular sort of consciousness. This is not that consciousness which:

> ... refers to a particular kind of awareness: of being an object of the gaze of the other ... a realisation that I owe my existence to a reflection in the mirror that the other is holding out for me.
>
> (Tseelon, 1995: 55)

Rather, it is a consciousness in which a woman is holding out the mirror for herself, for her gaze, using the latent image of herself which she wants to make manifest through her bodily inscriptions to judge her own physique, while being also aware of the limitations imposed by genetic inheritance on that physique:

> When I look in the mirror or get measured I know that I am still not quite right. Still not quite what I want to be. My legs are too under-defined, although my stomach and top half are okay. I'm pleased with those. I am amazed that people see me as so muscular when I am not as built as I used to be in terms of size.
>
> (Alma)

> I have come to terms – only recently within the last two years – that you *cannot* change your basic bone structure or genetic shape. My parents both have short stubby legs. Who am I to think that by training I can lengthen and sculpt them to a long, thin pair? Ridiculous! I have now resigned to the fact that I can only play with what I've got – not what I haven't got. So my aim now is a little different. The woman's physique I see in my mind is more realistic, more achievable. That's what I look for in the mirror.
>
> (Sasha)

Yeah, especially when you reach that *peak* and you know when you look in the mirror one day – *for ages* you don't notice anything – then one day you look in the mirror and you think *whoah*, hang on a minute, where did that come from?

(Carol)

The women become their own significant audience, mediating between the reflection in the mirror, their gains or losses when they are measured, what is butch and over the top and what isn't, and their latent image, in order to make decisions about what parts of their body to sculpt, to shape as *they* desire. They construct themselves almost as art forms, from the inside out. Their inscriptions on their bodies then come to represent them. Their identities are not ruled by the symbolic violence of the gendered habitus and the tyranny of slenderness. Their uniqueness is never likely to be undermined either, because their inner discourse of the self, genes, physiology, diet and training regime means that their inscriptions are theirs. A woman who weight-trains then does not buy into the beauty model described by Tseelon (1995: 89), but into a self-constructed transgressive one. She does not relate to men through practices designed to make her more attractive. She seizes power by operating outside the system which would judge her on the femininity of her appearance. Her inscription, her body becomes the site of struggle over the power to define beauty. This is a struggle which women win through becoming bodied as *they* have defined.

MANAGING THE STIGMA OF BODILY INSCRIPTIONS

The issue of stigma ... [arises] ... only where there is some expectation on all sides that those in a given category should not only support a particular norm but also realize it.

(Goffman, 1984: 17)

Stigma – being marked as different because of the body which they choose to create – forms part of the women's views of how others see them:[3]

I tell you what I can't cope with right? Some of the women at the gym, they kind of look at you and you can see them thinking *flipping heck*, she's so *muscular*. Why does she want to look like that? I know I look better this way.

(Sasha)

Yeah, they look at you as if you're some sort of *freak*. I mean I take no notice of them because as far as I'm concerned it's what I want. But I *did* at *first* feel like a *freak*, especially when we went out and people were touching me and things. They still do touch me. At first I used to say, don't touch me. But now I know they're only appreciating what I've done. Okay I say thank you. You know it's a compliment. I used to think they were pointing and staring, but I've got over that now because what is more important is that I have chosen to change *me* and I like it.

(Carol)

The women get these reactions to their bodies because the definition and expansion of musculature, becoming bodied through hard training and a high-protein, high-carbohydrate, low-fat diet, are not positively represented within popular culture. To aim for muscles and definition, then, is to go beyond the realm of the feminine, to transgress, to go beyond the bounds of the socially acceptable.

As Goffman's analysis of stigma suggests, we tend to perceive our bodies as if looking into a mirror which offers a reflection framed in terms of society's views and prejudices. How do the women then manage stigma and still maintain a view of themselves as feminine, given their inscriptions? Both Carol and Sasha, above, give us some clue here. Each is comfortable with herself because: 'I have chosen to change *me* and I like it', and because 'I know I look better this way'. Further, they feminize the reality of what they see as their bodies evolve. After all, they are women, and this is what they have chosen to be, so whatever they are must be feminine. Essentialism is here, then, used strategically in defining their politics of the body. Being muscular, yet still a woman and still feminine, becomes central to their sense of self, as can be seen by looking at the women's views in the section on latent images above. The power of these images to define feminine beauty and thereby manage stigma, feminize and eroticize muscles now becomes manifest:

And don't you look *sexy*? Can't you dress around your body? I mean that's why I wear off the shoulder things. A woman with flabby arms and flabby shoulders just can't wear that. And believe me we do *look sexy*.

(Carol)

In managing stigma through the latent images of their body projects, muscles come to be redefined and feminized, removing the stigma of the 'butch' label produced by the gaze of the other. In Goffman's terms, although the women fail to live up to the prevailing ideals of 'the woman', to what is effectively demanded of them by the gendered habitus, they seem to be relatively untouched by this failing:

> insulated by [their] alienation, protected by identity beliefs of [their] own, [they] feel that [they are] … fully-fledged, normal human being[s] and that we are the ones who are not quite human. [They] bear a stigma but do not seem to be impressed or repentant about doing so.

(Goffman, 1984: 17)

In this way the women transgress by reflexively redefining the social world and their place as women who embody power within it.

PHYSICAL CAPITAL: EROTICIZING 'THE UNEROTICIZABLE' AS TRANSGRESSION

Despite the rise of the athletic body in consumer culture a clear division remains between acceptable and unacceptable forms of the female body. Large muscles remain unacceptable.

(Shilling, 1994: 66).

'Unacceptable' means unerotic to the male gaze as the woman's body with the most physical capital is thin, occupying as little space as possible, vulnerable and non-threatening. So why create physical capital which is value-less in heterosexual relationship stakes?

For women who weight-train and watch the changes in their bodies year on year there is a challenge to be faced. As their latent image of the body becomes manifest through their inscriptions, how do they eroticize muscles and zero body fat? Eroticizing 'the masculine' and feminizing it is not easy within a society in which transgressive femininities are not presented for public consumption except within the constructed boundaries of stereotype and caricature. Women with hard bodies appear within popular culture at the level of 'the warrior woman' as in *Terminator 2* and *Alien 3*; 'the predatory dyke' as in the leather-clad woman bodyguard 'Kara' in *Double Impact*; 'the extreme transgressive female' as with Grace Jones in *Conan the Destroyer*, *A View to a Kill* and *Boomerang*, and 'the woman who still looks like a guy even in a bikini, with long hair and makeup' as with Kimberley Ann Jones in the 1993 Volkswagen advertisement. A hard body is not yet 'girlie' enough and may never be considered erotic within popular culture.

It could be the case though that the 'body-builder's v' – which is to some degree the outcome of the training the women are involved in – which was once thought of as masculine, is now no longer gendered in such a clear way. Wide shoulders and narrow hips have been with us for some time in the power dressing of the 1980s which emphasized wide shoulders and de-emphasized breasts and bottoms. 'Tight buns' and 'buns of steel' are marketed repeatedly on exercise videos and exercise routines in books, magazines and friends' tips. Wide shoulders and narrow hips have become a possibility for latent and manifest images of a 'feminine' body, available for consumption by women. However, the women's experiences of the body unclothed is that it draws looks of dismay (e.g., Sasha, above) or amazed approval from both men and women because it is 'too masculine':

> I was out a couple of weeks ago with a friend of mine who I went to school with. Janet's tall, she's probably about 5′ 11″, slimmish but not muscular. Just *tall* and slim. She's beautiful. We were in this club. I had a suit on and I kept my jacket on until it was time to dance and I took my jacket off. The *amount* of people that I had come over to me and say, you look good, you look fantastic, yuh know, men and women. Women in the toilets were saying to me your body really looks good. I thought, yeah, at least they know the training I'm doing.
>
> (Carol)

Perhaps the key factor here is *whose gaze* and *whose image* is more significant to the woman in terms of defining her identity. Here Carol chooses the gaze of those who know the training she is doing to develop such a body. Their image and gaze are important considerations because 'in the capacity of an image the woman is placed as an object of male desire (to be idolised and either conquered or destroyed)' (Tseelon, 1995: 67). The women, though, create themselves as their own objects of desire, as is shown in the previous quote where Carol constructs her body in opposition to that of her beautiful friend's, as the body with the most physical capital in the club. The women also seem to be involved in making themselves their own objects of desire; they state that they are doing all this training for themselves:

> I mean I'm not doing it for the fellas, I'm doing it for myself.
>
> (Carol)

I couldn't have insisted on having a low fat diet all these years. I couldn't have insisted on having a diet which is like carbohydrate rather than sweet stuff all these years. I couldn't have done it if I wasn't doing it for myself.

(Sheila)

When the women's latent images of the physical self lead them to create transgressive femininities their relationships with men also change. The women decide on the sort of man with whom they are prepared to have relationships, usually ones who train or appreciate the work that has gone into producing their bodies. Men are, thus, placed as the object of the female gaze:

The guys I date though have to train as well. It's changed my outlook on men, I won't even look at one who doesn't participate in a sport of some kind. I know it sounds a bit selfish, but my thoughts are that I train my little heart out to look like this (no, I am not happy with the way I look), so if you think I'm going to date a couch potato or someone who props the bar up in a pub all the time, you've got another think coming! I really don't want to know at all if they don't do anything, no matter how good looking they are'.

(Sasha)

A woman, then, has to idolize herself, become the object of her own gaze, in order to maintain her commitment to training to achieve her body project given her production of the negative physical capital of bulky muscles:

Oh I'm confident to slip on a mini-skirt and walk down the road and feel good about it – even if I'm not as *slim* as the girl next door – because my legs aren't flabby, I've controlled it.

(Carol)

That's the thing though because I think that to a lot of women, right, women with muscles like us aren't sexy. So they think how can we dress so revealingly, you know what I mean? But we are sexy aren't we? We're *more sexy* because we have nothing *flabby* around and we are not emaciated looking.

(Sheila)

Her 'feminine erotic', then, is about being lean, muscular, able to wear what she wants, being in control and embodying that. Her inscription is partially in opposition to the category woman, thus disrupting the gaze of the other. In becoming the object of her own gaze she becomes powerful in being 'invisible as the source of gaze (that is, the one who is looking without being looked at)' (Tseelon, 1995: 68). She constructs herself through the power of her own gaze and in so doing eroticizes the uneroticizable. Women weight-trainers thus deny the importance of the male gaze in eroticizing them, as well as denying themselves as performers for these spectators. They perform for themselves and accept the gaze of those few men who know about being dedicated to a particular body project.

CONCLUSION

Bartky reminds us that:

> Femininity as a certain 'style of flesh' will have to be surpassed in the direction of something quite different, not masculinity, which is in many ways only its mirror opposite, but a radical and as yet unimagined transformation of the female body.
>
> (1990: 78)

Perhaps the women in my research are helping us to begin to see what this radical transformation could be like. Located within the discourse of femininity and musculature, women have to negotiate and challenge its style of the flesh in order to develop the bodies they desire. In making their bodies their signature, women take a view of the world which is one in which they give themselves the power to choose how to be. They decide what is feminine and 'the masculine' becomes a sliding signifier. Their signatures show their control over their physical being, their representation of their image is self-produced through the power of their gaze. In making these inscriptions women weight-trainers create a space where they attempt control over nature by co-opting an-other body. They defy the beauty model by being the objects of their own gaze, using as a judgement of worth their own latent images of the body. They manage stigma and negate their negative physical capital by identifying with their own latent images so that muscles are seen as erotic and feminine. Further, as women with physical strength and muscularity, which are traditional symbols of male power, they have power actually and symbolically invested in their bodies (Hargreaves, 1994). Through these bodily practices women are transforming the gendered habitus and thus creating identities for themselves which transgress the boundaries of 'masculine' and 'feminine'.

NOTES

1.   This research was undertaken through personal interest in 1996. The women who participated in the research ranged in age from 26 to 41 years and trained in gyms in Bradford, England. I would like to thank them for giving me access to their 'space' and allowing me to use their ideas and words. Pseudonyms are used for confidentiality.
2.   Gendered habitus – Habitus refers to the 'schemata of perception, thinking, feeling, evaluating, speaking and acting that structures all the expressive, verbal and practical manifestations and utterances of a person ... Habitus refers to a generative principle, not to a set of finite rules ... gender identity is a deeply rooted, bodily anchored dimension of an agent's habitus. It affects the individual in the most "natural" parts of his or her identity, as it concerns his or her body' (Krais, 1993: 169–70).
3.   Stigma – 'Society establishes the means of categorizing persons and the complement of attributes felt to be ordinary and natural for members of each of these categories' (Goffman, 1984: 11). 'The normal and the stigmatized are not persons but rather perspectives. These are generated in social situations during mixed contacts by virtue of the unrealized norms that are likely to play upon the encounter' (Goffman, 1984: 163–4).

REFERENCES

Bartky, S. (1990) *Femininity and Domination: Studies in the Phenomenology of Oppression* (London: Routledge).

Bordo, S. (1995) *Unbearable Weight – Feminism, Western Culture and the Body* (London: University of California Press).

Bourdieu, P. (1978) 'Sport and Social Class', *Social Science Information*, 17, pp. 819–40.

Bourdieu, P. (1984) *Distinction: A Social Critique of the Judgement of Taste* (London: Routledge).

Chernin, K. (1983) *Womansize: The Tyranny of Slenderness* (London: Women's Press).

Giddens, A. (1991) *Modernity and Self Identity: Self and Society in the Late Modern Age* (Cambridge: Polity).

Goffman, E. (1984) *Stigma – Notes on the Management of Spoiled Identity* (Harmondsworth: Penguin).

Hargreaves, J. (1994) *Sporting Females – Critical Issues in the History and Sociology of Women's Sports* (London: Routledge).

Henry, L. (1996) 'Evolution of an Ideal', *Muscle and Fitness*, September, pp. 162–6 and 207.

Krais, B. (1993) 'Gender and Symbolic Violence: Female Oppression in the Light of Pierre Bourdieu's Theory of Social Practice', in C. Calhoun, E. LiPuma, and M. Postone (eds), *Bourdieu: Critical Perspectives* (Cambridge: Polity).

Lloyd, M. (1996) 'Feminism, Aerobics and the Politics of the Body', *Body and Society*, 2(2), pp.79–98.

Mansfield, A. and McGinn, B. (1993) 'Pumping Irony: the Muscular and the Feminine', in S. Scott and D. Morgan (eds), *Body Matters: Essays on the Sociology of the Body* (London: Falmer Press).

Pugh, J. (1993) 'The Social Perception of Female Bodybuilders', in C. Brackenridge (ed.), *Body Matters: Leisure Images and Lifestyles* (London: Leisure Studies Association Publication No. 47).

Shilling, C. (1994) *The Body and Social Theory* (London: Sage).

3D (1996) Yorkshire Television, 20 June.

St Martin, L. and Gavey, N. (1996) 'Women's Bodybuilding: Feminist Resistance and/or Femininity's Recuperation?', *Body and Society*, 2(4), pp. 45–57.

Tseelon, E. (1995) *The Masque of Femininity* (London: Sage).

White, P., Young, K. and Gillett, J. (1995) 'Body Work as a Moral Imperative: Some Critical Notes on Health and Fitness', *Society and Leisure*, 18(1), pp. 159–82.

4 Marked Bodies, Oppositional Identities? Tattooing, Piercing and the Ambiguity of Resistance
PAUL SWEETMAN

INTRODUCTION

The last twenty to thirty years have seen a considerable resurgence in the popularity of tattooing and body piercing in the West, with tattooing, for instance, undergoing what some have called a renaissance (Tucker, 1981; Rubin, 1988; Sanders, 1989; Curry, 1993). This refers not only to the development of new designs and techniques, but also to tattooing's growing popularity amongst an increasingly diverse clientele. Although they may still form a large proportion of many professional tattooists' clients, the stereotypical image of the tattooee as young, male and working class is increasingly outdated as more and more men *and* women, of various age-groups and socio-economic backgrounds, choose to enter the tattoo studio (Rubin, 1988; Sanders, 1989; Curry, 1993; Blanchard, 1994; DeMello, 1995).

Body piercing, too, has become more and more popular over the last couple of decades, and again amongst an increasingly diverse clientele. In both cases, these trends have accelerated since the late 1980s, with increasing numbers of tattooees and piercees becoming heavily involved in either one or both forms of body modification. Such 'hardcore' body modifiers – some of whom have been termed 'Modern Primitives' (Vale & Juno, 1989; Myers, 1992; Curry, 1993; Dery, 1996; Eubanks, 1996; Klesse, 1997; Pitts, 1998) – have done much to popularize the new styles of tattoo and piercing which have emerged in recent years. On the tattoo side, these include Celtic and

Native American motifs, as well as a variety of other 'neo-tribal' designs based more or less directly on the indigenous tattoo traditions of Polynesia and elsewhere (Sanders, 1989; Curry, 1993; Dery, 1996) (see Plate 1). The last five to ten years have also seen tattooing and piercing partially incorporated into the world of fashion (Curry, 1993; Craik, 1994; Steele, 1996; Bellos, 1996). Numerous celebrities now sport tattoos and piercings, related imagery has featured in the work of designers such as Jean-Paul Gaultier, and advertisements in the style press frequently include photographs of tattooed or pierced models (Plate 2). In spite of this exposure, comments in the press and elsewhere suggest that such practices retain their widely held deviant connotations.[1]

The rise in the popularity of tattooing and piercing, and their adoption by an increasingly diverse clientele, has been paralleled within academia by an increasing interest in the body amongst social and cultural theorists. Within sociology, for example, writers such as Anthony Giddens (1991) and Chris Shilling (1993) have argued that the current popularity of practices such as dieting, 'keep-fit' and aerobics reflects a growing tendency to treat the body as a 'project' (Shilling, 1993) through which a sense of self-identity is both constructed and maintained. Whilst in traditional or pre-modern societies identity was relatively fixed, and the size, shape and appearance of the body accepted more or less as given, in late-, high-, or post-modernity, identity is increasingly fluid, and the body is mobilized as a plastic resource onto which a reflexive sense of self is projected in an attempt to lend solidity to the narrative thus envisaged. We are, in other words, increasingly responsible for the design of our bodies and selves (Giddens, 1991: 102).[2]

From this perspective, the rise of dieting, 'keep-fit' and other corporeally oriented practices or activities is a manifestation of the increasing tendency to treat the body as constitutive or expressive of the reflexively constructed self, and the growing popularity of 'nonmainstream body modification' (Myers, 1992) might similarly be argued to reflect this trend.[3] While certain writers have recently stressed the increasingly tight relationship between the body and identity, however, others have focused more on the body's status as a, if not *the*, primary site of disciplinary power relations in contemporary society, and, concomitantly, on the potential for embodied strategies of resistance (Bordo, 1992: 167).

Following Michel Foucault and others, numerous contemporary theorists have argued that it is the operation of power on and through the body, and its effects on the way in which the body is used, experienced and displayed, that leads to the creation of the normalized or disciplined 'body-subject' (Bartky, 1988: 71). Coercion is less important in this regard than the various forms of self-regulation or 'voluntary' inscription by which 'bodies are made amenable to the prevailing exigencies of power' (Grosz, 1994: 142).

This is arguably of particular importance from a feminist perspective. Sandra Bartky, for instance, notes that practices such as aerobics and making-up 'are part of the process by which the ideal body of femininity – and hence the feminine body-subject – is constructed', and that such 'voluntary' behaviours 'produce a "practised and subjected" body, ... *a body on which an inferior status has been inscribed*' (Bartky, 1988: 71; emphasis added). She also notes that: 'normative femininity is coming more and more to be centred on woman's body – not its duties and obligations, ... but its sexuality, more precisely its presumed heterosexuality and its appearance' (1988: 81). For Bartky, practices such as 'pumping iron' may be seen as an example of the 'experimentation with new "styles of the flesh"' (1988: 83) that is needed in order to resist 'conventional standards of feminine body display' (1988: 78).[4]

Rather than rehearse the theoretical arguments alluded to above, this paper will instead explore whether tattooing and piercing might also be seen as somehow resistant or subversive: whether, like Bartky's women body-builders, tattooees and piercees might also be said to be resisting normalized forms of appearance and subjectivity through the creative 'reinscription' of the body. In this way, such activities could be said to differ significantly from other forms of contemporary 'body project' (Shilling, 1993) – dieting, 'keep-fit' and so on – which, though also increasingly popular, are arguably intended, for the most part, to move those involved closer towards, rather than further away from, the hegemonic Western ideal, at least where the latter is conceived of as the youthful, slim and *unmarked* body at the heart of Western (consumer) culture (Lloyd, 1996; Bartky, 1988).

Drawing in part upon semi-structured interviews with a variety of male and female body modifiers,[5] this chapter focuses primarily on tattooing and piercing as a means of altering one's *appearance*. It should be noted, though, that in investigating the potentially resistant or subversive nature of such practices, a number of other areas might also be examined. These include the nature of the transaction between tattooist and tattooee, or piercer and piercee – which necessarily involves pain, blood and the penetration of the skin in a non-medicalized setting[6] – and, equally importantly, the functional side of body piercing (Sweetman, forthcoming: a). In contrast with tattoos, piercings are not only decorative, but can also significantly affect bodily sensations during sex or otherwise, potentially remapping the body's 'erotogenic sensitivity' (Grosz, 1994: 139) through the creation of newly sensitized surfaces, edges, ridges and orifices. In this sense, certain piercings might be said to lead to the creation of new 'bodies and pleasures' (Foucault, 1981: 157) – *outside the realms of normalized sexual discourse* – in the manner that theorists such as Foucault have suggested (see also Foucault, 1988).

As already noted, however, I intend here to focus primarily on tattooing and piercing as a means of altering one's appearance, asking whether contemporary body modification of this sort might be seen as resistant or subversive of normalized forms of appearance in the way that writers such as Bartky have advocated. For some commentators this would appear to be the case. David Curry (1993), for example, argues that the increased popularity of tattooing and piercing can be linked to a wider 'revolution in claiming the freedom to explore one's own body and to claim the territory discovered as one's own' (Curry, 1993: 76), suggesting that, as such, becoming tattooed or pierced can be seen as 'a political act and a sign of dissent' (1993: 82). Margo DeMello, looking more specifically at women's tattoos, argues that the decision to become tattooed is: 'a political as well as a personal statement, ... tattooed female bodies are an attempt to liberate the objectified body, literally inscribing it with alternative forms of power' (DeMello, 1995: 79).

The following, then, seeks to interrogate the assertions of Curry (1993) and DeMello (1995), first by asking whether tattooing or piercing may be said to be resistant or subversive *per se* and then by questioning the extent to which such practices might be argued to resist or subvert normative forms of *gendered* appearance.

TATTOOING AND PIERCING AS RESISTANT *PER SE*?

To begin with, it could be argued that *all* contemporary tattooing and piercing is in some ways subversive, regardless of additional factors such as the gender of the tattooee or piercee. In the first place, the tattooed or pierced body arguably stands in counter-hegemonic opposition to the 'natural', *unmarked*, bodily ideal at the heart of Western (consumer) culture (Featherstone, 1991; Falk, 1995: 100) which stigmatizes wrinkles, scars and other marks on the skin as signs of ageing, disease or decay. Permanent or 'semi-permanent' (Curry, 1993) modifications to the body are still regarded by many as a form of mutilation rather than decoration (Gamman and Makinen, 1994: 87), and in this sense, as has already been noted, practices such as tattooing and piercing could be said to differ significantly from such 'self-disciplinary' activities as dieting and 'keep-fit', each of which arguably represents a form of self-monitoring or self-regulation intended to move the body closer towards the youthful, slim, athletic ideal (Lloyd, 1996). It also places tattooing and piercing in marked contrast to cosmetic surgery, for instance, which is dedicated towards 'correcting' perceived imperfections in as invisible a manner as surgical techniques allow (Davis, 1995).

The explicit nature of the markings themselves means that the tattooed or pierced body might also be said to highlight the partially socially constructed nature of *all* bodies, thereby acting as a reminder that we all bear the inscriptions of gender, race and class, whether we chose purposefully to modify our bodies or not being beside the point. In this way, such forms of body modification can be said to resist or subvert the myth of the 'natural' body upon which a number of fundamental dichotomies of Western thought depend, not least the sexual binarism that constructs and naturalizes an unbridgeable chasm between male and female corporeality. This point is problematic, however, as the reverse might also be the case. In other words, it might also be argued that *in* explicitly marking the body, tattooing and piercing instead reinforces the notion that, as Frances Mascia-Lees and Patricia Sharpe put it, 'the unadorned, unmodified body is an unspoiled … surface on which culture works' (Mascia-Lees and Sharpe, 1992a: 3). This is also the opinion of Virginia Eubanks (1996), who argues that: '[t]he practices of Modern Primitivism – tattooing, piercing, branding, scarification – literalize the vision that the body is an unmarked surface on to which meaning can be inscribed and, therefore, must assume that all bodies are initially unmarked' (Eubanks, 1996: 79).

As indicated above, however, I would argue that as forms of self-inscription, tattooing and piercing might instead be taken as highlighting the way in which the body is always already a marked surface. Nevertheless, statements by various commentators on 'Modern Primitivism' do support Mascia-Lees and Sharpe's and Eubanks' position. Writing in V. Vale and Andrea Juno's highly influential text from 1989, for instance, David Levi Strauss suggests that: '[t]he unmarked body is a raw, inarticulate, mute body. It is only when [it] acquires the "marks of civilization" that it begins to communicate and becomes an active part of the social body' (Levi Strauss, 1989: 158; see also Myers, 1992: 299).

Whether or not such practices question or reinforce the notion of the body as a 'blank slate', however, tattooing and piercing can also be said to question or subvert a wide range of cultural boundaries and dichotomies, both literally and in a more metaphorical sense. Both practices, of course, violate the integrity of the body, questioning the notion of a bounded, enclosed self. Tattooing, for example, has been described by Elizabeth Seaton as a practice that involves 'visibly defiling boundaries, mixing ink with skin, shattering frames' (Seaton, 1987: 18; see also Blanchard, 1994). As one of my interviewees pointed out, it is thus 'a fairly surreal process': 'you know, you're sticking ink under somebody's skin and it's there for ever.' In this way, the practice can be said to raise serious questions over such fundamental oppositions as nature/culture, naked/clothed, and, in relation to the body, inside and outside. It also means that the tattooee can be seen as both subject and object of the modificatory procedure, worker and raw material, and – to at least some degree – 'artist and ... work of art' (Falk, 1995: 99).[7]

Piercing, too, in its penetration of the body with inert substances, which may then become, *in a felt sense*, part of the body, can be seen to question such distinctions as organic/inorganic, body/technology, natural and artificial (Wilson, 1990: 243; Falk, 1995: 99). In both cases, as 'matter out of place' (Douglas, 1984: 36), tattoos and piercings can be argued to represent 'dirt' as defined by Mary Douglas, their disquieting effect in this respect helping to explain the strong distaste both practices commonly arouse within Western culture, and why they are widely 'conceived of as a profanation of the flesh' (Falk, 1995: 100; see also Grosz, 1994: 192; Lupton, 1995: 110; Wilson, 1995: 249).[8] As Elizabeth Grosz points out, 'dirt' for Douglas, is anything that 'is not in its proper place, that ... upsets or befuddles order', and thus 'signals a state of possible danger to social and individual systems' (Grosz, 1994: 192).

In relation to specific forms of contemporary tattoo and piercing rather than tattooing and piercing across the board, it should also be noted that the increasing popularity of styles of body modification derived from non-Western cultures may signal more than simply a rejection of contemporary norms of appearance or the subversion of certain key dichotomies as outlined above. For many of those involved, particularly those who might be termed 'Modern

Primitives', the adoption of indigenous' tattoo motifs and piercings may be interpretable as an implicit rejection of contemporary cultural values, indicated by a desire to identify with, and be seen to identify with, the values and beliefs ostensibly associated with pre-modern European, Polynesian and/or North American cultures (see, for example: Levi Strauss, 1989: 158; Musafar, 1989: 9) (Plate 1). Amongst my own interviewees, one lightly tattooed informant, for example, noted that her feather design was a reflection of her admiration for 'Native American culture' and her 'disillusionment with the way the world's going at the moment', while another, heavily tattooed, but lightly pierced male interviewee told me: 'it is really a sympathy with tribal societies and some of the simpler ways of thinking that they have which has caused me to take up tribal tattooing'.

Once again, however, this position is not without its ambiguities. As Mascia-Lees and Sharpe point out in relation to the use of Japanese imagery in the film *Tattoo*, 'this use of the East in a naïve ideology of authenticity is part of the same tradition in the West which has constructed '"the Orient" as the exotic' (Mascia-Lees and Sharpe, 1992b: 154). Rather than representing a simple and unqualified celebration of non-Western culture, 'neo-tribal' tattooing might instead be seen as a form of cultural imperialism, such plundering of other cultures itself reinforcing the notion of the non-Western as 'other'. The appropriation of techniques and imagery from a global scrapbook of design sources and procedures might also be argued to represent little more than the continued incorporation of 'the exotic' into the 'supermarket of style' (Polhemus, 1995; see also: Craik, 1994: 25; Steele, 1996: 160–1). According to Virginia Eubanks: 'Modern Primitivism is Benetton multi-culturalism, "I'd like to buy the world a Coke" liberalism, the brotherhood of consumption' (Eubanks, 1996: 87; see also: Klesse, 1997; Pitts, 1998).

For Eubanks, 'Modern Primitivism's' naïve appeal to an 'authentic', non-Western Other is problematic in part because it relies on 'the conception of One History, that of the West, overpowering and destroying the Eden that is the rest of the world' (Eubanks, 1996: 76). The movement can also be criticized for its essentialism, statements in key subcultural texts suggesting, for example, that contemporary tattooing and piercing represents the *'return of the repressed primitive'* (Dery, 1996: 278; original emphasis).

Whilst these criticisms are valid, however, a couple of additional points should also be made. In the first place, the views of key figures such as Fakir Musafar (see, for example, Musafar, 1989)[9] are not necessarily shared by the majority of contemporary body modifiers: the influence of 'Modern Primitivism' as a philosophical position is far more obvious in the United States than in the UK, for instance, and few of the British body modifiers interviewed during the course of this research had much of an interest in the term or what it implies. In addition, of those who did express an interest in the term, several also offered their own criticisms along similar grounds to those voiced above. The interviewee quoted earlier, who saw his tattoos as an expression of his 'sympathy with tribal societies', for instance, also noted that his feelings about such societies were 'probably quite wrong and idealistic'. Another, heavily tattooed and pierced interviewee told me that she considered it 'very dangerous' to think that a 'tribal' design would in any way connect the tattooee with those amongst whom such forms of body modification were traditionally practised, adding that, for her, the appropriation of such designs was a form of cultural 'tourism'.[10]

There are, then, considerable ambiguities associated with the notion of tattooing and piercing as resistant or subversive *per se*. Before moving on to consider tattooing, piercing and questions of gender, it is also worth noting the sense in which tattoos and piercings, particularly those placed on easily visible areas, might on the one hand be said to be resistant of normalized forms of appearance, but on the other be seen as a form of self-limitation (e.g., writing oneself out of particular employment prospects or other forms of social interaction). As before, however, this point retains a certain ambiguity in that such *self-imposed* limits may also be seen as a way of taking control of one's situation. Dick Hebdige, for instance, refers to facial tattooing as a way of 'throwing yourself away *before They do it for you*' (Hebdige, 1988: 32, emphasis added; see also Seaton, 1987: 21), while, in his novel *Miracle of the Rose*, Jean Genet notes that:

> in days of old, on the galley, pirates had those frightful ornaments all over their body, so that life in society became impossible for them. *Having willed that impossibility themselves, they suffered less from the rigour of fate. They willed it, limited their universe in its space and comfort.*
>
> (Genet, in Brain, 1979: 159–60; emphasis added)

Few interviewees saw their tattoos or piercings in *precisely* these terms, but several noted, for example, that if their tattoos prevented them from entering certain occupations, or forestalled potential relationships, then those were jobs, or partners, that they wouldn't have wanted anyway. A number of interviewees also emphasized the way in which tattoos, in particular, acted as an indelible connection with their own past. One lightly tattooed, 21-year-old interviewee, for example, told me that he regarded the two Native American designs on his upper-arms as 'a commitment to [him]self' in that 'you cannot run away from them, you can't stop being a tattooed person'. He explained that:

> By marking yourself I thought I could ... keep ... what I felt when I was eighteen, nineteen, for the rest of my life, 'cause I'd always re-member the time. Because having a tattoo done is such a special thing ... [and] just looking at them reminds me of that time. And hopefully it will stop me from forgetting who I am, when life starts to get, you know, kick the door in a bit more. The older you get, mortgage, kids, whatever.

In this sense, becoming tattooed can be argued to commit the tat-tooee to a particular narrative, and another interviewee described his numerous tattoos as an indelible 'diary' that 'no one can take off you'. The permanence of tattoos is important in this regard, helping to explain their popularity as a way of fixing or anchoring the self in late-, high-, or post-modernity (Blanchard, 1994: 296; Mellor and Shilling, 1997: 61; see also Sweetman, forthcoming: b), but equally pointing to the limits becoming tattooed imposes upon further attempts to reflexively revise one's sense of self through attention to the body's surface. Interviews with various young body modifiers suggest that this is one of the main reasons for *piercing's* growing popularity in relation to tattooing: most piercings leave little trace once the jewellery is removed.[11] When asked whether he had ever considered getting a tattoo, one lightly pierced, 20-year-old student, who was concerned about the image he might project to future employers, replied:

> No. [And] that was another consideration for getting the [nipple] piercing done over something like a tattoo, in that if I ever get fed up with it, it just comes out and heals over. Whereas if I had a tattoo, it's not really something I can just, at a moment's notice, ... just take off, and be rid of completely.

TATTOOING, PIERCING AND *GENDER*

Moving on to questions of gender, while all tattoos and piercings may to some extent be said to be resistant of contemporary norms of appearance, the predominantly masculine connotations of tattooing in Western culture mean that certain forms of tattoo might equally be argued to reinforce, rather than subvert, traditional gender distinctions, albeit along class-specific lines. This is perhaps particularly true of the 'traditional' designs characteristic of the 'International Folk Style' (Rubin, 1988), the masculine connotations of tattooing in general being heightened in the case of 'macho-motifs' such as panthers or eagles applied to the biceps or forearms. Following Grosz, one might argue that such forms of tattoo 'are oppositionally used to produce male bodies as virile [and] strong ... in relation to women's passive [and] weak ... bodily structure' (Grosz, 1990: 73; see also Seaton, 1987: 20).

This is certainly the reading suggested by much contemporary advertising material, such as the Katherine Hamnett advertisement shown in Plate 2, and that traditional tattoos retain their longstanding masculine connotations, to the extent that they might be argued to be central rather than incidental to the construction of a particular form of masculine identity, is further evidenced by their appropriation by many female-to-male (FTM) transsexuals. As photographs in a recent edition of the gay magazine *Attitude* demonstrate, along with beards and appropriate clothing, extensive upper-arm tattooing can allow the wearer to present a strongly codified masculine exterior, whatever his prior identity (Smyth, 1995).

Several of my own male interviewees also suggested that their tattoos were motivated in part by a desire to enhance their masculinity. As one heavily tattooed, professional informant in his early forties put it:

> I don't think getting tattoos [is] going to make me Charles Atlas, of course [it's] not, but it rather takes the attention away from the err, less desirable parts of my physique.

Others were less sanguine in acknowledging that such considerations formed part of their motivation to become tattooed. One heavily tattooed and pierced interviewee in his mid-twenties, for instance, noted that 'a big sort of design, like a tribal design, can make a man look a bit more masculine', but added 'not that that's ... a good reason to get it done'. To the extent that tattooing *is* employed as a means of bolstering the tattooee's own sense of masculinity, however, it might be argued to represent a form of 'homoevestism' (Gamman and Makinen, 1994: 65), and the rising popularity of tattooing, like body-building, be linked to the oft-cited 'crisis in masculinity'. At least one interviewee explicitly regarded tattooing as an alternative to working-out in terms of its effect on one's appearance:

> you know like, you can to the gym for years and get big and muscly, and [have] everyone say, 'Oh, he's beautiful', or you can just go and get a tattoo. ... So, you known, you don't have to be some big gym queen to look good, you can just get tattooed instead.

That is not to suggest that all male tattooing reinforces rather than subverts prevailing notions of masculinity however. The camp appropriation of 'traditional' tattoo motifs into gay iconography, for instance, might be interpreted as an ironic gesture, a parody of straight masculinity that subverts and undermines the conventional associations and connotations of this particular type of body modification. Such a reading is clearly implied by a series of recent advertisements for Jean Paul Gaultier products, one of which (for 'Le Male' perfume) features two heavily eroticized, tattooed sailors, arm-wrestling over a bottle of the scent in question (*Guardian*, May 4 1996), and while certain of my gay interviewees, like the man quoted above, favoured bold, 'tribal' designs that might be described as 'hyper-masculine' in terms of their effect on the tattooee's overall appearance, others explicitly opted for homoerotic designs, or parodic variations on standard motifs (see Plate 3). One heavily tattooed and pierced interviewee, for instance, had recently acquired a large panther on his thigh, which – whilst a classic design in every other respect – had been coloured in pink rather than the standard black, thereby subverting the motif's otherwise macho associations.

It is also worth noting at this stage that *despite* Western tattooing's predominantly masculine connotations, there is an extent to which it might be described as subversive of *middle-class* conceptions of masculinity given the feminization of adornment and decoration that gathered momentum during the nineteenth century (Sawchuk, 1987: 64; Ewen, 1988: 129; Tseëlon, 1995). *All* tattooing can be regarded as irrational or 'extra-rational' ornamentation – and thus as 'feminine' – when viewed from the perspective of the rational, utilitarian aesthetic expounded, amongst others, by design critics such as Adolf Loos during the late-nineteenth and early part of this century. Indeed, Loos himself was expressly critical of tattooing, which – like Cesare Lombroso (1896) – he regarded as atavistic, and a mark of either cultural inferiority as practised in non-Western contexts, or of degeneracy or criminality as practised in the West (Ewen, 1988: 127–9).

Tattooing can thus be seen as a 'classed', 'raced', and gendered practice, its masculine connotations belying an association with the feminized 'other' (see Guest, 1992).

Such considerations notwithstanding, male *body piercing* is perhaps more unambiguously resistant of contemporary norms of masculinity than tattooing, in part because of its sexual uses and connotations, but also because of the predominantly feminine connotations of all forms of jewellery in Western culture. Certain piercings are arguably more resistant of masculinized norms than others, however. Whatever their potentially transgressive *effects* (Sweetman, forthcoming: a), male genital piercings, for instance, may be said to *symbolically* reassert the significance of the most heavily valorized zone of the phallically oriented body. Nipple and navel piercings, on the other hand, can be said to involve not only a remapping of the body's 'erotogenic sensitivity' (Grosz, 1994: 139), but also to symbolically highlight, or draw attention to, 'feminine' parts of the body that would otherwise remain 'phallically disinvested' (1994: 201) (see Plate 4). In considering Plate 4, however, it should be noted that the men's *facial* piercings also contribute to their feminized or androgynous appearance, and the feminizing potential of facial piercing is also suggested by a recent advertisement for Gap clothing, where a close-up of the face of a blonde, long-haired male model is juxtaposed with a photograph of the same figure standing amongst a group of remarkably similar looking women (*The Face*, October 1996). In this case, the male model's lip-piercing, or labret, is again associated with an almost androgynous appearance, or at least a relaxed form of masculinity that stands in opposition to the macho use of tattooing apparent in the advertisement of Katherine Hamnett Denim (see Plate 2).

As Plates 3 and 4 suggest, then, certain forms of men's body modification might be argued to challenge existing norms of masculinity. At first glance, women's tattooing is arguably far more resistant or subversive, however, not only because of tattooing's continued masculine connotations, but also because of the gendered nature of the hegemonic, unmarked body (see Plate 5). According to DeMello:

> Tattooed women overstep the physical boundaries of their bodies by permanently modifying them, and they overstep the boundaries of femininity by embodying a formerly masculine sign. ... Out of bounds and openly mocking categories of class and gender, the

tattooed female body represents a critique of middle-class values ... rejecting middle-class assumptions about the body, and in particular, female bodies.

(DeMello, 1995: 77)

Again, this reading can be supported by reference to contemporary advertising material, a recent advertisement for Smirnoff, for example, explicitly labelling women's tattooing as of 'the other side' (*Elle*, May 1994). More interestingly, perhaps, a recent advertisement for Calvin Klein's 'unisex' perfume, 'One', features the model Jenny Shimizu, her upper arm tattoo clearly visible, in a pose which clearly distinguishes her from the other men and women in the advertisement, strongly associating her, as a short-haired *tattooed* woman, with the 'unisex' perfume being sold (*The Face*, October 1995).

As DeMello further notes, women's tattoos can also be seen as resistant to the extent that they act as a means of controlling the viewer's gaze, 'forcing men (and women) to look at their bodies in a manner that keeps them in control' (DeMello, 1995: 74; see also Blanchard, 1994: 294–5). As one heavily tattooed and pierced interviewee in her early thirties put it:

> a lot of people say, 'Ooh, do you do that to shock people?' And I don't really do it to shock people, but I don't like being chatted up and stuff like that, yeah? And I like the feeling, when I go out and I look the way I do, that I get left alone, by, well not by everybody, but by the type of people that would normally chat women up. You know, they tend to sort of think, 'Oh Christ,' you know, 'I won't go and talk to her, she looks a bit mental or something.'

Having been asked whether she was, through her extensive tattoos and piercings, deliberately setting out to reject the conventionally feminine, the same woman replied:

> Yeah, I suppose I am really. It's like, in my particular case, ... I was made to be feminine, and to look like that, and wear the frilly dresses and skirts and stuff like that, as part of [my husband's] process of weakening me, yeah? And now, I perceive women, ... I perceive women that look like that to, to be weak.

As the above quote also indicates, like certain of Sanders' (1989: 43) and Myers' (1992: 282) informants, the interviewee in question saw her extensive body modification not simply as a rejection of the conventionally feminine, but also as a way of regaining control of, or 'reclaiming', her body, following the dissolution of a 'violent marriage' which had seen her denied the freedom to be who she 'really was' (see also Gallina, 1989: 105). Another, lightly tattooed but heavily pierced interviewee in her forties noted that, for her, becoming tattooed and pierced was a way of reasserting control over her body following adolescence and motherhood:

> I suppose it gives me a feeling of control over my body. I've been through all these, you know, all the adolescent things, and I've had my children, and now my body's just mine ... to do what I want with. And I think it's like a way of ... asserting control. And I'll do what I want, and I don't care if other people find it unpleasant or whatever.

Once again, however, there are difficulties in describing women's tattooing as subversive or resistant without further qualification. In the first place, while many contemporary female body modifiers choose designs that would generally be perceived as carrying masculine connotations, many do not, instead opting for what are explicitly regarded as either 'gender-neutral' or 'feminine' motifs. These include the traditional roses and butterflies of the 'International Folk Style' (Rubin, 1988), as well as contemporary designs that tend to be more 'ornate' than those favoured by most male tattooees (see Plate 6).

Indeed, most of the tattooed women interviewed for this study explicitly distinguished between masculine and feminine designs, with one young lightly tattooed and pierced community worker describing the feather design on her back as follows:

> it's not a feminine symbol, but it's not a definitely masculine symbol either. Whereas a rose would definitely be something I'd think of as being feminine. But 'cause it's helped me with my self-confidence and helped me with my looking on my body image as being something better than it was, then I think it's probably helped my femininity rather than hindered it or whatever.

As this quote suggests, a further difficulty with describing women's tattoos as resistant *per se* is that although they may be seen as empowering, a form of self-inscription that involves asserting control over the body, such marking is often sought or enjoyed not as a means of subverting hegemonic notions of femininity, but in order to detract from or disguise perceived deficiencies in relation to this hegemonic ideal.

1. Gail and Mark; tattoos by Steve Graves and others.

2. Katherine Hamnett Denim advertising campaign (1995); tattooist(s) and models unknown.

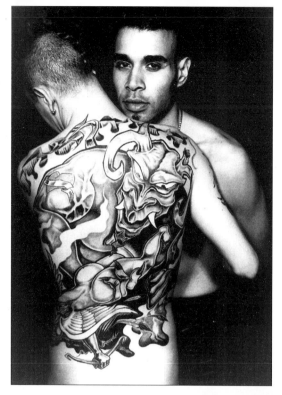

3. Steve and Sultrix; tattoos by Bugs.

4. Christian and Danilo; piercer(s) unknown.

5. Julie; tattooist(s) unknown.

6. Kathy; tattoos by Bugs (back) and Fiona Long (arm).

Like certain of the male interviewees, while several female body modifiers told me of their increased confidence as a consequence of being tattooed or pierced, many also referred to their improved body-image along the following lines:

> it gives you a bit more, as well, so ... you don't have to worry ... so much that you haven't got the catsuit figure, if you see what I mean. 'Cause ... you know, you've got other stuff for people to look at, so they don't have to look at your body.

As DeMello points out, then:

> it could be argued that, contrary to empowering women, tattoos contribute to their further objectification in a male-dominated society. Many women claim that their primary motivation for becoming tattooed is to make themselves more beautiful or sexy. Even as more women wear tattoos, many still only wear obviously 'female' tattoos so that their femininity (or heterosexuality) is not at risk.
>
> (DeMello, 1995: 76–7)

Two additional problems with describing women's tattoos and piercings as unambiguously resistant or subversive are, first, the way in which, instead of allowing the woman in question to 'control the viewer's gaze', they may instead place the body on display as an object of voyeuristic fascination (DeMello, 1995: 77). Interestingly, Robert Bogdan notes that part of the appeal of tattooed women in nineteenth- and early-twentieth-century freak shows 'was that in order to show their tattoos they had to expose parts of their bodies ... which under any other circumstances would have been lewd if not illegal' (Bogdan, 1988: 251). While the sense of illegality no longer applies, and while it is, I think, somewhat problematic to draw comparisons between contemporary tattoo conventions and the 'ten in one' shows of the past, my own observation at such gatherings in the UK confirms DeMello's point that the exposure of (female) flesh remains a strong attraction for many (male) attendees at tattoo conventions today (DeMello, 1995: 77).

Second, whatever the intention of the tattooee or piercee as author of her own embodied text, she will be unable to control the readings, or interpretations, ascribed to her body markings by the viewer in question. As Elizabeth Seaton notes in respect of tattooing:

> the ... tattoo is animated not only by the movement of the skin or the tension of contradictions which it embodies, but by the spectator's

active gaze; a gaze which not only receives passively that which is projected, but which actively contributes to that which is already there.[12]

(Seaton, 1987: 21)

Both of the above points are illustrated by the following quote from the heavily tattooed and pierced interviewee, who, as noted earlier, saw her various body modifications as a rejection of the conventionally feminine:

> if I go to like a bikers' pub, you know, it's OK 'cos it's perfectly accepted there. But, erm, ... suppose you're going out for a drive somewhere and you see a pub and think, 'I'll just pop in for a pint', ... you get all these people staring and making rude comments, you know, and they, sort of, keep looking at you. They're quite loud about their comments, you know, they don't, sort of, talk quietly, and I just find it really insulting.

The same interviewee told me that she found 'stereotyping very irritating', adding that 'a lot of people ... don't even bother to find out what sort of person you are, or listen to anything you've got to say, they just look at you and think "aggressive", and that's it'. She also noted that a lot of people immediately assume she is gay, which, whilst not problematic, she none the less finds rather strange: 'You know why? ... just because I've got like a shaved head and tattoos, ... why would that make me a lesbian? It's really odd.'

Such responses confirm the way in which the appearance of the interviewee in question embodies a challenge to conventional, heterosexual constructions of femininity. At the same time, however, they also illustrate Susan Bordo's point that 'most people ... have no problem accommodating data which *should* subvert their assumptions to *fit* their prevailing organization of reality' (Bordo, 1992: 173; original emphasis). The labelling of contemporary body modifiers in terms of their *presumed* character traits or sexuality, in other words, is illustrative of the way in which the tattooee or piercee's intended reading may be ignored, overlooked, or simply go unrecognized by those intent on pigeonholing them in a particular 'identity-category'.

Paradoxically, perhaps, this suggests that it may be more resistant or subversive for women to 'mix and match' tattoos and piercings with typically feminine items of dress, for example, than assume a wholesale transformation which, whilst apparently more dramatic, none the less allows the observer to slot the body modifier in question into an easily assimilated niche. Various writers have recently stressed the *power* of ambiguity, or of acts 'that challenge our practices of reading, *that make us uncertain about how to read*' (Butler, 1994: 38; emphasis added; see also Sawchuk, 1987: 75). At the same time, however, this point raises the whole difficulty of assessing the subversive or resistant potential of *any* form of body modification in isolation when the way it is read will depend in part upon the tattooee or piercee's *overall* appearance – or the syntagmatic relationship between the tattoo or piercing and those other features that contribute to the body modifier's look as a whole – *as well as* the attitude that the observer brings to bear upon the corporeal ensemble in question (Simon-Miller, 1985: 73).

A further but related point is that the subversive or resistant potential of such forms of body modification – as with any other aspect of one's appearance – will also depend upon the contexts in which it is displayed (Gamman and Makinen, 1994: 65). Whilst most interviewees – male *and* female – had developed a variety of strategies to ensure that they had some choice over when and to whom their tattoos or piercings were revealed, certain contexts demand that all but the most intimately sited forms of body modification are publicly displayed. One 25-year-old credit analyst told me that she frequently encountered what she perceived to be unpleasant reactions to her tattoos when getting changed in the gym after work. Another, heavily tattooed and pierced informant, also in his mid-twenties, told me that reactions to his tattoos depend 'on the environment', and that while they can be successfully concealed at work, he had been subject to particularly 'disapproving looks' when swimming with his four-year-old daughter at the local pool.

CONCLUSION

As I hope to have indicated then, while there are several ways in which contemporary forms of body modification might be described as resistant or subversive, such an interpretation is not without its problems. In part this is because of the polysemic nature of such forms of corporeal inscription (Blanchard, 1994: 290). Nevertheless, and in spite *or because of* the considerable ambiguities noted above, I would still suggest that, at present, the practices in question retain some potential to act as forms of counter-hegemonic self-inscription, resisting, subverting, or undermining contemporary gendered norms of appearance. In this way, tattooing and piercing stand in opposition to the wide nexus of practices – dieting, 'keep-fit', aerobics and the like – which, whilst potentially empowering, are arguably intended to move those involved closer towards, rather than further away from, the hegemonic bodily ideal (Bartky, 1988: 66; Lloyd, 1996).

While certain writers have criticized contemporary body modifiers for what is perceived to be their self-absorbed apoliticism (Dery, 1996: 276), and while such forms of bodily resistance might be seen as relatively minor expressions of 'dissent' (Curry, 1993: 82) when compared with other forms of political activity, I would argue, following Foucault, that such dismissals are misconceived: 'nothing will be changed if the mechanisms of power that function outside, below and alongside the state apparatus, on a much more minute and everyday level, are not also changed' (Foucault, 1980a: 60; see also Cohen and Taylor, 1992: 159–60).

In common with participants in other recent studies directed towards the investigation of 'spectacular style' (Muggleton, 1997: 5), few of the informants interviewed during the course of this research were willing to label their own involvement in contemporary body modification as expressly 'political' (Gottschalk, 1993: 368; Muggleton, 1995: 3–4; Muggleton, 1997: 5). As David Muggleton also points out, however, '[t]o claim that one's appearance is a "message" would, in fact, be tantamount to an admission of in-authenticity' (Muggleton, 1997: 7; see also Muggleton, 1995: 4), and *whether or not it is expressly viewed as such*, the adoption of an unconventional or nonconformist appearance can still be regarded as an example of the 'small-scale postmodern resistance which [has] emerged in the decline of political metanarratives' (Muggleton, 1997: 9).

It should also be noted that whilst the 'politics of aesthetic representation' may share few affinities with more conventional forms of political struggle, the two are by no means 'mutually exclusive' (Butler, 1994: 38; see also Cohen and Taylor, 1992: 25). Indeed, as writers such as Elizabeth Wilson have suggested, it may be that the one leads to the other, in part through the establishment of 'a space in which the normative nature of social practices ... may be questioned' (Wilson, 1990: 233). Either way, like Jeff Ferrell's (1993) graffiti writers, contemporary tattooees and piercees are certainly involved in a creative cultural practice, which 'confronts the aesthetics of authority' (Ferrell, 1993: 178), through the construction of 'an alternative, street-wise aesthetic' (1993: 173).

In conclusion, however, it should be noted that, in addition to the various ambiguities noted above, a further difficulty in labelling tattooing and piercing as potentially resistant practices concerns their ongoing 'recodification [and] recolonization' (Foucault, 1980b: 86). No cultural field is ever static (Seaton, 1987: 22), and in the case of contemporary tattooing and piercing, continued changes in status are arguably ensured not only by what Ted Polhemus and Lynn Proctor would refer to as the process of 'fashionalization' (Polhemus and Proctor, 1978: 64), but also, in the case of tattooing, by the continued and deliberate effort of many involved to have the practice re-appraised as a legitimate form of art (Blanchard, 1994: 292; Sanders, 1989: 35).

As well as illustrating certain dominant readings of such practices, the advertisements discussed above are also illustrative of the continued incorporation of tattooing and piercing imagery into the world of fashion, and to the extent that they *are* becoming fashionable, contemporary tattooing and piercing might be described as just another element in the 'supermarket of style' (Polhemus, 1995). This is certainly the opinion of one or two commentators (Craik, 1994: 25; Steele, 1996: 160–1), and numerous writers have recently suggested that 'in postmodern times ... the proliferation and commodification of "difference"' (Bordo, 1992: 172) is all but inevitable (see also Emberly, 1987: 59; Sawchuk, 1987: 73; Cohen and Taylor, 1992: 138). Whatever the popularity of relevant *imagery*, however, and however much such practices are divorced from their marginal or deviant connotations, certain features intrinsic to both tattooing and piercing arguably militate against their full incorporation into Baudrillard's 'carnival of signs' (Tseëlon, 1995: 124). As American tattooist Don Ed Hardy points out, whilst 'there *are* elements of fashion to it' (Hardy, 1989: 58), '[i]t's on your body, it's permanent; you have to live with it; and it hurts' (1989: 61; see also Sweetman, forthcoming: b).

Finally, however, I would also suggest, following Seaton (1987: 22–4), that there are considerable problems involved simply with naming cultural practices as resistant or subversive, however cautious one is in so doing, and however alive to the inevitable ambiguities involved. In writing about such practices, in naming, delineating, and incorporating such practices into academic discourse, one inevitably limits their potential as polysemic, creative and semi-autonomous fields of cultural production.

ACKNOWLEDGEMENTS

I would like to thank Graham Allan, Simon Blyth, Sasha Roseneil and Chris Schilling for commenting on earlier versions of this chapter (or parts thereof), and the Department of Sociology and Social Policy at the University of Southampton for supporting the wider study of which it forms a part. Thanks are also due to those who raised comments or suggestions at the various sessions during which the paper was first presented (including the 1997 BSA Annual Conference), to all the interviewees quoted above, and to numerous others who have helped with my research in some way, shape or form. Special thanks go out to Ashley, and to Nick Vinson at Katherine Hamnett, for providing the photographs. The usual disclaimers, of course, apply.

NOTES

1. Amongst the police, for instance, Malcolm Young's 'An Inside Job' suggests that 'the very idea of "tattoo" equals' criminal (Young, 1991: 160), while the columnist Theodore Dalrymple argued recently in *The Sunday Times* that the association between tattooing and criminality 'is so strong that one suspects burglary, theft and assault are caused by a long-acting virus that lodges in the brain, having entered the body via the tattooing needle' (Dalrymple, 1995: 3). Less specifically, when showing my fieldwork photographs to colleagues and others, I have frequently encountered comments such as: 'I wouldn't want to meet them on a dark night', and 'Why would *anyone* do that to themselves?'
2. The turn to the body also reflects wider anxieties, and the sense, for example, that if we can't control our external environment, we can at least exercise some control over 'the size, shape and appearance' of our bodies (Shilling, 1993: 7). It has been exacerbated, moreover, by our increasing *ability* to manipulate the body through technological and other means, and by the body's growing importance as 'a bearer of symbolic value' within contemporary consumer culture (1993: 3).
3. Like the forms of 'body project' considered by Chris Shilling, for example, tattooing and piercing have the effect of transforming the

exterior surfaces of the body 'in line with the designs of its owner', and can also allow a 'wholesale transformation' of the body along these lines (Shilling, 1993: 3). When compared with traditional body modification in non-Western contexts, contemporary tattooing and piercing are also far more individuated practices, to which those involved are, for the most part, drawn as a matter of individual choice rather than out of conformity to established patterns of behaviour associated with either religious beliefs or tradition in a wider sense.

4. For more critical appraisals of women's bodybuilding, which raise a number of ambiguities surrounding the practice similar to those that this paper considers in respect of tattooing and piercing, see: St Martin and Gavey (1996); Mansfield and McGinn (1993). See also Tate (Chapter 3 of this volume).

5. The chapter forms part of a wider study on contemporary body modification, for which in-depth, semi-structured interviews were conducted with 35 tattooed and/or pierced informants, as well as with several professional tattooists and body piercers. The study also draws on observation conducted at a number of tattoo conventions and tattoo and/or piercing studios, as well as analysis of the popular literature devoted to the forms of body modification in question.

   15 of the 35 tattooees and/or piercees interviewed were women, and ages ranged from 19 to 40 amongst the women, and 20 to 60 amongst the men. The mean ages for each group were 24 and 32 respectively. Occupations ranged from the unemployed and students to credit analysts, local government officers and company directors. Around 40 per cent of the women and 70 per cent of the men were heavily tattooed and/or pierced, which generally implies that they had three or more of either form of body modification. This is a fairly loose definition, however: several standard ear-piercings, for example, would not place someone in the heavily pierced category, while someone with a full backpiece as their sole tattoo would certainly be counted as heavily tattooed.

6. As Marc Blanchard notes, for instance, 'there is something in tattooing which *escapes the flow of commodification*' (Blanchard, 1994: 292; emphasis added). Tattooing remains 'artisanal' because, while tattoo *designs* can be mass-produced, 'the replication of the tattoo [is] contingent upon its siting on the body of a specific subject' (1994: 292). In combination with increasing requests for one-off, *custom* designs, such factors limit

> the possibility that the relation between producer (the tattooist) and consumer (the tattooee) could be entirely subject to the laws of the market. On this point, at least for now and waiting for tattooing chains on the model of beauty parlor chains, *the modern tattooed body remains a precapitalist body*.
>
> (Blanchard, 1994: 292; emphasis added)

Whilst not describing his body as 'precapitalist', at least one of my interviewees appears to have been motivated to become tattooed for the these very reasons. Talking first about his relationship with the tattooist, he noted:

> it was like we were working together rather than just going and getting something done. Which is the way ... life is nowadays; you just go ... for what you want and it gets done. And someone else can get exactly the same thing. Everybody's got ... the same clothes, you know what I mean? ... There's no individuality any more. ... And, in a way, I had them done because they were ... the one personal thing I could ever have that was totally mine, that no one else could have.

7. The latter point should not be overemphasized: where standardized tattoo designs or piercings are employed, the tattooee or piercee plays little part in *this* stage of the creative process, and except in cases of self-tattooing or piercing, relies on the skill of the tattooist or piercer during the process of application.

8. Tattooing is expressly prohibited in the Bible (Leviticus 19:28; see Govenar, 1988: 210), and Pasi Falk (1995) notes that Kant, for instance, believed that 'primitive' body-marking might be considered beautiful were it not permanently etched into the flesh (Falk, 1995: 101). For their part, several interviewees told me that relatives and others had reacted disapprovingly to their tattoos or piercings, not simply because of their aesthetic qualities, their permanency, or the procedures involved, but because they considered such practices to be 'anti-Christian' and/or 'unnatural'.

9. For academic commentaries, see Myers (1992); Dery (1996); Eubanks (1996); Klesse (1997); Pitts (1998).

10. An additional point is that those who do position tattooing and piercing as in some way 'authentic' practices tend to refer to their inherent qualities – pain, blood and the penetration of the skin, for instance – over and above any association with non-Western cultures. Commenting on the diverse mix of 'subcultural types' present at annual conventions such as *Tattoo Expo*, for instance, one interviewee told me that he felt the lack of trouble could in part be attributed to the fact that everyone present had undergone the same process, and that all tattoos were thus equally 'authentic':

> you can't, well you *can* buy it, but you can't like, go to the shop and try it on and say, 'I'll have one of them', and just walk out with it. You've gotta sit there for hours and put up with the pain. So even if you're really rich, if you can't stand the pain, you can't get tattooed. So it's like something that everyone's been through, whether you've got loads of money or not.

11. This is not true, however, of 'stretched' piercings – where the diameter of the piercing is gradually enlarged and in the case of ear piercings, for instance, can reach upwards of three or four centimetres – and it should also be noted that many standard piercings leave a permanent scar, the extent of such scarring dependent on a variety of factors such as the success – or otherwise – of the initial healing process.

12. As Susan Bordo points out, the ' "subversion" of cultural assumptions ... is not something that happens *in* a text or *to* a text. It is an event which takes place (or doesn't) in the "reading" of the text' (Bordo, 1992: 171; original emphasis).

REFERENCES

Balsamo, A. (1995) 'Forms of Technological Embodiment: Reading the Body in Contemporary Culture', *Body and Society,* 1(3–4): 215–37.

Bartky, S. L. (1988) 'Foucault, Femininity and the Modernization of Patriarchal Power', in I. Diamond and L. Quinby (eds), *Feminism and Foucault: Reflections on Resistance* (Boston: Northeastern University Press).

Bellos, A. (1996) 'As British as S&M', *Guardian,* 6 November.

Blanchard, M. (1994) 'Post-Bourgeois Tattoo: Reflections on Skin Writing in Late Capitalist Societies', in Lucien Taylor (ed.), *Visualizing Theory: Selected Essays from V.A.R., 1990–1994* (New York and London: Routledge).

Bogdan, R. (1988) *Freak Show: Presenting Human Oddities for Amusement and Profit* (Chicago and London: University of Chicago Press).

Bordo, S. (1992) 'Postmodern Subjects Postmodern Bodies', *Feminist Studies,* 18(1), pp. 159–75.

Brain, R. (1979) *The Decorated Body* (London: Hutchinson).

Butler, J. (1994) 'Gender as Performance: an Interview with Judith Butler', *Radical Philosophy,* 67, pp. 32–9.

Cohen, S. and Taylor, L. (1992) *Escape Attempts: The Theory and Practice of Resistance to Everyday Life,* 2nd edn (London: Routledge).

Craik, J. (1994) *The Face of Fashion: Cultural Studies in Fashion* (London: Routledge).

Curry, D. (1993) 'Decorating the Body Politic', *New Formations,* 19, pp. 69–82.

Dalrymple, T. (1995) 'The Way of All Criminal Flesh', *Sunday Times,* 6 August.

Davis, K. (1995) *Reshaping the Female Body: The Dilemma of Cosmetic Surgery* (New York and London: Routledge).

Dery, M. (1996) *Escape Velocity: Cyberculture at the End of the Century* (London: Hodder and Soughton).

DeMello, M. (1995) 'The Carnivalesque Body: Women and Tattoos', in The Drawing Center, *Pierced Hearts and True Love: A Century of Drawings for Tattoos* (New York/Honolulu: The Drawing Center/Hardy Marks Publications).

Douglas, M. (1984 [1966]) *Purity and Danger: An Analysis of the Concepts of Pollution and Taboo* (London: Routledge).

Emberly, J. (1987) 'The Fashion Apparatus and the Deconstruction of Postmodern Subjectivity', in A. Kroker and M. Kroker (eds), *Body Invaders: Panic Sex in America* (New York: St Martin's Press).

Eubanks, V. (1996) 'Zones of Dither: Writing the Postmodern Body', *Body and Society,* 2(3), pp. 73–88.

Ewen, S. (1988) *All Consuming Images: The Politics of Style in Contemporary Culture* (US: Basic Books).

Falk, P. (1995) 'Written in the Flesh', *Body and Society*, 1(1), pp. 95–105.

Featherstone, M. (1991) 'The Body in Consumer Culture', in M. Featherstone, M. Hepworth and B. Turner (eds), *The Body: Social Process and Cultural Theory* (London: Sage).

Ferrell, J. (1993) *Crimes of Style: Urban Graffiti and the Politics of Criminality* (New York and London: Garland Publishing).

Foucault, M. (1980a) 'Body/Power', in C. Gordon (ed.), *Michel Foucault: Power/Knowledge – Selected Interviews and Other Writings, 1972–1977* (Brighton: Harvester Press).

Foucault, M. (1980b) 'Two Lectures', in C. Gordon (ed.), *Michel Foucault: Power/Knowledge – Selected Interviews and Other Writings, 1972–1977* (Brighton: Harvester Press).

Foucault, M. (1981) *The History of Sexuality*, vol. I: *An Introduction* (London: Penguin).

Foucault, M. (1988) 'Sexual Choice, Sexual Act: Foucault and Homosexuality' (interview), in L. Kritzman (ed.), *Michel Foucault: Politics, Philosophy, Culture – Interviews and Other Writings, 1977–1984* (London: Routledge).

Gallina, R. (1989) 'Raelyn Gallina' (interview by A. Juno), in V. Vale and A. Juno (eds), *Re/Search no.12: Modern Primitives – An Investigation of Contemporary Adornment and Ritual* (San Francisco: Re/Search Publications).

Gamman, L. and Makinen, M. (1994) *Female Fetishism: A New Look* (London: Lawrence and Wishart).

Giddens, A. (1991) *Modernity and Self-Identity: Self and Society in the Late Modern Age* (Cambridge: Polity Press).

Gottschalk, S. (1993) 'Uncomfortably Numb: Countercultural Impulses in the Postmodern Era', *Symbolic Interaction*, 16(4), pp. 351–78.

Govenar, A. (1988) 'The Variable Context of Chicano Tattooing', in A. Rubin (ed.), *Marks of Civilization: Artistic Transformations of the Human Body* (Los Angeles: Museum of Cultural History/University of California, LA).

Grosz, E. (1990) 'Inscriptions and Body-maps: Representations and the Corporeal', in T. Threadgold and A. Cranny-Francis (eds), *Feminine, Masculine and Representation* (Sydney: Allen & Unwin).

Grosz, E. (1994) *Volatile Bodies: Towards a Corporeal Feminism* (Bloomington and Indianapolis: Indiana University Press).

Guest, H. (1992) 'Curiously Marked: Tattooing, Masculinity, and Nationality in Eighteenth-Century British Perceptions of the South Pacific', in J. Barrell (ed.), *Painting and the Politics of Culture* (Oxford: Oxford University Press).

Hardy, D. (1989) 'Don Ed Hardy' (interview by A. Juno and V. Vale), in V. Vale and A. Juno (eds), *Re/Search no. 12: Modern Primitives – An Investigation of Contemporary Adornment and Ritual* (San Francisco: Re/Search Publications).

Hebdige, D. (1988) *Hiding in the Light: On Images and Things* (London: Routledge).

Klesse, C. (1997) 'The Representation of Primitivism in a Specialised Sexual Subculture', unpublished paper presented at 'Body Modification', at TCS conference, Nottingham Trent University, June 1997.

Levi Strauss, D. (1989) 'Modern Primitives', in V. Vale and A. Juno (eds), *Re/Search no. 12: Modern Primitives – An Investigation of Contemporary Adornment and Ritual* (San Francisco: Re/Search Publications).

Lloyd, M. (1996) 'Feminism, Aerobics and the Politics of the Body', *Body & Society*, 2(2)' pp. 79–98.

Lombroso, C. (1896) 'The Savage Origin of Tattooing', *Popular Science Monthly*, April, pp. 793–803.

Lupton, D. (1995) 'The Embodied Computer/User', *Body & Society*, 1(3–4), pp. 97–112.

Mansfield, A. and McGinn, B. (1993) 'Pumping Irony: the Muscular and the Feminine', in S. Scott and D. Morgan (eds), *Body Matters: Essays on the Sociology of the Body* (London: Falmer Press).

Mascia-Lees, F. E. and Sharpe, P. (1992a) 'Introduction: Soft-Tissue Modification and the Horror Within', in F. E. Mascia-Lees and P. Sharpe (eds), *Tattoo, Torture, Mutilation, and Adornment: The Denaturalization of the Body in Culture and Text* (New York: State University of New York Press).

Mascia-Lees, F. E. and Sharpe, P. (1992b) 'The Marked and the Un(re)Marked: Tattoo and Gender in Theory and Narrative', in F. E. Mascia-Lees and P. Sharpe (eds), *Tattoo, Torture, Mutilation, and Adornment: The Denaturalization of the Body in Culture and Text* (New York: State University of New York Press).

Mellor, P. and Shilling, C. (1997) *Re-forming the Body: Religion, Community and Modernity* (London: Sage).

Muggleton, D. (1995) 'From "Subculture" to "Neo-Tribe": Identity, Paradox and Postmodernism in "Alternative" Style', unpublished paper presented at 'Shouts from the Street: Culture, Creativity and Change' MIPC Conference on Popular Culture, Manchester Metropolitan University, September 1995.

Muggleton, D. (1997) 'Resistance or Difference? Expressive Individualism, Alienation and Subcultural Disengagement', unpublished paper presented at 'Power/Resistance', BSA Annual Conference, University of York, April 1997.

Musafar, F. (1989) 'Fakir Musafar' (interview by V. Vale and A. Juno), in V. Vale and A. Juno (eds), *Re/Search no. 12: Modern Primitives – An Investigation of Contemporary Adornment and Ritual* (San Francisco: Re/Search Publications).

Myers, J. (1992) 'Nonmainstream Body Modification: Genital Piercing, Branding, Burning, and Cutting', *Journal of Contemporary Ethnography*, 21(3), pp. 267–306.

Pitts, V. (1998) 'Provoking the Organic: Representations and Resistance in Extreme Body Marking', unpublished paper presented at 'Making Sense of the Body', BSA Annual Conference, University of Edinburgh, April 1998.

Polhemus, T. and Proctor, L. (1978) *Fashion and Anti-Fashion: An Anthropology of Clothing and Adornment* (London: Thames and Hudson).

Polhemus, T. (1995) *Streetstyle: From Sidewalk to Catwalk* (London: Thames and Hudson).

Rubin, A. (1988) 'The Tattoo Renaissance', in A. Rubin (ed.), *Marks of Civilization: Artistic Transformations of the Human Body* (Los Angeles: Museum of Cultural History/University of California LA).

Sanders, C. (1989) *Customizing the Body: The Art and Culture of Tattooing* (Philadelphia: Temple University Press).

Sawchuk, K. (1987) 'A Tale of Inscription/Fashion Statements', in A. Kroker and M. Korker (eds), *Body Invaders: Panic Sex in America* (New York: St Martin's Press).

Seaton, E. (1987) 'Profaned Bodies and Purloined Looks: The Prisoner's Tattoo and the Researcher's Gaze', *Journal of Communications Inquiry*, 11, pp. 17–25.

Shilling, C. (1993) *The Body and Social Theory* (London: Sage).

Simon-Miller, F. (1985) 'Commentary: Signs and Cycles in the Fashion System', in M. R. Soloman (ed.), *The Psychology of Fashion* (Lexington, MA: Lexington Books).

Smyth, C. (1995) 'What Makes a Man?', *Attitude*, January, pp. 32–6.

St Martin, L. and Gavey, N. (1996) 'Women's Bodybuilding: Feminist Resistance and/or Femininity's Recuperation?', *Body & Society*, 2(4), pp. 45–57.

Steele, V. (1996) *Fetish: Fashion, Sex and Power* (New York and Oxford: Oxford University Press).

Sweetman, P. (forthcoming: a) 'Only Skin Deep? Tattooing, Piercing and the Transgressive Body' in M. Aaron (ed.), *The Body's Perilous Pleasures* (Edinburgh: Edinburgh University Press).

Sweetman, P. (forthcoming: b) 'Anchoring the (Postmodern) Self? Body Modification, Fashion and Identity', *Body & Society*.

Tseëlon, E. (1995) *The Masque of Femininity: The Representation of Woman in Everyday Life* (London: Sage).

Tucker, M. (1981) 'Tattoo: the State of the Art', *Artforum* 19(9), pp. 42–7.

Vale, V. and Juno, A. (1989) *Re/Search no. 12: Modern Primitives – An Investigation of Contemporary Adornment and Ritual* (San Francisco: Re/Search Publications).

Wilson, E. (1990) 'These New Components of the Spectacle: Fashion and Postmodernism', in R. Boyne and A. Rattansi (eds), *Postmodernism and Society* (Basingstoke: Macmillan).

Wilson, R. W. (1995) 'Cyber(body)parts: Prosthetic Consciousness', *Body & Society*, 1(3–4): 239–59.

Young, M. (1991) *An Inside Job: Policing and Police Culture in Britain* (Oxford: Clarendon Press).

5 Active Women, Power Relations and Gendered Identities: Embodied Experiences of Aerobics
LOUISE MANSFIELD and JOSEPH MAGUIRE

This chapter draws on an ongoing research project which aims to further an understanding of the significance of sport and exercise in the lives of women. Our principal aim here is to examine the embodied experiences of women who participate in aerobics (exercise to music). Drawing on evidence from participant observation and interviews, the significance of the techniques, practices and rituals of women in an aerobics class are mapped out. In particular we discuss issues of gender power relations in the context of aerobic exercise and explore how women's identities are shaped and practised in and through the exercise experience. In this respect, our work confirms studies conducted over the past decade (Scraton, 1987; 1992; Cole, 1993; Hall, 1996; Morgan and Scott, 1993; Shilling, 1993; Birrell and Cole, 1994; Hargreaves, 1994; Tseëlon, 1995; Young and White, 1995; Woodward, 1997).

Our analysis is informed by aspects of feminist thought and figurational (process) sociology. In another paper we examine in more detail the contribution that a synthesis between feminist scholarship and figurational sociology can make to exploring complex questions of gender power relations (Maguire and Mansfield, 1999). Here, we emphasize that our pro-feminist position recognizes the active role that women play in interpreting the gender power networks generated by the aerobics class. We want to let these women speak about the significance of exercise in their everyday lives. Like Markula (1995) we recognize the importance of hearing their private voices and allowing them a more public place to express themselves. The fundamental principle of a figurational approach is that it is dynamic and relational. It focuses on studying social processes over time and is concerned with understanding the networks of human interaction in social contexts.[1] Framing the feminist questions in this chapter, several conceptual tools from figurational sociology have informed our analysis. These include a relational and dynamic conception of power, the theory of established–outsider relations and the concepts of habitus, identity formation and I/We images. We explore these concepts in more detail throughout the chapter.

We analyse the aerobics class as an exercise figuration. The concept of the figuration is a key analytical tool of figurational sociology. It represents a network of interdependent, mutually oriented people. We view aerobics as a social sphere where women's experiences and identities are contoured. That women are active in interpreting and maintaining this figuration and their sense of self-identity is important. But an intricate web of factors including the influence of education, the family, the media and commodification processes are at work both within the aerobics class and in the wider social context in which women live out their lives. A system dominated by a patriarchal ideology of which these women are relatively unaware, but which they nevertheless encounter, can be identified. We are well aware that we do not capture these complexities in their entirety but relevant aspects of this network of processes are addressed throughout our analysis. Emphasizing that 'aerobicizing' women (Markula, 1995) do not completely submit to the forces at work, the focus of the discussion is that they embody both the enabling and constraining features of aerobics. There is a sense in which aerobics is an enjoyable activity for some women. On a weekly basis, participating in aerobics is an opportunity for these women to meet their friends, talk and escape from the daily pressures presented to them at work and by their partners and children. But established ideals of femininity dominate the body work in which they engage. This was highlighted by Elaine, who explained how she felt about exercise and her body.[2] She said:

> I became so obsessed with the fact that I wanted to be thin and so I didn't hardly eat anything ... and I exercised a lot and I just thought that if I became thin everything would be a lot better. ... When I lost weight I did some fashion modelling and you become aware that you have to be really thin for the clothes and there is an emphasis on bodies from the media and expectations of what women

should look like and that made me want to prove a point and show that I could model clothes just like people thought was ideal.

This statement supports the notion that an exercise discourse such as aerobics can be a means through which women are persuaded to manipulate their bodies for the expression of patriarchal values (Cole, 1993). That is, to some extent, the exercise class is viewed by these women as a tool for achieving the acceptable slender, toned 'look' which we term the 'body beautiful'. Obtaining this 'look' is a fundamental part of these women's gendered identities. Achieving the body beautiful is inextricably interconnected with the construction, development and maintenance of a feminine identity. These women have an intense desire to look and feel feminine and they embody Western ideals of femininity which they encounter in and through aerobics and their wider lived experiences.

These introductory comments highlight that women are active in attaching meaning to the images and messages symbolized in the aerobics class in question. Not wishing to portray women as a homogeneous whole, we highlight differences in experience between the women in the group. All of these women embody both the repressive and liberating features of aerobics, but in varying degrees. For some there is a pleasurable dimension to aerobics. But the extent of resistance to dominant ideals of femininity is submerged by the reinforcement of the need for women to conform to the slender female 'look'.

Given these observations, the aims of this analysis are two-fold. First, we seek to examine the complex and dynamic network of gender/power relations generated by and characteristic of the aerobics class. We elaborate on a specific power dynamic occurring in the micro-context of the aerobics class. In doing so our analysis is informed by the Eliasian concept of established–outsider theory (Elias and Scotson, 1994). Contributing to our analysis of power balances between dominant and non-dominant groups, established–outsider theory is particularly useful in explaining the processual influences that afford greater power chances to particular groups within the aerobics class. Using this concept we explore the balance of power between the sexes and trace the pattern of gender/power relations in a broader social framework. In addition we highlight that body image, use and appearance are interrelated with the construction of gendered identities. Analysing the development of gendered identities we make connections between established–outsider relations, I/We images and aerobic exercise. We emphasize that aerobics is significant in the construction and practice of an exercise identity and is intertwined with the development and maintenance of feminine identities. Before presenting our interpretation and analysis of the significance of aerobics to the women in our study, we explore some of the literature that is concerned with women's bodies, exercise and gendered identities.

FEMALE BODIES, EXERCISE PRACTISES AND GENDER/POWER RELATIONS

Traditionally the body has been overlooked in sociology and the sociology of sport (Loy, 1991; Maguire, 1993). Sociological analyses have tended to adopt a disembodied approach and until recently bodies have remained a secondary concern in social theory (Loy, 1991; Turner, 1991; Shilling, 1993). However, several authors highlight that sociological explorations of the body are important if we are to further an understanding of the relationships between nature, culture and society (Featherstone *et al.*, 1992; Turner, 1992, 1996; Morgan and Scott, 1993; Shilling, 1993, 1997; Lupton, 1996).

Individuals in society are continually judged by their appearance, and our everyday experiences present us with all manner of ways to alter and control our bodies. The exercise regime is one practice of the 'self' that 'inscribes' or 'writes' upon the body, marking it with sociocultural messages that are interpreted by others (Lupton, 1996). Deborah Lupton's work on food, embodiment and subjectivity explains that bodily practices are adopted as part of an individual's project to contour, shape and express the self. Responding to external messages concerning bodily control people recognize specific discourses as crucial to self-regulation. For Lupton (1996) food habits are central to the disciplining of the body. Strict dietary routine, often in connection with a specific exercise programme, demonstrates high self-control. The achievement of a slimmer body is the outward sign of self-discipline. In discussing the body, health and eating disorders, Benson (1997) also highlights that the body is intertwined with the development of gendered identities. Emphasizing that the most powerful image of femininity in Western culture is that of the thin, lithe and tight body she explains that women discipline their bodies in accordance with social norms of femininity. Slender female bodies are inscribed with a feminine identity. The slim, toned woman is held in high regard in contemporary society. Poorly disciplined bodies 'do not count for much' (1997: 41) and fat bodies symbolize a failure to achieve an ideally feminine self. Cole (1993) explores the way in which bodies and exercise practices are rooted in a type of biopolitics. Female bodies reflect societal power and gender relations. Cole (1993) highlights that the significance of exercise is to optimize the internal and external female body according to dominant patriarchal norms of femininity. Sport and exercise regimes define femininity in narrow terms according to societal ideals of thinness and tone.

There are certainly connections between a feminine appearance and the construction of a feminine identity. Women's bodies are disciplined and controlled and provide a foundation on which to construct a sense of self and indeed group identity (Maguire, 1993; Shilling, 1993). Identity is developed in reciprocal relationships between individuals and social contexts (Burkitt, 1991). Exploring the interdependent relationships between human beings Shilling (1993) explains that it is only in relation to others that a sense of self can be developed. He harnesses the concept of the 'civilizing process' in understanding what it is to be an embodied person. The historical development towards more controlled behavioural and emotional acts involves wide and diverse changes in standards of conduct for the body. In particular there has been an increase in thresholds of shame, embarrassment, and repugnance. 'Civilized' bodies are characterized by internal pacification, rationalization, self-restraint and regulation. We wish to suggest that these historical transformations are illustrative of specifically gendered civilizing practices. Symbolizing societal values, female bodies are 'civilized' within a patriarchal organizing framework. Shilling's (1993) account of civilized Western bodies makes it readily apparent that female bodies and feminine identities are socially managed. 'Civilized' female bodies are symbolized by a rationalized command of the techniques, practices and rituals of exercise and by bodily appearance (Shilling, 1993). In addition, the way in which people perceive themselves to be similar to and different from others in a group is influenced by reflection and articulation of emotional feeling towards pertinent group characteristics (Mennell, 1992). The women in this study internalized a dominant and common aspiration to be slim and toned. This is fundamental to becoming an established aerobics participant. Slenderness speaks of femininity. These women's sense of feminine self is contoured by a group desire to achieve the body beautiful. As Bordo (1993) notes, slenderness is intertwined with the 'inner state of the self'. Bodily appearance is symbolic of personal order and disorder. On this basis a woman's body size and shape is a sign of her emotional, moral or spiritual self-identity (Bordo, 1993).

Several other studies have explored the experiences of women in physical activity. In their conversations with female body-builders, Miller and Penz (1991) highlight that women's expertise in 'body work' can be used as a political tool to colonize a male preserve. To some extent these women rejected conventional ideals of feminine beauty. Perceiving their bodies as their own terrain, they remodelled their appearance in their own image. Nevertheless, Miller and Penz (1991) note that female body-builders do conform to the traditional pressure that uses female bodies as a site for 'corrective action'. These women still engage in the rational reconstruction of their bodies. That body-building is a site of feminist resistance and feminist recuperation is explored by St Martin and Gavey (1996) and Obel (1996). Obel (1996) agrees with St Martin and Gavey (1996) and Miller and Penz (1991) that the muscled bodies of women who body-build challenge traditional notions of femininity. Yet, at the same time, differential rules and judging criteria for women reinforce dominant notions of what it is to be feminine. For St Martin and Gavey (1996) there is a transgressive potential in this type of female activity. But in competitive events, female body-builders cannot be 'too bulky'. Judging criteria for women incorporate the notion that the size of their muscles must be balanced with displays of feminine deportment, shape and attitude. To stay within the bounds of femininity competitive women body-builders wear extensive amounts of make-up, dye their hair blond and often undergo surgery for breast augmentation (Obel, 1996; St Martin and Gavey, 1996). Despite displaying highly muscled bodies which can be interpreted as resistant to feminine ideals, these women were still 'shaped into femininity' via the rules of competitive body-building.

In her work on women and aerobics, Markula (1995) confirms that the motivation for women to participate is to achieve thinness. 'Aerobicizing' women control their bodies within narrow limits because they are persuaded that the thin body is liberating. Her study is insightful because she identifies a complex of ambiguities in the 'postmodern aerobicizing female body'. For Markula, participating in aerobics classes it is not *simply* a case of attaining a thin body. These women's bodies must also possess enough muscularity to look athletic. Like Lloyd (1996), Markula (1995) explains that women are not able to ignore the sociocultural images of feminine beauty. That is, women are controlled by their own awareness of the privileges of the body beautiful. This supports the ideas of Featherstone *et al.* (1992) in their work on the body in consumer culture. The view here is that the body beautiful has exchange value. It is status-enhancing and brings with it the perception of youth, health, happiness, heterosexual attractiveness and longevity. Agreeing that understanding the discourses of diet and exercise is complex, Lloyd (1996) views aerobics as one practice of feminization that contributes to women's sense of self-identity. Although Lloyd (1996) recognizes that there are many reasons for women's participation in aerobics, the focus on weight loss and the construction of a slender body is oppressive. This is what Kim Chernin (1981) calls the 'tyranny of slenderness' and it is this notion that negates the pleasure of physical activity.

OBSERVING AND INTERVIEWING ACTIVE WOMEN

In this study we set out to understand what aerobics meant to women in the context of their everyday experiences. As we have previously noted, women are active in interpreting their experiences in social settings. On this basis our analysis of the aerobics exercise class gives priority to what these women have to say. The research aimed to achieve a balance and blend between involvement and detachment (Maguire, 1988; Dunning, 1992). That is, we recognize that it is not possible to produce research which is detached in an absolute sense (Dunning, 1992). Social scientists cannot escape being 'involved' in social life. Indeed, in order to understand how social actors view their social world, they have to be involved. Yet by being too involved the researcher can 'go native'. As a way of understanding the views of different group members located in the aerobics class (figuration) in question, the researcher must adopt a 'detour via detachment' approach. A two-way dialogue between involvement and detachment is required. The initial formulation of the research idea was grounded in discussions of research on the body, the emotions, sport and society. Several key theoretical concepts from figurational (process) sociology and feminist scholarship guided the female researcher's initial involvement. She actively participated in the aerobics classes, observed the exercise practices that the women engaged in and talked to some of them informally as well as in the more formal interview sessions. A degree of detachment from the research context also occurred when both authors conducted an ongoing exchange of views about observation and interview material and of theoretical concepts and issues. There was a dynamic and shifting relationship between involvement and detachment throughout the study. This allowed theoretical themes to emerge from the data which informed our discussion of the exercise experiences of these women.

The evidence in this study was obtained by combining the strategies of in-depth interviews and participant observation. The women interviewed and observed participated in aerobics at a public leisure centre in a small market town in the English East Midlands. Both interviewing and observing were conducted by the female author. Mindful of the need to ensure internal dialogue, the authors conducted regular reviews concerning observation and interview technique, and undertook frequent examinations of emerging themes and issues. A participant as observer role ensured an openness about the intention to observe, report and publish an account of what was seen (Bryman and Burgess, 1994). This role also allowed the female observer to 'stand back' from the research setting. That is, she was detached in order to establish a more precise pattern in the actions and emotions of the women.

A total of 35–40 women were observed during 6 months of research. Performing some of the classes, the researcher took frequent breaks for further observation at different positions in the dance studio and for fieldwork note-taking. The themes and theoretical insights that emerged from the observer field notes were interwoven with the themes and issues of the interviews. The interview transcripts presented confirming and additional evidence which helped to clarify observation data. Rather than being preoccupied with specific interview rules, a semi-structured style of interviewing was adopted, aiming for a two-way conversational flow. Depersonalized interviews restricted to a one-way flow of responses were felt to be intimidating to the interviewees and would create a barrier to the acquisition of information (Roberts, 1983). Like other feminist writers we recognize that interactive interviewing acknowledges the subjective experiences of women and allows them to express their opinions in their own words (McRobbie, 1982; Hargreaves, 1994; Hall, 1996; McDermott, 1996). Two major themes were explored via interviewing. The first focused on body image and included questions about ideal images, self-perceptions and the perception of others. The second concerned body management, and more specifically the practices, techniques and rituals of bodily control that the women adhered to. Five pilot interviews were conducted with women from the aerobics class in question. This enabled the female researcher to 'get a feel for' building a rapport with the women, to ensure a logical flow of questions and to assess the duration of interviews. Sixteen interviews, lasting between 45 minutes and 1 hour each, were completed during the 6-month observation period. The respondents presented different perspectives concerning their embodied experiences. Therefore, the agenda of questions was not followed in a strict order, but allowed a flow appropriate to each case. The process was flexible and aimed to develop a rapport with, and confidence in, those who were interviewed, so that they could develop full and honest answers. Each interviewee gave permission to record the interviews and these were transcribed verbatim. Recurring themes and contradictory data were examined, allowing an interweaving between theory and evidence. Our grounded analysis is presented in the following sections where we analyse the characteristics and nature of the aerobics class and the significance of this exercise discourse in the daily lives of the women who were interviewed and observed.

AEROBICS AND ESTABLISHED–OUTSIDER BODIES

The established–outsider concept was derived from a study of two neighbourhoods in the English East Midlands (Mennell, 1992; Elias and Scotson, 1994). The ideas pertaining to power balances between dominant and non-dominant groups are particularly useful to studying the power dynamics in the micro-context of the exercise class. Examining aerobic exercise, established–outsider relations explain the processual influences that afford greater power chances to specific groups of 'aerobicizing' women. Established women are relatively empowered in the aerobics context via access to exercise knowledge, increased fitness and the achievement of acceptable bodies. These characteristics differentiate higher-status women from lower-status women in the group. Yet the women who participated in this exercise discourse were not isolated human beings. Their exercise experiences were interconnected with the way in which they lived out their lives. Higher-status women hold a relatively privileged position in the dance studio. In addition, the achievement of the body beautiful is revered in a broader social landscape. Empowered by obtaining an ideal appearance, however, these women are also oppressed in their pursuit of the social body They are involved in the reconstruction and improvement of their 'imperfect' bodies. They are persuaded that thin, toned bodies signify femininity and they embody established patriarchal values concerning what women's bodies should look like (Hargreaves, 1994; Benson, 1997).

The established group in the exercise class we observed comprised 10 women, whereas the outsider group consisted of 25–35 women. The established women formed a relatively stable unit showing little diversity in its composition. The women in question were predominantly 'white', and the established unit consisted entirely of 'white' women. There was one Chinese and one Indian woman in the classes observed. The women interviewed represented both the established group and the outsiders. They ranged in age from 19 to 50 years, with the insider group aged between 22 and 36 years. Of the women interviewed, six were married and two were divorced. Seven stated that they were single, although each of these spoke of current or previous boyfriends, reflecting the dominance of heterosexuals. The socioeconomic background of these women was diverse. Those who exercised in the established group stated their occupations as: tanning shop assistant; student; housewife; gym instructor; teacher; safety officer; and personnel manager. The occupations of the outsider group interviewed were: shelf filler; personnel assistant; library assistant; student; receptionist; and executive.

The dominant group represented an elite clique of individuals who gravitated towards each other, striking up conversations in sub-cliques. Yet these cliques were not static or fixed. A fluid set of relations existed within the established group. These women mingled and 'danced' with different established members. One could almost see them forming a dynamic figuration of bodies (Elias and Dunning, 1986). They communicated verbally and acknowledged each other with smiles, nods and waves, engaging in a 'reciprocal exchange' of signs and symbols (Maguire, 1995). Exploring the dance studio in terms of what Maguire (1995) has described as a 'living labyrinth', we interpret this space as a stage for the expression of these women's embodied feelings and actions. To an extent this female space provides the performers with a sense of place in which there is the possibility that they can freely experience their bodies. Yet this space is by no means isolated from the broader social messages about female body ideals. These wider social influences impact upon the way in which these women strive to contour and shape their own bodies. The dominant aspiration is for the slim, tanned, toned 'look'. Intensely aware of their own and others' bodies they gazed at others and surveyed themselves in the mirror. Moving in close proximity to each other, established individuals also distanced themselves from outsiders by congregating in a close-knit group, which dominated the front of the dance studio. This was illustrated by Jane, an established member of the group who stated that: 'I always stand in front of the instructor ... and that's my position now and those at the front work harder. ... You get "picked up" by those working hard.' Their determination to 'work out' their bodily imperfections was an unspoken bond between these women and is a unifying feature of the established group. 'Establishing' their positions at the front, close to the mirrors, a smile, verbal greeting or eye contact with the instructor signalled a greater access to her expert knowledge. Their unique, personal body space was reserved and protected by exercise equipment (hand weights, exercise bands, 'steps' and mats), a bag, towel, or water bottle. Identifying 'ownership' of their body–work space reflected their dominance in the exercise figuration. The fact that they were able to secure their own dance space supports the notion that the dance studio is partitioned along established–outsider lines.

As Massey (1994) observes, one's sense of space and place is gendered. Indeed, the 'health' club reveals a separation of space along gender lines whereby women dominate the aerobic dance classes and men more usually dominate the gym. The exercise class in question consisted entirely of women. For men, perhaps, the images and messages connected with aerobic exercise classes speak of feminization. We speculate that this activity is, in the main, perceived by men as one that women 'do'. Men seem to be ideologically barred from the dance studio space via the networks of relations between the sexes both in the micro-context of the class and in the wider sociocultural sphere. In part this female place represents a successful attempt by these women to 'close out' their space to the presence of men. But, paradoxically, this female solidarity is marked by a series of power hierarchies between women and by the presence of dominant social messages concerning what women's bodies can look like and what they can do. Asked about securing her location in the dance studio, Ruth, herself a high-status, established insider, highlighted a specific ritual:

> Sometimes I get there early if I think there is going to be a dash for the steps. Although in theory there are enough, I do like my space ... also you know people won't want to move over because I wouldn't want to. ... I tend to get a bit territorial if someone goes where I normally go. It's like if someone parks outside my house. I get unreasonable. Sometimes I do think that's my place. ... You see I walk in the door and drop my bag that side of the room and take

my ticket to the front. But if all the others went to the other side I think I would.

This statement clearly alludes to the privileges of established group members. Outsiders must perform furthest from the instructor and the mirrors. Dominating the space around the instructor, the established group excluded outsiders from seeing the routines effectively. This hindered the outsiders' mastery of movement patterns and was one power tactic which helped to maintain the dominance of the established group. Dominance was also secured via embodiment of societal values of thinness and tone. 'Established' bodies revealed their skin surface in the clothing that was worn and drew attention to their bodies by adorning themselves with jewellery and make-up. At the front of the class a 'chorus line' of tanned, toned breasts, bottoms, legs, and backs performed for the viewing of outsiders. Setting the standards of appearance, these bodies reminded outsiders of their (the 'outsiders') 'imperfections'. Yet established insiders in no way considered their bodies to be finished. Illustrating their continual adherence to narrow limits of female bodily display, Jane, an established aerobics participant, remarked:

> I like to wear longer leggings, not short ones really because I don't use a sunbed or tan easily. If I was tanned I probably would wear short leggings. Also I have some scars on my legs that I've got a thing about. But I wear a thong leotard because I think it gives me the best shape.

This comment suggests that achieving the ideal body is connected with the internalization of embarrassment about bodies which do not conform to social norms. Jane expanded on this idea, saying that 'you feel more intimidated by women if they look better or are fitter'. These women embodied the class rules of display which reflected societal values of femininity, and we therefore are able to see the exercise figuration as a means of contouring women's bodies according to dominant ideals of slimness and tone.

ESTABLISHED–OUTSIDER RELATIONS AND GENDERED IDENTITIES

There is a link between the development of a gendered identity and established–outsider relations. It was evident from observing and talking to the women in this study that a 'We' image is developed within the established group. Outsiders fall into a 'They' image within the aerobics class. Displaying their slim toned bodies, the insider women know the routines and the music and they work out together at the front of the dance studio. They incorporate an energetic and vocal group charisma into their performance. At every session they sing to the words of the music, they shout, cheer and clap enthusiastically as they perform the routines. Their actions and emotions seem to be second nature to them. They have developed what we would term an 'exercise habitus'. Although Bourdieu is most closely associated with the term habitus he was not the first to use it. Mauss (1973) notes that body techniques involve habitual actions. The concept of habitus has been utilized extensively within figurational sociology (Elias, 1987; 1996; Maguire, 1994; Dunning and Maguire, 1996). According to Eliasian thinking a person's habitus is the enduring disposition that suffuses their way of living. Individual habitus is inextricably connected with a shared social habitus evident in specific social settings.

Aerobics represents an activity with a common language, dress code and shared actions and emotions. The personal development of a feminine identity is constructed via the meanings that the women attach to the ideology and practices of the exercise class. Ruth explained that she loved to be a part of the established clique, saying 'I flow and I have a spring in my step at the front . ... I've got to keep up with the girl next to me. ... It makes me feel alive doing my bit of singing and shouting.' Cathy also took part in this animated and exuberant display. 'We just clap along and sing all the time', she said. Elaine confirmed that a 'We' image was developed and internalized by established group members and that a 'They' image was attached to outsider women when she highlighted that 'I'd rather see myself put in a lot of effort, energy and enthusiasm. ... I know the routines and come out sweating. ... I always put a lot of energy in myself.' Cathy also noted that 'some people at the back are just quiet', and Ruth emphasized that some women at the back of the class 'just do small movements and conk out . ... There isn't much point for them.' Falling into a 'They' image, outsiders are aware of the dress, gesture and language codes that would allow them to develop an established exercise habitus. Penny did not stand at the front of the class. She preferred to 'hide' at the back. Referring to the established women she said 'I don't know the routines like they do. ... I was at the front once and I didn't know the routines and I felt a bit stupid.'

Perpetually surveying each other, the women imitate acceptable actions and appearance. They internalize the correct techniques, practices and rituals of the exercise activity, formulating and learning an appropriate emotional and behavioural vocabulary in the development of a self-conscious mind and the construction of an exercise habitus. The pertinent group characteristics are embodied by the established group and reflect a dominant exercise identity. The significance of aerobics to these women is based upon its influence in controlling bodily appearance and function. Seeing their reflections in the mirrors, and gazing at others, they realize the gap between their existing form and an ideal appearance. They make themselves into objects, scrutinizing and adapting their bodies within specified social limits. They also construct an exercise identity via processes which lead to their development as subjective social beings. These processes are based on their social interactions and interpretations of environmental messages within the exercise figuration. The agency factor involved here is interwoven with the structural power and communication networks of the aerobics figuration. That is, women consciously shape their bodies according to the social norms of femininity perpetuated by aerobics.

In several respects the personal development of these women's identity and their social development are interconnected. The hidden agenda governing the development of a feminine identity via the practice of aerobics is shaped by a patriarchal ideology. Several of the interviewees highlighted that achieving and maintaining their bodily ideals would provide them with an improved sense of confidence in their everyday experiences because it would allow them to feel attractive. Judy explained that a body which assumed the ideal shape and size would give her 'more self confidence to go walking around in really short shorts and not worry about it. ... I'd be able to think I've got really nice legs and no one is going to say you look awful.' Penny explained: 'I could wear all the clothes in my wardrobe and I'd be more confident with men in certain clothes that showed more skin.' These comments illustrate that there is a specific logic to the discourse of exercise tied up with the construction of a feminine identity. While exercise *is* perceived by some women as an enjoyable, exhilarating and personally satisfying way to achieve the body beautiful, there is also a somewhat distorted sense of gratification experienced in obtaining the social body. Illustrating this point, and highlighting that women see their whole selves reflected in bodily appearance, Sheila remarked that:

It's just something I know I've got to do. I don't mind my body now but I just keep thinking this isn't my normal weight. I'm 10 stone now and I was 9 stone when I used to run and I just keep thinking I want to be there. It would make me happier and I'd feel more confident and it would give me personal satisfaction.

Being judged on appearance, women are under pressure from societal images reinforced within the 'exercise–body beautiful complex' to stay young, slim and healthy. They do aerobics in response to this pressure. However, the pleasure of physical activity is submerged because its primary purpose is to achieve a body shape and size that is unrealistic. As Sarah revealed:

I feel angry that women are under so much pressure to conform to a fashionable shape. ... It's difficult to maintain. ... It's a constant battle. ... I don't like it, it's irritating. I'm going on holiday at the weekend. ... I want to look a bit respectable in a bikini. ... There isn't a day goes by when I don't think about it. I feel guilty when I don't do my stomach exercises and it becomes deeply ingrained.

For these women, aerobics is a way to achieve the social body. They sculpt their bodies in line with dominant messages about femininity. Yet in doing this they embody the inequalities and conflicts of the wider contemporary society. The routines based on the movement of dance are feminized in the sense that they require grace, balance and control. In addition, the exercises which constitute the aerobic workout tone and slim the female figure, rather than develop strength. These exercise techniques, usually completed on mats on the floor, consist of small repetitive movements focusing on isolated body parts. These are the parts of the female body identified by the key groups and social institutions such as exercise instructors, the fitness industry, diet technologies and media images, and by the women themselves, as problem areas. We commonly heard that these women were distressed about the size and shape of their stomach, hips, thighs, bottom and breasts. Chris explained that 'there are lots of women here who are trying to lose weight ..., to get rid of this or that bit of fat or lose their tummy'. 'I don't like the usual', sighed Ruth, 'bum, thighs and tummy.' Maggie despaired saying 'It's my stomach. ... The muscles really need toning. ... I'd like to be a bit slimmer on the waist and legs.' And Judy expressed a similar body problem, saying 'I'd prefer to have less weight on my hips. I think everyone would say that. Every woman I know wants to lose weight. I think it is part and parcel of society today.' Judy highlights that a feminine body ideal is expressed via social messages. These are reflected in the aerobics regime and through the institutionalized images represented to women in a wider social context. Jane confirmed the influence of media representations of ideal femininity when she explained 'I don't like my stomach and the general things that most women don't like ..., cellulite on thighs and bottoms ... yuk! Everyone wants to look like the super-models don't they? ... The clothes that are out at the moment are designed for waif-like girls and I can't get into things like that. ... I'm doing aerobics to try and change my body.' Typically, these women perceived specific parts of their bodies to be too big, too fat and too fleshy. They were deeply dissatisfied with those parts of their body which are uniquely female. Aspiring to tighten, tone and reduce the thighs, hips, bottom, stomach and breasts, they adhere to a distorted notion of femininity that is defined by dominant social ideologies (Markula, 1995).

Exploring the construction and practice of female exercise identities, we highlight the impact of power relations. Clearly there are power inequalities at work within the aerobics class but power inequalities in wider social relations are also important to consider in seeking to understand the construction of feminine identity. Dominant patriarchal values control and constrain female bodies through the creation of ideal images of female bodies, and these values are often expressed by male partners. These values can affect women, enabling and constraining the construction of particular identities. For example, admitting that she faced criticism about her body from her ex-boyfriend, one interviewee, Gill, said: 'sometimes I am criticized but it's only on a joke basis like – oh you've got a fat arse!' However, she emphasized that she took this extremely seriously, saying: 'yes, yes I do take it seriously. I have to sort it out. It is a bit fat.' Two other women gave detailed accounts of the direct influences that their male partners had upon their perceptions of their body. Amrinda described how she had experienced dramatic weight loss:

> Last year I got too thin. ... I went down to six stones from eight stones. But I had problems with a man who forced me to be thin and watch my food which I had to share with him and he forced me to run. I mean I was a prat for doing all that for a man but you don't notice at the time, it was all so gradual. Stupid really.

Penny explained the impact that her boyfriend had on her self perceptions by saying that:

We used to go to the cinema and I'd go and get sweets and he'd say you don't need them and stop me buying them and that made me annoyed and upset with him because I want to do what I want. Also we were on holiday last year and I wasn't eating much and I had a bikini on and he looked at me for a while and said you really should lose weight shouldn't you and I just went mad and berserk.

These men's views clearly restate the underlying patriarchal ideology of aerobics. Intertwined with a complex network of gender/power relations, we feel that it is difficult for women to realize a purely self-defined identity. This is because they experience an embodied psychological alienation via the socially constructed behavioural and emotional codes of the exercise class. A rational control of action is undermined by a strong personal anxiety about the sanctions of the established group. We emphasize here that women who do not conform to ideal images fear that they are unattractive, worthless and socially undesirable. Power relations are apparently internalized and actions are structured by fear, shame and embarrassment. Individual conscious choice is, therefore, shaped by the social construction of the feminine habitus within the aerobics figuration and the various social setting and power relations within which these women live out their lives.

'OUTSIDER' WOMEN AND ESTABLISHED IDENTITIES

Having examined the way in which dominant group members embody relatively greater power chances in the exercise figuration, we wish to make clear that their ability to reduce the power chances of the outsider group is not absolute or static, but subject to change. Cultural exercise capital can be gained by more astute outsiders. Those aspiring to attain the bodily standards of the established group are also active in empowering themselves. Knowledge and skill may be acquired by watching, listening to and talking to those 'who know'. Having themselves experienced the intimidation and discomfort of being outsiders, dominant group members show a degree of flexibility and tolerance towards the exercise attempts of less powerful participants.

Mirroring our analysis, that the 'We' image of the established group creates a 'They' image into which outsiders fall, one interviewee,

Sharon, who had gained her exercise knowledge from fitness consultants, explained, 'I am part of the fixtures and fittings. ... It takes time. ... It looked a nice little clique when I came to my first trial. I was really nervous thinking everyone knew each other. It took about four months before I got to know people, and now I see new people who look uncomfortable.' This sense of discomfort in non-dominant participants seemingly becomes part of the embodied self. Wendy was located in the outsider group. She said that she wore: 'Just a t-shirt and track suit bottoms', and then continued 'I can't see myself in any of those leotards. I haven't got the body for it.' Jane echoed Wendy's feelings, saying 'it would be nice to look like that ..., toned. ... I wish I could'. And Jo stated 'I look in the mirrors and see slimmer people than me and think God I wish I could be like that.' Jane, Wendy and Jo had not achieved the 'body beautiful'. They remained a part of the outsider group.

Not having acquired appropriate exercise knowledge, or competency in the movement patterns, outsiders are also too timid to move to the front. Such women are 'in limbo' as they gradually engage in rites of passage in an attempt to become part of the established insider group. Over time, some women come to perform with greater skill and technique. Some may also achieve the expertise which can afford them a place in the established space of the dance studio. Illustrating these empowering processes one woman, Judy, explained her exercise experiences, saying:

> My performance is average. I mean lots of people are much fitter than me and don't seem to be gasping for air. So I look a bit tired by the end of it and especially after the stomach exercises. I look at others who aren't so fit and who are overweight and I wonder if they go to lose weight themselves. You can see people at the back and the super-fit people at the front and the intermediate people in the middle. I used to always want to go at the back and not be noticed and just mingle in but now I like to be in the middle and I'm not bothered at being at the front. ... I'm used to the routine and the exercise and I don't mind making mistakes now. People do tend to have their own little spot.

To the extent that participation in the 'in-house' exercise regime turns their bodily aspirations into 'reality', some women begin to uncover their bodies and gradually identify appropriate clothing for the exterior body. Not having achieved established, insider status, Judy commented further on her participation in the exercise class:

When I first came I just wore shorts and a t shirt and then I thought 'look at all these people with leotards on ..., they look good ..., I think I'll get one'. I'd prefer to wear a leotard now which is about wanting to belong in the class and be part of the same group and I feel more comfortable.

Maureen also explained her process of migration towards the front of the class, saying 'when I was first here I stood at the back so people didn't see me. But now I'm not too worried. I've got used to the class. I look a bit better and I go more to the front now. Still you are always trying to look better.' Climbing the hierarchy of relations within the dance nexus some outsiders are received into the established group. They 'dance back' and begin to succeed in the battle for power with regard to the perceived control of their bodies and the social space of the dance studio.

AEROBICS: A DOUBLE-BIND ROUTINE

Empowered by exercise knowledge and appropriate appearance, established bodies claim privileged positions at the front of the dance studio. Yet we have shown that outsiders can gain access to knowledge, skill and acceptable appearance. Manoeuvring into more advantageous positions, they can begin to 'exercise' more power. It is important here to locate this set of interdependent relations within a wider labyrinth exploring the broader established–outsider relations between men and women in society. In this section we suggest that the relational nature of power generated in the aerobics class illustrates a prevailing gender inequality in society in which the overall balance of power favours the values of men. We wish to make clear that the embodiment of power symbolized in the appearance and skill of 'established' women's bodies in the exercise class setting is interconnected with long-term hegemonic processes connected to the balance of power between the sexes.

Permeating the network of gender/power relations evident in the aerobics class are hegemonic ideals supported by the media, fitness industries, diet and health technologies and fitness sciences. These social institutions are underpinned by patriarchal codes determining acceptable uses and displays of female bodies. Commercial exercise classes are a legitimate way for women to sculpt a petite, passive ideal, and embody the myth that women's bodies are inferior to men's.

There is, however, a possibility that exercise can empower female bodies (Gilroy, 1989; Bùnel, 1991; Young and White, 1995). But the findings of this study lead us to believe that while some women *think* or *feel* that they are improving their bodies for themselves, they modify their bodies according to legitimated ideas of appearance.

We want to re-emphasize that these knowledgeable women also find themselves in a double-bind situation. That is, they desire to freely experience their bodies via exercise, but they perpetuate and embody the dominant norms of femininity. To some, such comments may appear unduly pessimistic and serve to overlook the 'liberating' dimension of physical activity. For some women, aerobics may be more enabling than constraining. But for many of the women in this study the commercial aerobics class is more oppressive than liberating.

We would want women to make choices about their bodies based on their own informed terms rather than ideological wishful thinking provided by the dominant ideologies reflected in the aerobic exercise discourse. In this sense one of our tasks involves being 'destroyers of myths' (Elias, 1978). The aerobics class involves women in a set of routines which keep female bodies within narrow permissible limits. The 'aerobic' workout is advocated as a means to reduce the size of women's bodies. Women are encouraged to believe that the continuous rhythmic exercise will help them to lose fat, to slim down and to achieve a more slender form. The toning exercises include repetitive movements using isolated areas of the body which we have previously highlighted as 'problem' parts. In the aerobics class, and at home, these women perform repetitive exercises which do not use heavy weights because they are persuaded that the former method is the way to correct the problem areas of their bodies. Amrinda noted that she needed to lose fat from her stomach: 'I do my stomach exercises everyday at home. ... It's hard ... and sometimes I think that whatever I do my stomach just won't go.' Apparently women continually aim to reduce the size of their bodies and have a particular dislike of fat. Penny explained her desire to achieve a thin, toned body, saying:

> Ultimately I do exercise for weight reasons. ... I hate my legs and my bum and my arms because they are really horrible and fat. ... I was happier when I lost weight at the beginning of the year. I go to the gym every day. ... I wouldn't want to stop. I want the class to be hard. I want to come out of a class and feel that I've worked out and burned fat. ... If I was really thin I don't think I'd go at all.

Bev also highlighted the ideal image of the body beautiful, saying: 'there is one picture only, a slim, toned physique. I don't want to be bigger. I've been bigger and I don't want to go back to that. I don't do heavy weight work because I don't want to build muscles.' Elias's theory of 'double-bind impediments' (Mennell, 1992) furthers an understanding of the meaning women attach to this exercise regime. That is, the wider figuration in which women find themselves operates to *impede* their growth of knowledge over time (Mennell, 1992). Women internalize insecurities about their bodies which prevent them from forming detached explanations of their experiences. A female infatuation with the body appears to be based upon dominant patriarchal ideals. Women remain emotionally involved with their preoccupation about appearance and they do not realize a self-defined image. Sharon explained that her ideal body image was structured by media images, saying:

> God, I live in a blinking dream world when I work out. ... I'm watching MTV, I'm thinking ... I could do those routines. You know Salt and Pepa on MTV? That's my ideal woman. Muscley arms, black leotard, black short shorts, black knee pads, black boots you know, that kind of thing. ... I've half got the hair style. ... But I can't really express myself properly here. ... It's like your body is a machine. In the classes you can let your hair down a bit ... but the moves are still quite mechanical aren't they?

We emphasize here that patriarchal ideologies about women's bodies are reproduced and maintained by the figurational dynamics of the aerobic exercise class in question.

CONCLUDING REMARKS

We have sought to highlight the pervasiveness of patriarchal ideals within the aerobics figuration which we connect with women's experiences in a wider social framework. The aerobics figuration is conceptualized as perpetuating the 'We' image of men who hold an established position in society. Women fall into an outsider category determined by a 'They' image. In contemporary patriarchal society we view commercial aerobics classes as a normalizing technique for the embodiment of ideal femininity and feminine identities (Cole, 1993). We have discussed here that 'aerobicizing' women embody

dimensions of power symbolized by a feminine appearance and expertise in the movement patterns of aerobic exercise. It is these aspects
which contour and shape 'established' bodies in the dance studio. The
power dynamics of the exercise class are interconnected with hegemonic ideals about women's bodies and are supported by key groups
and institutions in society. We have also examined how rationalized,
managed female bodies are interconnected with a network of patriarchal power relations. Exercise perpetuates the objectification of
female bodies, organizing the reshaping of their bodies so that they
are (hetero)sexually appealing. Maintaining patriarchal standards of
femininity, exercise regimes reinforce the notion that women's bodies
are somehow deficient, and contribute to the maintenance of the subordination of women. Exploring processes of gender identity construction we see that feminine identities are developed through specifically
feminized exercise practices like aerobics. It is difficult to tell whether
these women experience a 'total' freedom of bodily and emotional
expression or a self-defined sense of identity via aerobic exercise.
Apparently they experience deferred gratification from the exercise
regime when their bodies begin to conform to perceived ideals of
shape and size. This leads us to view commercial exercise practices
like aerobics as tools for legitimizing slender female bodies as the
ideal image. However, rather than thinking of these exercise practices
as either totally constraining or totally liberating, we wish to suggest
that there is an interdependence between these features and that
women experience both freedom and restraint via this exercise practice. That is to say, active women, to some extent, represent a degree
of resistance to traditional definitions of femininity.

For some of the women interviewed in our study, expressions of
defiance towards codes of self-control were evident in those who
spoke of exercise as a pleasurable release from the everyday pressures
of life and as a place where they could 'let themselves go'. Yet the
dance studio is but a temporary haven from their children, partners
and work. Their experiences seem to be transient rather than long-
lasting. There are small gains to be made from exercising in relation to
personal esteem. These feelings of self-possession spill over into the
way in which these women live out their lives and they express feelings
of improved self-confidence and an energetic zest for life. But longer-
lasting feelings about the body and the self are dominated by images
and messages connected to the wider social messages reflected in the
'exercise–body beautiful complex'. The pursuit of the 'body beautiful'
is intertwined with a cultural distaste of fat and the desire to control

the body according to social norms of femininity. Drawing on Lupton's (1996) ideas on food, the body and the self we highlight that there is a paradox in the relationships between food, bodies and physical activity. Many of the women in this study exercised in order to counter their calorie intake and to discipline their bodies. For some there were feelings of pleasure associated with exercising, but these were located in a complex web of emotions. The exercise habit evoked a cluster of feelings including excitement, enjoyment, shame, guilt and self-disgust. What seems to be apparent is that exercise is both a pleasure and a pain. On this basis exercise represents a struggle between the rationality of self-control and expressions of inner 'free' impulses (Lupton, 1996).

Women are active in attaching their own meanings to the images and messages reflected in aerobics. They are also instrumental in the development of their own sense of self-identity. But the interdependent network of processes that they encounter and interpret in and through aerobics is marked by dominant sociocultural ideals of femininity. The women interviewed intended to empower themselves via their exercise experiences but they found themselves subject to the unintended consequences of conforming to social norms. Participating in aerobics is not the problem. It is the pursuit of the social body that is a negative strategy for women. The evidence of personal distress in women is connected with internalization of shame and guilt about their bodies. This negates the pleasure of the physical activity experience. Illustrating this point Sheila said: 'When I put on weight I wouldn't buy new clothes. I felt I didn't deserve it because I had put on weight. For six months I honestly hated myself and I wouldn't exercise because I felt that self-conscious. I just felt awful.' What is required is a rethinking of the unrealistic images presented to women if they are to experience their bodies more freely via aerobics and realize a self-defined sense of identity.

ACKNOWLEDGEMENTS

We examine, in more detail, the themes and issues that are raised in this chapter in a forthcoming journal article. We are grateful to two anonymous reviewers who provided detailed suggestions on earlier drafts of this work. We thank Cynthia Hasbrook for her continued support. In addition, the comments and advice from Sasha Roseneil and Julie Seymour in the preparation of this chapter have been extremely helpful.

NOTES

1. In this chapter we do not present a detailed account of the form of sociological reasoning and enquiry argued for by figurational sociology. The work of Goudsblom (1997) and Mennell (1992) is recommended as further reading.
2. The names of the women quoted in this chapter are pseudonyms. They stated their age, marital status and occupation at the interviews and the data are listed below: **Amrinda** – 50, divorced, one child, librarian; **Bev** – 25, single, safety and environment officer; **Cathy** – 33, one child, mother; **Chris** – 36, married, three children, mother; **Claire** – 23, single, one child, mother/student; **Elaine** – 29, single, student; **Gill** – 19, single, receptionist; **Jane** – 33, single, advertising executive; **Jo** – 28, single, student; **Judy** – 28, married, personnel manager; **Maggie** – 30, married, one child, assistant accountant; **Maureen** – 41, divorced, two children, shelf filler; **Penny** – 21, single, student; **Ruth** – 35, one child, teacher trainer; **Sarah** – 43, divorced and re-married, one child, executive; **Sheila** – 22, single, fitness instructor; **Wendy** – 31, single, personal assistant.

REFERENCES

Benson, S. (1997) 'The Body, Health and Eating Disorders', in K. Woodward (ed.), *Identity and Difference* (London: Sage), pp. 121–83.

Birrell, S. and Cole, C. L. (eds) (1994) *Women, Sport and Culture* (Champaign, IL: Human Kinetics).

Bourdieu, P. (1978) 'Sport and Social Class', *Social Science Information*, 17, pp. 819–40.

Bordo, S. (1993) *Unbearable Weight: Feminism, Western Culture and the Body* (Berkeley, CA: University of California Press).

Bryman, A. and Burgess, G. (1994) *Analysing Qualitative Data* (London: Routledge).

Bùnel, A. (1991) 'The Recreational Physical Activities of Spanish Women: a Sociological Study of Exercising for Fitness', *International Review for the Sociology of Sport*, 26, pp. 205–13.

Burkitt, I. (1991) *Social Selves: Theories of the Social Formation of Personality* (London: Sage).

Chernin, K. (1981) *Womanize: The Tyranny of Slenderness* (London: Woman's Press).

Cole, C. L. (1993) 'Resisting the Canon: Feminist Cultural Studies, Sport and Technologies of the Body', *Journal of Sport and Social Issues*, 17, pp. 77–97.

Dunning, E. (1992) 'Figurational Sociology and the Sociology of Sport', in E. Dunning and C. Rojek (eds), *Sport, Leisure and the Civilising Process* (London: Macmillan), pp. 221–84.

Dunning, E. and Maguire, J. (1996) 'Process Sociological Notes on Sport, Gender Relations and Violence Control', *International Review for the Sociology of Sport*, 31, pp. 295–323.

Elias, N. (1978/1982) *The Civilising Process*, vol. 1: *The History of Manners* (Oxford: Blackwell).

Elias, N. (1987) 'On Human Beings and their Emotions: a Process Sociological Essay', *Theory, Culture and Society*, 4, pp. 339–61.

Elias, N. (1996) *The Germans: Power Struggles and the Development of Habitus in the Nineteenth and Twentieth Centuries* (Cambridge: Polity).

Elias, N. and Dunning, E. (1986) *Quest for Excitement: Sport and Leisure in the Civilising Process* (Oxford: Blackwell).

Elias, N. and Scotson, J. (1994) *The Established and the Outsiders* (London: Sage).

Featherstone, M., Hepworth, M. and Turner, B. (1992) *The Body, Social Process and Cultural Theory* (London: Sage).

Gilroy, S. (1989) 'The Embody-ment of Power – Gender and Physical Activity', *Leisure Studies*, 8, pp. 163–71.

Goudsblom, J. (1977) *Sociology in the Balance* (Oxford: Blackwell).

Hall, A. (1996) *Feminism and Sporting Bodies: Essays on Theory and Practice* (Champaign, IL: Human Kinetics).

Hargreaves, J. (1994) *Sporting Females* (London: Routledge).

Lloyd, M. (1996) 'Feminism, Aerobics and the Politics of the Body', *Body and Society*, 2, pp. 79–98.

Loy, J. (1991) 'Missing in Action: the Case of the Absent Body', *Quest*, 43, pp. 119–22.

Lupton, D. (1996) *Food, the Body and the Self* (London: Sage).

Maguire, J. (1988) 'Doing Figurational Sociology: Some Preliminary Observations on Methodological Issues and Sensitising Concepts', *Leisure Studies*, 7, pp. 187–93.

Maguire, J. (1992) 'Towards a Sociological Theory of Sport and the Emotions: a Process Sociological Perspective', in E. Dunning and C. Rojek (eds), *Sport and Leisure in the Civilising Process* (London: Routledge), pp. 96–121.

Maguire, J. (1993) 'Bodies, Sport Cultures and Societies: a Critical Review of Some Theories in the Sociology of the Body', *International Review for the Sociology of Sport*, 28, pp. 33–50.

Maguire, J. (1994) 'Sport, Identity Politics and Globalization: Diminishing Contrasts and Increasing Varieties', *Sociology of Sport Journal*, 11, pp. 398–427.

Maguire, J. (1995) 'Sport, the Stadium and Metropolitan Life', in J. Bale and O. Moen (eds), *The Stadium and City Life* (Keele: Keele University Press), pp. 45–57.

Maguire, J. and Mansfield, L. (1999) '"No-body's Perfect": Women, Aerobics and the Body Beautiful', *Sociology of Sport Journal* (forthcoming).

Markula, P. (1995) 'Firm but Shapely, Fit but Sexy, Strong but Thin: the Postmodern Aerobicizing Female Bodies', *Sociology of Sport Journal*, 12, pp. 424–53.

Massey, D. (1994) *Space, Place and Gender* (Cambridge: Polity).

Mauss, M. (1973) 'Techniques of the Body', *Economy and Society*, 2, pp. 70–88.

Mennell, S. (1992) *Norbert Elias: An Introduction* (Oxford: Blackwell).

Miller, L. and Penz, O. (1991) 'Talking Bodies: Female Bodybuilders Colonise a Male Preserve', *Quest*, 43, pp. 148–64.

Morgan, D. and Scott, S. (1993) *Body Matters: Essays on the Sociology of the Body* (London: Falmer Press).

McDermott, L. (1996) 'Toward a Feminist Understanding of Physicality within the Context of Women's Physically Active and Sporting Lives', *Sociology of Sport Journal*, 13, pp. 12–30.

McRobbie, A. (1982) 'The Politics of Feminist Research: Between Talk, Text and Action', *Feminist Review*, 12, pp. 46–59.

Obel, C. (1996) 'Collapsing Gender in Competitive Bodybuilding: Researching Contradictions and Ambiguity in Sport', *International Review for the Sociology of Sport*, 31, pp. 185–201.

Roberts, H. (ed.) (1983) *Doing Feminist Research* (London: Routledge).

Scraton, S. (1987) 'Boys Muscle in where Angels Fear to Tread: Girls' Subcultures and Physical Activity', in J. Horne and D. Jary (eds), *Sport, Leisure and Social Relations* (London: Routledge), pp. 160–86.

Scraton, S. (1992) *Shaping up to Womanhood: Gender and Girls' Physical Education* (Buckingham: Open University Press).

Shilling, C. (1993) *The Body and Social Theory* (London: Sage).

Shilling, C. (1997) 'The Body and Difference', in K. Woodward (ed.), *Identity and Difference* (London: Sage), pp. 65–120.

St Martin, L. and Gavey, N. (1996) 'Women's Bodybuilding: Feminist Resistance and/or Femininity's Recuperation', *Body and Society*, 2, pp. 45–57.

Tseëlon, E. (1995) *The Masque of Femininity* (London: Sage).

Turner, B. (1991) 'Recent Developments in the Sociology of the Body', in M. Featherstone, M. Hepworth and B. Turner (eds), *The Body: Social Processes and Cultural Theory* (London: Sage).

Turner, B. (1992) *Regulating Bodies: Essays in Medical Sociology* (London: Routledge).

Turner, B. (1996) *The Body and Society* (London: Sage).

Woodward, K. (ed.) (1977) *Identity and Difference* (London: Sage).

Young, K. and White, P. (1995) 'Sport, Physical Danger and Injury: the Experience of Elite Women Athletes', *Journal of Sport and Social Issues*, 19, pp. 45–61.

6 Contingent Masculinities: Disruptions to 'Man'agerialist Identity
STEPHEN WHITEHEAD

INTRODUCTION

The management arena may not appear at first sight the most obvious place in which to explore the contingency of identity, for surely management speaks of control and certainty. Indeed, if management cannot speak with certainty, how does it speak? Is certainty not the essence of leadership? To believe in one's self and, from that, to be able to articulate and publicly communicate an appropriate and convincing organizational vision, is this not the very stuff of the 'modern manager'? Certainly it would appear so. If you aspire, for example, to educational leadership then having a 'vision' is now *de rigueur*, as a cursory scan of the job advertisements in the educational journals will reveal. But there is, of course, an additional aspect to management – it is gendered. Management is gendered through both the sheer numerical dominance of men as managers (Institute of Management, 1995; Marshall, 1995, Collinson and Hearn, 1996), and, importantly, through the masculinist cultures which prevail in most organizational settings (Roper, 1994; Connell, 1995; Cheng, 1996). When men managers speak then, they speak from a position of *double certainty*; as men and as managers. And it is from this position, one historically and culturally substantiated, that much of men/managers' identity work is acted out. However, as this chapter reveals, despite the appearance of being fixed and concrete, the identities of men/managers are highly contingent, in no small part because they rest on a *double illusion*: the singularity of masculinity and the omnipotence of managerialism. The aim of this chapter is, then, to critically explore this double illusion, in the process exposing both the moments of disruption that occur in men/manager's investment in masculinism/managerialism, and the

107

discursive resistance to dominant organizational culture that can arise from such contingency and multiplicity of being (a man).

EXPOSING THE 'MAN'AGER

This research reveals that, as men, the managers interviewed have an ambiguous yet symbolic relationship to the arena of managerialism (Saco, 1992; Gherardi, 1995). It is a complex and symbiotic connection involving men as gendered subjects, management discourse and masculine identities. This relationship is arresting the attention of an increasing number of critical gender theorists. Not surprisingly, the earliest interventions in this field were those of feminist scholars, notably Acker and Van Houten (1974), Kanter (1977) and Wolfe (1977). These researchers into organizational behaviour not only raised a long-overdue challenge to 'malestream theory' (O'Brien, 1981) they actually began to emphasize, and deconstruct, the 'man' in manager. The invisibility, yet centrality, of this connection was made even more explicit in the 1980s and 1990s through an increasing number of publications and research projects which focused on, for example: the gendered organization (Mills and Tancred, 1992); sexuality and organizational dynamics (Hearn and Parkin, 1987); new managerialisms and new masculinities (Kerfoot and Knights, 1993); the reproduction of men's power in work practices (Cockburn, 1991); and the links between gendered organizational power and practices of discrimination (Collinson *et al.*, 1990). As Collinson and Hearn (1996) succinctly put it, the 'silence' is finally being broken on men, masculinities and managements. Drawing on these and other works, this chapter aims to contribute to the breaking of this silence, in so doing revealing the paradoxical and contradictory character of the man/manager.

FURTHER EDUCATION

The empirical site for this investigation into men's identity work is education, specifically further education (FE), the largest education sector in the UK with close to 4 million students and an annual budget in excess of £3 billion. This research into FE was undertaken during a period of rapid if not frantic transformation, affecting each and every employee in the sector. The pivotal moment in FE's restructuring came in April 1993 when all 465 FE colleges in England and Wales became, overnight, independent corporations. Known as 'incorporation', this was the date when colleges were released from Local Education Authority (LEA) control, in the process becoming responsible for their own budgets, staffing and, ultimately, survival in a new competitive, postcompulsory education marketplace. The research informing this chapter was conducted over the 3-year period following incorporation. In all, 24 men managers were interviewed using qualitative research methods. Because the focus was men managers, no women managers were formally interviewed. This chapter draws selectively on four of the interviews, in the process providing a narrative account of these men's often tenuous relationship to the world of management.

Despite its size and perceived importance, FE is generally understood to be the Cinderalla sector of UK education, attracting little attention beyond those few journals and newspapers which specialize in education and related issues. FE is, however, a particularly pertinent site in which to critically study masculinities and managerialism, given the dramatic restructuring that has occurred across the sector over the past decade.[1] As this chapter suggests, a central consequence of this restructuring has been the emergence of new managerialist discourses: languages and practices which seek to privilege competition, aggression, entrepreneuralism, and a more instrumental approach to the management of people. In coming to prominence these new managerialist discourses have displaced paternalistic management codes; created new forms of work organization; challenged workplace democracy; and ushered in new management control strategies (Whitehead, 1996, 1999). What has not changed however, is the numerical dominance of men in FE management (Murray, 1995; Coleman, 1997).

PERFORMATIVITY AND EDUCATION MANAGEMENT

While the gendered constitution of FE management has remained unchanged, with men still occupying 70 per cent of senior management positions,[2] the style and ethos of management has not. Altogether there has been a marked upgrading in the value and importance of management/managers across the sector, and a noticeable shift from a paternalistic management style to an overtly competitive and entrepreneurial one (see Whitehead, 1999, for elaboration). FE managers are subjected to the same surveillance and measurement techniques now imposed on all staff,[3] and are also increasingly expected to be proponents and articulators of this competitive and entrepreneurial work culture, a culture which has come to largely define postcompulsory education.[4] The cold instrumentality of these new work practices is neatly encapsulated in the notion of 'performativity', a concept utilized by Usher and Edwards (1994) in their interrogation of contemporary education and postmodernity.

In their study Usher and Edwards refer to the work of the postmodern theorist Lyotard (1984). Drawing on Wittgenstein's philosophy of 'language games', Lyotard suggests that the knowledge sector of society has, in the postmodern era, undergone a shift of interest from concerns with human life, to pragmatic concerns interested only in the optimal performance of means; a move to performativity. Within this understanding it is possible to see how education discourse has shifted from one that might be described as 'human orientated', to one in which the only question of concern is: is it efficient? Once this question becomes the dominant, privileged question, then the task, direction and very ethos of education shifts. Management is obviously central to this movement and this privileging of new knowledge, for the manager is the key fulcrum in the articulation and reification of this discourse. The discourse of performativity in education then finds its expression and narrative in terms which have already become prominent and privileged across the private sector and other public sector sites such as the National Health Service, the Post Office and Civil Service. Such terms include total quality management, human resource management, competency statements/objectives and performance indicators. As these terms and associated practices proliferate and become ascendant, so the work culture and ethos of education shifts. This shift is to a set of organizational practices primarily concerned with measurement, performance, targeting, and 'objective' assessment and appraisal, embedded within a framework of competition (internal and external), and a funding and financial system which requires government-inspired growth together with simultaneous 'efficiency gains'. However, the expansion of FE has not been matched by a corresponding increase in government funding; consequently most FE colleges are rapidly sinking into financial chaos. At the time of writing, two-thirds of all English and Welsh FE colleges are 'trading at a loss', and one in five is technically bankrupt (Further Education Funding Council, 1997). As a result, some informed commentators fear that, failing government intervention, the FE sector faces wholesale collapse (Ainley and Bailey, 1997).

FE is, then, currently characterized by conditions of extreme uncertainty despite the appearance of control which attends the articulation of new managerialist discourses. Consequently, the new FE places men/managers in a particularly interesting light, for it throws into critical focus many of the masculinist assumptions of control and rationality that abound and are replicated within contemporary organizations, and which continue to inform much of managerial rhetoric and theory (see Watson, 1994; Kerfoot and Whitehead, 1996). These gendered stereotypes are, however, not confined to the managerial arena. As gender theorists have long noted, culturally specific notions of the male as naturally rational, reasoned, logical and task-orientated have an extensive history, being explicit in many of the common-sense assumptions surrounding men and masculinity in most areas of social interaction.[5] But how singular is masculinity, and how fixed and grounded are the 'male attributes' it alludes to?

THE CONTINGENCY OF MASCULINE IDENTITY

In common-sense, everyday parlance, masculinity is usually considered to be something that 'men have'. It is generally seen as the natural expression of the male and can be readily located in those gendered stereotypes which purport, as do all stereotypes, to anchor, pin down, and make sense of difference, complexity and change with the minimum of critical examination. More obvious examples of this are notions of 'man the hunter', the 'male breadwinner', men's 'innate' competitiveness and aggression, and the 'male sex urge' (Segal, 1990). However, the first stage in the deconstruction of the term masculinity from any essentialistic, biological grounding occurs when we examine how definitions and expressions of masculinity and manliness have shifted historically, coming to represent wider social and cultural concerns and understandings. For example, Mangan and Walvin (1987) describe how the concept of manliness in the UK metamorphosed through the Victorian and Edwardian eras, as the needs of empire became more acute, from being closely associated with a Christian ethic of selflessness and integrity to emerging as a 'neo-Spartan virility, hardness and endurance' (1987: 1). Moving on from an ethnocentric examination of the term, it becomes apparent that masculinity, or what is considered culturally and socially appropriate in men, has always been different across cultures and through space. Ethnographic research by anthropologists reveals the diversity encompassed by the term, its fluidity, multiplicity and amenability to cultural norms, taboos and expectations.[6] Any attempt to pin down masculinities, and male identities, in Euro/American/Australasian countries at the end of the twentieth century, is similarly problematic. It can be argued that, in part at least, this is due to the pluralism of consumption (identity) patterns, and associated (gendered) signs, symbols and images (Saco, 1992), all competing for attention in the postmodern era (Bauman, 1992). For whatever reason, it appears to be the case that masculinity is now more than ever pluralistic in expression, including within its boundaries a wide range of contrasting identities and meanings: from the ever-suited politician, to the androgynous David Bowie or Boy George; from the leathered biker, to the company man in a company car; from the gay athleticism of 'gym queens', to the raunchy hetero-sexuality of the Chippendales; from the domestically traditional to the househusband.

Not surprisingly, much of the literature on men's identities has sought to grapple with the multiple, yet illusory and amorphous, character of masculinity, while simultaneously seeking to illuminate some of the contextual arenas within which masculinities come to appear 'real'.[7] One of the writers laying the foundation for this critical investigation is Brittan (1989). Stressing the variability and ambiguity of men's identity, Brittan argues that masculinity, and femininity, should not be seen as inevitable outcomes of a functional socialization process dictated by dominant and 'appropriate' gender role models. Nor, he suggests, should erosion of male power in either the workplace or home be seen as somehow inevitably leading to a 'crisis of masculinity' (see, for example, Pleck, 1981). Rather, Brittan questions any notion of a collective identity of men, whilst recognizing that the political consequences of the gendered embodiment of male and female bodies favour men, at least materially.[8]

This recognition by Brittan that men, whilst not a biologically grounded gender class, are implicated in a collective *gender politics* of identity, is one discussed by a number of (pro)feminist writers (e.g. Hearn, 1992; Cornwall and Lindisfarne, 1994). An aspect central to this 'politics by association' is men's material advantage in paid work – the public sphere (O'Brien, 1981). This setting for the construction of men's identities and exercise of gendered power has been explored by, amongst others, Tolson (1977), Cockburn (1991), Morgan (1992), Hearn (1992), and Seidler (1994). Seidler (1994) for example, suggests that the (gendered) public and private dichotomy encourages a process of 'depersonalization' in men, whereby emotional self-control

and mechanistic instrumentality towards self and others are fundamental to the capitalist work ethos. Discussing the inter-relationships
of work, class and men's identity, Tolson (1977) argues that while
working-class men may be victimized by class and work conditions, for
many their sense of identity remains heavily invested in being the
family breadwinner, a concept which posits man as powerful and in
ascendancy. Recognizing the ideological features of the 'male breadwinner', Morgan (1992) suggests that while unemployment may well
disrupt some men's sense of male identity, the acuteness of this may
be mediated by variables such as age, class and (marital) relation-
ship(s). Supporting this argument is the work of Thompson (1994),
which reveals some of the strategies used by men in maintaining a
sense of (potent) self when confronted with the inevitability of ageing.
Related studies, looking at the settings and consequences of male
youth identity construction, include Mac an Ghaill's (1994) research
into black English masculinities, and Messerschmidt's (1995) investigation into crime by young white males.

One aspect that emerges as prominent, in the above and similar
studies, is the importance of language as a core contributor to men's
sense of masculine identity: the texts and narratives engaged in by
men of all classes and ages in order to reify an ultimately amorphous
and elusive masculine identity. Language plays an important role in,
for example, rituals of male bonding, fraternity, the exclusion of
women and 'others', and gay and heterosexual identities through the
use of codes, labels, certain expletives and other gendered signifiers.
However, as empirical studies into 'men's language' have revealed
(Johnson and Meinhof, 1997), while many men may well utilize those
texts and narratives seen as representative of an idealized masculine
paradigm, meaning (in language) is 'not guaranteed by the subject
which speaks it' (Weedon, 1987: 22).[9] Indeed, meaning in language is
always context-specific and never finally fixed (see also Jefferson,
1994). This point emphasizes the centrality of cultural and social
influences in the formation of gendered identities: the (masculine)
speaking subject being a product of the social world rather than a
unified self.

Masculinity, having no base in biology, is, then, no more and no less
than that which can be spoken of, about, and by men (and women) at
any given moment in time and space. Therefore, the potential multiplicity of masculinities is inexhaustible; what the term means to whom,
here and now, is its only fixedness. Yet there is a further aspect to
masculinities. As feminists and pro-feminist scholars have long

argued, men's power, or at the very least their potential to have power over women and 'others', is substantially invested and accommodated within *dominant* notions and expressions of masculinity (see, for example, Carrigan *et al.*, 1985; Brittan, 1989; Morgan, 1992; Brod and Kaufman, 1994). In their seminal 1985 work, Carrigan *et al.* offer three models of masculinity which they argue exist, usually in tension with each other, in all arenas within Euro/American/Australasian countries (see also Connell, 1993). These they describe as hegemonic, subordinated and conservative. In seeking out hegemonic masculinities one would notice the prevailing, dominant and most acceptable expression of being a man in a particular situation or location. Its hegemonic character would then suggest itself through the marginalization and subordination of other ways of being a man; for example, in gayness, paternalism, lack of aggression/assertion, and so on. To be a man and to be a 'powerful' man in many situations (for example, sport, politics, business), becomes then an almost Goffmanesque display of self in which the subject engages in, partly chooses, and is inculcated by, contesting notions of masculinity.[10] The (gendered) power, or its promise, is invested in the particular practices of masculinity that are acted out.

While the concept of hegemonic and subordinated masculinities is a useful shorthand for identifying differences between men, the concept is itself flirting with some essentialistic notions. For example, it subcategorizes men and tells us little about those women who might display masculine ways of being. Nor does it provide us with a means to understand or analyse the actual processes of inculcation, power and resistance that might occur in a given location or arena. Like most sociological typologies it is too tidy.

MASCULINITY, DISCOURSE AND POWER

A number of critical gender theorists have, by contrast, chosen to utilize the work of Foucault (see McNay, 1992, for elaboration), and adopt a poststructuralist understanding of identity formation, power/resistance dynamics and the actions of the subject within intersubjective occurrences (see, for example, Butler, 1990; Weedon, 1987; Game, 1991; Sawicki, 1991). In brief, Foucault understands discourses as: what can be spoken of at a given moment; privileged knowledges and 'truths effects' (Foucault, 1988), made real only through and by the dynamics of the social network and various and contesting power regimes which are its constitution. For Foucault, one of the prime effects of power is that 'certain bodies, discourses, come to be identified and constituted as individuals' (1973: 18). Following this, the individual should not be understood as an elementary nucleus, but as constituted and identified through discourse (either dominant or subordinate). 'Man' and 'woman' thus become discursive subject positions (Hollway, 1984). The subject position of 'manager' can be seen as produced in a similar way. Although Foucault did not write about gender his analysis makes possible the study of masculinities as discursive constructs, for masculinities have no existence outside the social, their existence being made 'true' and 'real' only in their inculcation of, and articulation by, the subject. Any power that men, or women, may exert, is made possible only through the taking-up of, and being in, dominant discourses, themselves in flux. This understanding of identity formation again alerts us to the very fragility of masculinity – and its illusory characteristics. Similarly, as Foucault stresses, the power dynamics that constitute the social network and intersubjective processes are sustained in moments when resistance might materialize: there being no fixed or absolute position on which to have or to exert power (Foucault, 1977, 1982). Following this, power and identity are both understood to be contingent. Rather than being grounded in the 'certainties' of power, status and biology, the managerial subject in organizational life is, then, revealed to be a contingent subject working at, and seeking, identity constitution. As will be elaborated below, this can be understood as an existential project of becoming, one constantly exposed to points of discursive resistance and disruption.

(MASCULINE) IDENTITY AT WORK

Having recognized and accepted what Foucault describes as the discursive (ungrounded) subject, it then beholds the sociological enquirer to fathom how subjects acquire a *sense* of being concrete and grounded. By what means do individuals achieve their ontological security in a social environment characterized by contingency, risk and disruption? As will now be discussed, it is in the tensions between contingency and ontological security, and the existential anxiety arising from such disruption, that work and organizational life become important for all subjects, but particularly men.

Briefly, ontological security can be understood as the shared reality of people and things bracketed and framed in the recognizable conventions of everyday social interaction (Giddens, 1991). Work, and the boundaries, codes and orthodoxes of organizational life, can be seen to provide the sense of grounding sought by all subjects (Casey, 1995; Pahl, 1995). This search might be termed the 'existential quest' whereby the subject, through his/her inter-subjective moments and everyday associations, seeks to achieve a 'cognitive and emotional anchor' (Giddens, 1991: 36), in the face of the chaos and disorganization lurking beyond the trivial, the routine and the apparently banal. Work can thus be seen to provide both spatial and temporal boundaries, framed in multiple discourses and subject positions, in the process providing the subject with a means to alleviate the constant and ever-present existential questions surrounding purpose, identity, validity and human self-sufficiency. Rather than being overwhelmed by anxiety, the organizational subject achieves a sense of rootedness, of 'being in the world', through their association with a particular organizational arena, one which they, as discursive subjects, help re-constitute and re-form (Smircich, 1983). This is not to suggest that paid work is the only remedy available to the subject for alleviating existential anxiety (see, for example, Bauman, 1997), though it is one which nestles comfortably with other late or postmodern obsessions regarding consumerism and conspicuous consumption (Goffman, 1974). What work does achieve so effectively, especially in the modern 'frantic organization', is the filling of time and space, and, accruing from this, the sense of purposeful action as we hurry and busy ourselves with detail, deadlines and delivery. Our sense of self, and our sense of importance and relevance, is thus re-confirmed daily – in our overflowing diaries. Consequently, there is less time to think, reflect and question (our selves). It is a seductive phenomenon.

   It can be argued that work organizations have oppressive characteristics, linked to, for example, alienation, bullying, deskilling and authoritarianism (see, for example, Thompson and McHugh, 1990; also Sturdy *et al.*, 1992). Furthermore, it can be suggested that the modern, frantic and high-speed corporate workplace is a site with potentially pathological consequences for those who might invest in the 'career self' (LaBier, 1986). However, recognizing such does not negate the point that work provides us with a pre-given arena in which to experience a sense of identity. Moreover, as an arena with particular historical and gendered associations for men (Collinson and Hearn, 1996), organizational life offers multiple opportunities for men to achieve a sense of *masculine identity*. This is not to suggest that self-identity, for either women or men, is ever fully achieved, nor that the process and experience is unproblematic (see Shotter and Gergen, 1994, for elaboration); but, rather, to recognize that, for all discursive human subjects, the inherent tension between ontological security and existential anxiety appears as the only pre-given 'fact' of being.

POWER/RESISTANCE

In elaborating this understanding of self-identity processes, the emphasis is on the discursive, continuous and contingent character of identity work, while also recognizing the influence of dominant gender(ed) discourse in work and organizations (Kondo, 1990; Gherardi, 1995). The 'project of self-construction' through work (Casey, 1995), is, then, perceived as possible through the subject's immersion in the dynamics of power and resistance, and the multiple discourses consolidating the social field (Foucault, 1988). In keeping with a poststructuralist analysis of the subject at work (see, for example, Jermier *et al.*, 1994), this chapter seeks to stress the (inter)subjective processes as pivotal in constituting a sense of identity within organizational life, as opposed, that is, to a structuralist under-standing of power and resistance which fails to provide an adequate account of the subject's simultaneous inculcation and re-configuration of discourse (see, for example, Thompson and Ackroyd, 1995). Consequently, power/resistance is understood as both creative and subversive: the disruptive moments within, and alternatives to, domi-nant organizational and gendered discourse. These possibilities emerge and are in part constructed by the subject, not necessarily as rational strategies, but as the very effects and consequences of the multiplicity and fragility of self (Kondo, 1990). As has been discussed, the discursive arena (Ball, 1990) of education management is itself understood as no less fragile, subject as it is to the unpredictable play and counterplay of discursive subjects and macro-influences. This is not to discount the power effects of privileged knowledges within the organization, but rather to point to the moments when privileged knowledges shift, become unsustainable or are reconstituted by the subject within, yet also outside of, prevailing power structures. As a consequence, the organizational arena remains exposed to subversive moments and practices, largely outside the control of any predeter-mined management strategy – or dominant managerial discourse.

To summarize, not only has FE undergone a significant cultural shift, but those individuals charged with 'managing' this shift are themselves constructed, in their discursivity, through a fragile and unpredictable process, one involving constant change. It is a process of becoming which is made possible only by the complex dynamics of power/resistance which constitute all subjects and intersubjectivities (see Foucault, 1977, 1988). As a result, the notion of the rational, grounded man/manager becomes problematized and exposed as concrete only in the moments and practices of gendered discursive signification (Butler, 1990; Saco, 1992), and these moments are themselves unpredictable and largely unmanageable. While all of the managers described in this research are at some pains to present themselves as successful managers, that is, in control, rational and purposive, their narratives reveal a more complex reality. It is a reality of contrasting and contradictory masculinities, where resistance to a particular dominant discourse is always possible, indeed in some instances likely. Yet, in order to maintain their position and identity within the organization as able managers, these men must constantly police their language and movements. They are subjects working hard at trying to manage the contradictions of their own multiple identities within their particular discursive organizational arena. As the research below reveals, to present themselves as able to 'stand the heat' in the new atmosphere in education management, these men must take in and take on the discourses of managerialism. Only by so doing can they even begin to contemplate a future in a sector and profession many had confidently expected to remain in for their working lifetimes. Yet, at the very moment of expressing these dominant discourses, these men also reinscribe and reconstitute them in different ways.

EXCERPTS FROM THE INTERVIEWS

This section will draw on four specific interviews undertaken as part of the larger project. The four men/managers referred to below, while all individuals, do reflect the wider constituency of FE managers; they are all white, middle-class and university-educated. The relationship of each to FE, is however, subtly different. Jim, the youngest at 32, is an ambitious manager who considers himself to be a high-flyer with senior management potential. A single man, he has a middle management position heading up a growing team of leisure and sport lecturers. Moving to a large Yorkshire college to take up this new post 4 months prior to the interview, Jim has been in FE just 4 years. By contrast, Greg, 45 and married with four children, has much more experience of FE. His 16 years in the sector have been spent in the one college. Previously an accountant, Greg began his career in FE as a lecturer in communications. Four years ago he moved to a junior management position in student support. At the time of interview he had just accepted a new contract – not entirely out of choice. In this new post he is a middle manager responsible for an aspect of student services. The outcome of internal restructuring, Greg's new contract is for only one year in the first instance. He assured me that he 'will do enough to make it permanent'. The third manager, Paul, has also been directly confronted with some of the harsher aspects of the new FE work culture. Aged 41, and married with two children, he has been in FE over 14 years, moving ever-upwards from basic lecturer to, now, divisional manager in one of the largest colleges in the UK. As his narrative reveals, much of Paul's early enthusiasm for the job has, however, turned to anxiety and anguish as his workload has been steadily but surely increased, linked ever-closely to externally imposed targets. This has resulted in him questioning both the validity of the job and his ability to cope with it. Finally, Neville, at 48, is the eldest. He has a senior management position in a small college in the north-east of England, a post he has held for three years. Neville is one of two assistant principals in this college, with responsibility for curriculum affairs. He has been in FE for 21 years. Having started out as an assistant lecturer, he no longer considers himself ambitious. He is married with a year-old daughter and has two older children from a previous marriage.

The discourses of new managerialism in education are apparent in each of these men/manager's narratives, yet each articulates it in a slightly different way, reflecting his own unique subjectivity and history. For example, Jim, in keeping with his presentation of self as a man who is comfortable with the entrepreneurial culture in FE, discusses his career to date as one of continuous effort combined with instrumental control:

> The thing to remember now is that the number of students equals income and income equals power. I have worked hard at setting up this new department but moving to this college was part of a clearly defined career path. There are more changes (to the structure) yet to take place here, I'm keeping my eye on things but the next rung up, Head of School, is what I'm looking for in say two years.

Jim's understanding of power is that, as a manager, one has power over others, this being a discourse reflected by all of the men/managers interviewed. Yet he fails to acknowledge that his own access to this power is partly circumscribed by other factors, not least his age. At 32, Jim is one of the youngest middle managers in the college. His rapid move from lecturer to manager has meant that he has had to work at 'being the manager' in the face of his youthfulness and relative inexperience. One of the ways in which he sets about achieving this gravitas is through separation and presentation:

> Being promoted from lecturer to management means that you go from being one of the lads to being in a position of no man's land. You are a bit piggy in the middle. I have learnt not to confide in people so much, not to give too much away. It can be dangerous. I have to be more professional ... I always wear a suit and tie at work now.

Whilst Jim acknowleges that incorporation has brought stress and uncertainty to the sector, he believes that the way forward is to manage it like a business. There is no place, he says, for the 'enthusiastic amateur' doing marketing or personnel functions. He works long hours but takes the weekend off 'to recover'. Apart from active sport, his life revolves around his work. For him being a manager is very much about managing the pressures. As he expresses it: 'those that can't stand the heat – you know the rest'.

One way in which Jim attempts to maintain this presentation of himself as the able, competent and thrusting manager, is to keep his emotions 'under wraps'. Jim spoke of the need to, at all times, be in control of himself, his feelings and emotions. In so doing, Jim is acting out a quite stereotypical image of masculinity: the man/manager as the rational, controlled and logical agent.

By contrast, the second manager, Greg, has a somewhat different relationship to work. Very much a family man, changes in FE have placed him and his family under pressure. He is quite open about the consequences, for himself and for others:

> The 'flexibility' of the new contracts will damage family life. I've discussed it with the kids you know, regarding holidays and so on. It is going to mean changes for all of us.

Greg has already been witness to many changes in FE over the years, beginning with his first post in the 1970s:

> I am not a romantic, I had few illusions about FE, but I believed, I still do, in student-centred ideas and so on. I wanted to contribute.

In the interview Greg struck me as a sensitive and reflective man, who had found himself in a middle management position, not a careerist who had aimed for this. Although quite a large institution, his college had been a pleasant place to work:

> It's a college where change has happened very slowly. It's been very comfortable here – nobody leaves.

But inevitably change had come. New management structures had been imposed and many staff, including Greg, had to re-apply for positions, many of which were for a year in the first instance. Greg had to 'get on the bus', but in so doing had gone onto a new contract; more money, but longer hours, shorter holidays, and it was for 12 months only. It was a big risk and he knew it, but the alternative, as he saw it, was to be left behind:

> I felt it right to apply. I can hack it. I'll do something in the next twelve months to get it made permanent.

The new managerialist discourse of performativity in FE has impacted on all staff. As Greg notes, the risks for everyone are now that much greater, and it appears that many who contributed to the sector in the past will now be marginalized as the *pace of work intensifies.*

> In the old days you could tolerate people's weaknesses; you could make space for those not coping but who contributed in different ways. Now you can't do that. The new culture doesn't allow that support or space. It's much more rigorous and stressful. If I'd been a younger man I'd have resigned. I couldn't have faced the years of insecurity and uncertainty. It's much more threatening now.

This open recognition, by each of the managers, that FE life is 'much more threatening now', belies, somewhat, the degree of involvement, indeed intensity, with which each man has been immersed in the organizational culture, and how, by their own actions, they have contributed to the very culture they now feel to be 'threatening'. This has not been an accidental process, nor one they have necessarily been pushed into as passive actors. For example, the third manager, Paul, found it relatively easy to move up the FE career ladder from fairly inauspicious beginnings, his background in industry preparing him quite well for many of the changes taking place in his college during the 1980s. College restructuring in 1990 opened up further opportunities and he moved to a management position, responsible for income-generation activities across a faculty, an area of work increasingly valued in the newly competitive FE. Reflecting on these changes, Paul revealed the enthusiasm he once had for his work, but also how this enthusiasm became a burden once the pressure on him to deliver more increased.

> Four years ago the new faculty decided it would be nice to get involved in income generation. There was no target, just the remit to get it started and develop it in the best way I could. I felt in control then, and to be honest, there was much more enthusiasm because it was new and because I felt it was achievable. I put a lot of energy into it.

The emergent funding crisis, plus the increasingly competitive nature of FE, encouraged colleges like Paul's to adopt some of the harder aspects of private sector culture. Consequently, where once Paul had been an enthusiastic and dedicated 'amateur' in terms of income generation, he now found himself on the receiving end of an entirely different culture.

> A new Vice Principal for marketing and finance was appointed in 1993 who thought that the college needed to be more successful in income generation. Therefore we went down the route of targets. The target was decided simply by taking what we had achieved the previous year and upping it. There was no discussion or negotiation. In the first year of this 'system' it went up by 50 per cent. So it has gone on every year since.

Originally the product of his own expectations, Paul's target is now dictated by someone further up the hierarchy. The target income to be achieved has steadily grown and now exceeds £1 million per year, garnered from every possible avenue of commercial activity including restaurants, shops and conferences. Consequently, the pressure on Paul is immense, for the faculty is increasingly reliant on this money – lecturers' jobs depend on it. However, in spite of strenuous efforts, these targets are proving difficult if not impossible to meet. Yet Paul still maintains a close investment in the job, and is still looking at climbing the career ladder, in spite of clear warning signs that all is not well, either at work or at home.

> I do get a buzz out of it [the job] and I have been very successful. I might want to go for a Vice Principal's post in marketing, but I have to consider the effect on my family life. The trouble is, the job has changed now. Last year for example, the faculty didn't achieve its student target and we had a deficit. They were hoping I would

exceed my target to meet this deficit. I didn't. There is a real sense of crisis… . I've a lot less control now over my work.

Whilst Paul is still anxious to portray himself as a 'player' in the new FE culture, his response to these crises, his personal one and the college's, is both to retreat into himself, thereby becoming less visible at work, and to adopt an almost secretive stance, one which inevitably pervades and intrudes into his home life.

There is stress at home. I find it difficult to unwind, so I'm much shorter with the kids – more irritable. I work at home in the evenings but I don't discuss work issues with my wife as I don't want work to intrude into my home life. But then it becomes secretive. The family criticize me for this!

As Paul becomes more reflexive about the tensions between home and work the importance to him of his home life becomes more apparent; he admitted that family life is increasingly replacing, albeit slowly, the space previously occupied by paid work.

I suppose I've got to be honest and say that family is replacing work for me, I am more comfortable at home. The job is stressful but I am increasingly finding that I'm distancing myself from it. I find the rituals of home life reassuring, you know, set times for meals, television, weekend routines, shopping. I guess I'm re-thinking my future.

Paul's comments reflect those made by all the research respondents regarding changes in the work patterns of FE. Yet, clearly, each has a slightly different relationship to these cultural shifts. For, as Paul's narrative reveals, while there are dominant patterns, there are also other influences at work. The tensions between work and family and, as has been discussed earlier, between the individual's sense of identity investment in work and/or family, was also acutely visible in the interview with Neville.

As an assistant principal, Neville is one of those senior managers referred to by Greg and Jim, who are pivotal in bringing about local institutional change in the FE sector. Yet, as with the others, Neville's relationship to the new discourses of management has an air of ambiguity about it. At the begining of the interview Neville presents himself as the senior manager, charged with ushering in the new work culture, and 'making things happen':

Yes, there is a change in the work culture, but we need more flexibility from the staff if we are to survive. The new structure we are introducing will require some staff to retrain. There may be some redundancies.... . We see the ourselves (the college and senior managers) as entrepreneurial, progressive and growing.

When the interview moves to staff responses to all this change, Neville's comments indicate that staff resistance is firming up.

No, we are not going to introduce the new contracts. We are taking a fairly relaxed view of this. We don't want to lose goodwill ... there used to be a lot of staff goodwill.

A number of managers discussed this particular aspect of the changing work culture of FE; the decline in goodwill of most staff and a hardening of attitudes towards management. These responses by staff represent one of a number of aspects of organizational resistance[11]. Some of the management in the bigger colleges tended to have a 'take it or leave it' response to this, but smaller colleges appeared more vulnerable to negative staff attitudes. Neville's college is a minor player in the region it serves, and as such will have to forever be on its guard against 'predatory' colleges, intent on moving into its 'patch':

We must grow to survive, we can never rest, it's a bit like sharks moving forward, to survive ... consolidation is not an option. I do recognise that the college is under threat.

The interview with Neville progressed to talk about his family life, in particular his relationship with his 1-year-old daughter. At this point the contradictions in Neville's narrative emerge. From presenting himself as the ambitious, progressive manager, he goes into an alternative discourse of 'family man':

Since Joanna was born my attitude to work has changed. I am much less ambitous. We weren't expecting a child, it all came as a tremendous shock. Work is of much less importance now.

From being a mouthpiece for the new masculine/managerialist discourse, Neville actually moves to position himself in opposition to it:

There is an an unhealthy work culture in FE now. It is somehow macho to be here until 7.30/8.00pm, but I won't join in. My wife works full-time and I collect Joanna from the creche. I leave at 5.30 p.m, sometimes in the middle of meetings. I don't find it a problem, in fact I find it a tremendous discipline.... . Having Joanna has caused me to reflect on things, especially as an older father. Also, I feel I have become more secure in myself I suppose, much more serene.

From this point in the interview, Neville went on to describe the emotional experience of having a daughter and how this unexpected but welcome event had caused him to reflect upon and reconsider his position in work and management. Practical outcomes of this reevaluation included taking his full holiday entitlement, spending less time at work, and less time at home on work-related activities. As an 'older' father, Neville appeared anxious to invest time and effort in this role, his work role suddenly seeming less important to him. Yet this self-reflection had only gone so far. Whilst his relationship with his daughter had touched him deeply, this experience had not significantly changed his understanding of emotions in the organization, for he continued to believe in them being manageable and in good managers being unemotional and somewhat distant from others. His understanding of himself as man/manager in relation to the organization might have shifted but his location of self remains gendered, reflecting conventional understandings of masculinity. This location of self is revealed in Neville's articulation of the gendered discourse of the rational, reasoned man/manager. What becomes apparent, then, are the various expressions of being a man and being masculine now available to Neville, his understanding of himself as a gendered subject being no more apparent to him following the recent reevaluation of his work and personal priorities.

CONCLUSION

Whilst occupying various subject positions, these four men/ managers have a number of important areas of commonality in their relationship to work. All acknowledged the stress and increased pressure they experience as a result of the competitive, market-driven culture now abroad in FE. Yet each was also at pains to demonstrate, in various ways, that he could 'hack it'. For all four men there is a significant investment of gendered, masculine identity in their work as managers. Their belief that they can control the potentially threatening circumstances in which they find themselves, and thereby can manipulate their way through the uncertainty and insecurity of contemporary managerial life: these are extremely important self-determinants, gender signifiers (Kerfoot and Whitehead, 1996). Located in the subject position of manager, the narrative that is articulated reflects, not surprisingly, the dominant discourses of the new managerialism: competition, growth, survival of the fittest, instrumentality, measurement against objectives, winning against the odds. As managers, men who wish to continue being in some position of power, authority and control over their work situation, Neville, Greg, Paul and Jim must display and act out, indeed believe in, their innate ability to survive if not prosper – for managerial discourse requires nothing less of its articulators.

Their inculcation in the discourses of performativity is of course further embedded and reinforced by the gendered dimension of this discourse. For performativity, the quest for efficiency and instrumental achievement carries the added message of masculinity; the common-sense expectations of men's behaviour. That is, the competition, aggression, the functionality of performance measurement, all framed within notions of emotional control, rationality and endurance, have a distinctly masculinist dimension. These four men are simultaneously inculcated by, and expressive of, these masculine/managerialist discourses.

Yet their individually different and fragile relationship to work and masculine/managerial identity is also evident, underlining the potential each subject has for subverting and reconstituting discourse. For Jim the potential disruption to this identity, this uncertainty of self, is revealed by his desire to appear 'managerial'; his youthfulness and inexperience being, he feels, disadvantageous in a work environment where most managers are over 40. He has to labour at acquiring the power that, he believes, is inherent in the symbiotic subject positions of man/manager. Greg, likewise, has an ambiguous relationship to the masculine/managerial discourses of the new work culture. While he appears aware of the contradictions and consequences for him in this culture, he remains anxious to display commitment to it. Yet throughout the interview his was scathing and critical of the changes taking place in FE, and at times bitter about the effects on himself and his family. Whilst being a manager, Greg remains significantly personally removed from this position. His is an almost schizophrenic-like state of being in, yet outside, this particular subject position. Only just in post, Greg already has a relationship of resistance to the dominant discourses of the new FE. Similarly, Paul's relationship to his job and associated career aspirations seems less than solid if not increasingly disrupted by the insecurity and uncertain work conditions now apparent in his college. From being a keen articulator and enthusiast of the new entrepreneurial and competitive work culture within his faculty, Paul now finds himself on the receiving end of 'sharp practice', whereby externally dictated targets are imposed on him with little negotiation, yet always with the carrot of further promotion to mitigate some of his anxiety and frustration. Consequently, Paul's narrative contains the elements of contradiction, tension and resistance so apparent in all these men's accounts. Somewhat inevitably, fundamental and highly personal questions have now emerged for Paul as he faces the re-examination of his previously unquestioned identity investment in work and organizational life: Can I hack it? Can I survive? Do I want to continue up the career ladder? What happens to me if I don't? Yet while the family setting might appear safe, benign and reassuring, to what extent is it a realistic alternative, as an arena of identity investment, for men such as Paul, individuals who, over many decades, have invested so much in the assumptions of control and certainty symbolized in the (masculine/managerial) subject position of 'man/manager'?

Similar questions to those raised in Greg's and Paul's narratives have emerged for Neville, though the work and family histories of these three men are quite dissimilar. The almost traumatic experience of being a father again, at what he considers to be an 'old' age, has ushered into Neville's life a new set of unexpected circumstances. This event carries with it new discourses of identity, discourses which do not fit so easily with the subject position of manager as it is practised in the new entreprenuerial work culture. For Neville, as his narrative suggests, there is a firm resistance to being the man/manager before all else, a resistance which emphasizes the power he exercises as a subject in the organizational arena, albeit constrained somewhat by the complexities and ambiguities of (gendered) identity work. For Neville, as with all these men/managers, success in paid work is not merely about material, extrinsic reward. For as has been discussed, the degree of ontological security that comes from being immersed in the 'frantic organization' is not insignificant. To move out of the organization, mentally and/or physically, puts the discursive (masculine) subject under some strain. It is not simply a case of transferring one's identity work to the private sphere and becoming more involved with home and family.

To conclude, this chapter has suggested that the organization can be best understood as an arena of multiple subjectivities, a site for the propagation and dissemination of contesting discourses: a gendered environment, but one which does not preclude the creation of different identities. Furthermore, I have argued that, in their diversity, some identities may well come to exist in a state of resistance to conventional ways of being (a manager). In keeping with similar research which has sought to make more visible the man in management, I have argued that the dominant discourse of performativity, now widespread in education management, has distinctly masculine characteristics which offer to men/managers a means of exhibiting manliness. Following this, the seduction and attraction of management becomes easier to understand. It provides a ready-formed arena for men in which to engage in identity work, and, subsequently, a means by which to possibly achieve the sense of ontological security sought by all human subjects: the 'double certainty' (of being) contained in the man/manager. Yet this is not to discount the possibilities of disruption and subversion to this dominant discourse, a poststructuralist perspective being particularly useful here in illuminating the points of power/resistance in discourse, and the relationship between the subject and practices of self.

Whilst the new work culture of FE is, for a variety of reasons, somewhat entrenched in these colleges, it is the case that its reconstitution and reconfiguration by subjects will be a constant aspect of (FE) organizational life. Resistance is, then, understood as continuous, often subtle, sometimes hidden, yet still an aspect of power. However, to reiterate, the examples described in this chapter, of the subject's resistance to, and/or tension with, dominant discourses should not be read as the strategic acts of rational individuals. Rather, these narrative accounts reveal the moments wherein subjects reconstitute and become reconstituted in discourse, not in any strategic fashion, but as a result of the very contingency of identity; the fragility and unpredictability of being. Thus can be seen the double illusion awaiting those men who would invest identity in masculinity/managerialism, for lurking beyond the given assumptions of control, certainty and fixedness is an ever-present insecurity. Moreover, I would suggest that these moments of disruption to dominant masculine/managerial discourse are increasingly likely. In the so-called postmodern era the different ways of being open to men are multiple and multiplying. In this respect the conventional, common-sense understanding of masculinity, expressed in much of managerial practice and language, whilst powerful and seductive, is increasingly anachronistic. Recognizing the ever-shifting historic and cultural dimensions of masculinity, the time may be approaching when 'managerial man' is less an exemplar of masculinity, more an isolated outpost.

ACKNOWLEDGEMENTS

I thank the editors for their helpful comments, and also Deborah Kerfoot, Sheila Scraton and Jeff Hearn for their advice and support during the larger research project. This chapter draws on and develops work begun in: S. Whitehead, (1998) 'Disrupted Selves: Resistance and Identity Work in the Managerial Arena', *Gender and Education*, 10(2).

NOTES

1. See Cantor *et al.* (1995), Avis *et al.* (1996), Ainley and Bailey (1997) for further discussion and elaboration of the political, economic and cultural shifts influencing and constituting post-incorporated FE.
2. FE is a sector in which women are over-represented both as students and staff. However, despite a recent increase, women represent less than 30 per cent of senior managers and just 18 per cent of all principals (Murray, 1995; 1997).
3. See Wilkinson and Willmott (1995) for discussion of organizational change in respect of surveillance, control and measurement, and practices of total quality management across both the public and private sectors.
4. See Morley and Walsh (1995), Hall (1996) and Prichard (1996), for discussion of similar changes and developments in schools and higher education.
5. See Morgan (1992) and Seidler (1994) for examination of the historically and socially specific relationship between rationality, reason and dominant codes of masculinity.
6. Gilmore (1990) and Cornwall and Lindisfarne (1994) provide some interesting insights into the cultural diversity of masculine 'norms'.
7. Recognizing that masculinity is not 'real', both Hearn (1996) and MacInnes (1998) consider the concept to be problematic in terms of its usefulness in critically understanding, and changing, men's practices.
8. See Hassard and Holliday (1999) for discussion of the relationship between gender, (managerial) embodiment, bodies and organizational life.
9. My understanding of language is one which locates it, in Foucaldian terms, as an effect of discourse; where subjectivity and a sense of self are defined, constructed, but amenable to transformation. This is in contrast to Lacan's post-Saussurean model which argues for a notion of the subject as being a product of language, fixed in the 'symbolic order' of a primary signifier – the phallus.
10. My use of the term 'Goffmanesque' refers to Goffman's (1959) use of the theatrical metaphor to describe the actions of the self in masked performance, reified by the gaze of the other, in this case the audience

(of masculinity). See Manning (1992) for critical discussion of Goffman's theories.
11.   See Jermier *et al.* (1995) for poststructuralist analysis of organizational resistance and counter-cultural subjectivities in the workplace.

REFERENCES

Acker, J. and Van Houten, D. R. (1974) 'Differential Recruitment and Control: the Sex Structuring of Organisations', *Administrative Science Quarterly*, 19(2), pp. 152–63.
Ainley, P. and Bailey, B. (1997) *The Business of Learning* (London: Cassell).
Avis, J., Bloomer, M., Esland, G., Gleeson, D. and Hodkinson, P. (1996) *Knowledge and Nationhood* (London: Cassell).
Ball, S. J. (ed.) (1990) *Foucault and Education* (London: Routledge).
Bauman, Z. (1992) *Intimations of Postmodernity* (London: Routledge).
Bauman, Z. (1997) *Postmodernity and its Discontents* (Cambridge: Polity).
Brittan, A. (1989) *Masculinity and Power* (Oxford: Blackwell).
Brod, H. and Kaufman, M. (eds) (1994) *Theorizing Masculinities* (Thousand Oaks, CA: Sage).
Butler, J. (1990) *Gender Trouble* (New York: Routledge).
Cantor, L., Roberts, I. and Pratley, B. (1995) *A Guide to Further Education in England and Wales* (London: Cassell).
Carrigan, T., Connell, R. W. and Lee, J. (1985) 'Toward a New Sociology of Masculinity', *Theory and Society* 4(5), pp. 551–604.
Casey, C. (1995) *Work, Self and Society* (London: Routledge).
Cheng, C. (ed.) (1996) *Masculinities in Organizations* (London: Sage).
Cockburn, C. (1991) *In the Way of Women* (London: Macmillan).
Coleman, M. (1997) 'Managing for Equal Opportunities: the Gender Issue', in T. Bush and D. Middlewood (eds), *Managing People in Education* (London: Paul Chapman).
Collinson, D. L. and Hearn, J. (eds) (1996) *Men as Managers, Managers as Men* (London: Sage).
Collinson, D. L., Knights, D. and Collinson, M. (1990) *Managing to Discriminate* (London: Routledge).
Connell, R. W. (1993) 'The Big Picture: Masculinities in Recent World History', *Theory and Society*, 22, pp. 597–623.
Connell, R. W. (1995) *Masculinities* (Oxford: Polity/Blackwell).
Cornwall, A. and Lindisfarne, N. (eds) (1994) *Disclocating Masculinity: Comparative Ethnographies* (London: Routledge).
Foucault, M. (1971) *L'Ordre du Discours* (Paris: Gillimard).
Foucault, M. (1973) *The Birth of the Clinic* (London: Tavistock).
Foucault, M. (1977) *Discipline and Punish: The Birth of the Prison*, trans. by A. Sheridan (London: Tavistock).
Foucault, M. (1982) 'The Subject and Power', in H. L. Dreyfus and P. Rabinow (eds), *Michel Foucault: Beyond Structuralism and Hermeneutics* (Chicago: University of Chicago Press).

Foucault, M. (1988) 'Power and Sex', in L. D. Kritzman (ed.), *Politics, Philosphy, Culture: Interviews and Other Writings, 1977–1984* (New York: Routledge).

Further Education Development Agency (FEDA) (1997) *Women at the Top in Further Education* (London: FEDA).

Further Education Funding Council (FEFC) (1997) *Annual Report 1996/97* (Coventry: Further Education Funding Council).

Game, A. (1991) *Undoing the Social: Towards a Deconstructive Sociology* (Milton Keynes: Open University Press).

Gherardi, S. (1995) *Gender, Symbolism and Organizational Cultures* (London: Sage).

Giddens, A. (1991) *Modernity and Self-Identity* (Cambridge: Polity Press).

Gilmore, D. G. (1990) *Manhood in the Making: Cultural Concepts of Masculinity* (London: Yale University Press).

Goffman, E. (1959) *The Presentation of Self in Everyday Life* (Harmondsworth: Penguin).

Goffman, E. (1974) *Frame Analysis: An Essay on the Organization of Experience* (New York: Harper & Row).

Hall, V. H. (1996) *Dancing on the Ceiling* (London: Paul Chapman).

Hassard, J. and Holliday, R. (eds) (1999) *Body and Organizations* (London: Sage).

Hearn, J. (1992) *Men in the Public Eye* (London: Routledge).

Hearn, J. (1996) 'Is Masculinity Dead? A Critique of the Concept of Masculinity/Masculinities', in M. Mac an Ghaill (ed.), *Understanding Masculinities* (Buckingham: Open University Press).

Hearn, J. and Parkin, W. (1987) *Sex at Work* (Brighton: Wheatsheaf).

Hollway, W. (1984) 'Gender Difference and the Production of Subjectivity', in J. Henriques, W. Hollway, C. Urwin, C. Venn and V. Walkerdine (eds), *Changing the Subject* (London: Methuen).

Institute of Management (1995) *National Salary Survey* (Kingston upon Thames: Institute of Management).

Jefferson, T. (1994) 'Theorising Masculine Subjectivity', in T. Newburn and E. A. Stanko (eds) *Just Boys Doing Business?* (London: Routledge).

Jermier, J. M., Knights, D. and Nord, W. R. (eds) (1994) *Resistance and Power in Organizations* (London: Routledge).

Johnson, S. and Meinhof, U. H. (eds) (1997) *Language and Masculinity* (Oxford: Blackwell).

Kanter, R. M. (1977) *Men and Women of the Corporation* (New York: Basic Books).

Kerfoot, D. and Knights, D. (1993) 'Management, Masculinity and Manipulation: From Paternalism to Corporate Strategy in Financial Services in Britain', *Journal of Management Studies*, 30(4), pp. 659–79.

Kerfoot, D. and Whitehead, S. (1996) '"And So Say All of Us"? The Problematics of Masculinity and Managerial Work', *Gender and Life in Organizations*, Occasional Papers in Organizational Analysis no. 5 (University of Portsmouth).

Kondo, D. K. (1990) *Crafting Selves: Power, Gender, and Discourses of Identity in a Japanese Workplace* (Chicago: University of Chicago Press).

LaBier, D. (1986) *Modern Madness: The Hidden Link between Work and Emotional Conflict* (New York: Simon & Schuster).

Lyotard, J. F. (1984) *The Post-Modern Condition: A Report on Knowledge* (Manchester: Manchester University Press).

McNay, L. (1992) *Foucault and Feminism* (Cambridge: Polity).

Mac an Ghaill, M. (1994) 'The Making of Black English Masculinities', in H. Brod and M. Kaufman (eds), *Theorizing Masculinities* (Thousand Oaks: California).

MacInnes, J. (1998) *The End of Masculinity* (Buckingham: Open University Press).

Mangan, J. A. and Walvin, J. (1987) *Manliness and Morality: Middle Class Masculinity in Britain and America, 1800–1940* (Manchester: Manchester University Press).

Manning, P. (1992) *Erving Goffman and Modern Sociology* (Cambridge: Polity).

Marshall, J. (1995) *Women Managers Moving On: Exploring Career and Life Choices* (London: Routledge).

Messerschmidt, J. W. (1995) 'Schooling, Masculinities and Youth Crime by White Boys', in T. Newburn and E. A. Stanko (eds), *Just Boys Doing Business?* (London: Routledge).

Mills, A. J. and Tancred, P. (eds) (1992) *Gendering Organisational Analysis* (London: Sage).

Morgan, D. H. J. (1992) *Discovering Men* (London: Routledge).

Morley, L. and Walsh, V. (eds) (1995) *Feminist Academics: Creative Agents for Change* (London: Taylor & Francis).

Murray, L. (1995) 'Women Academic Staff in Further Education', paper presented at the *Men in Management: Changing Cultures within Education Conference'*, Thomas Danby College, Leeds, 24–5 May.

O'Brien, M. (1981) *The Politics of Reproduction* (London: Routledge & Kegan Paul).

Pahl, R. (1995) *After Success* (Cambridge: Polity).

Pleck, J. H. (1981) *The Myth of Masculinity* (Cambridge, MA: MIT Press).

Prichard, C. (1996) 'Managing Universities: Is It Men's Work?' in D. Collinson and J. Hearn (eds), *Men as Managers, Managers as Men* (London: Sage).

Roper, M. (1994) *Masculinity and the British Organisational Man since 1945* (Oxford: Oxford University Press).

Saco, D. (1992) 'Masculinity as Signs: Poststructuralist Approaches to the Study of Gender', in S. Craig (ed.), *Men, Masculinity and the Media* (London: Sage).

Sawicki, J. (1991) *Disciplining Foucault: Feminism, Power and the Body* (London: Routledge).

Segal, L. (1990) *Slow Motion* (London: Virago).

Seidler, V. J. (1994) *Unreasonable Men* (London: Routledge).

Shotter, J. and Gergen, K. J. (eds) (1994) *Texts of Identity* (London: Sage).

Smircich, L. (1983) 'Concepts of Culture and Organizational Analysis', *Administrative Science Quarterly*, 28: 3, pp. 339–59.

Sturdy, A., Knights, D. and Willmott, H. (eds) (1992) *Skill and Consent: Contemporary Studies in the Labour Process* (London: Routledge).

Thompson, E. H. (ed.) (1994) *Older Men's Lives* (Thousand Oaks, CA: Sage).

Thompson, P. and Ackroyd, S. (1995) ' "All Quiet on the Western Front?": A Critique of Recent Trends in British Industrial Sociology', *Sociology*, 29(4), pp. 615–33.

Thompson, P. and McHugh, D. (1990) *Work Organisations* (London: Macmillan).

Tolson, A. (1977) *The Limits of Masculinity* (London: Tavistock).

Usher, R. and Edwards, R. (1994) *Postmodernism and Education* (London: Routledge).

Watson, T. J. (1994) *In Search of Management: Culture, Control and Chaos in Managerial Work* (London: Routledge).

Weedon, C. (1987) *Feminist Practice and Poststructuralist Theory* (Oxford: Basil Blackwell).

Whitehead, S. (1996) 'Men Managers and the Shifting Discourses of Post-Compulsory Education', *Research in Post-Compulsory Education*, 1(2), pp. 151–68.

Whitehead, S. (1999) 'From Paternalism to Entrepreneuralism: the Experience of Men Managers in UK Postcompulsory Education', *Discourse: Studies in the Cultural Politics of Education*, 20(1).

Wilkinson, A. and Willmott, H. (eds) (1995) *Making Quality Critical* (London: Routledge).

Wolfe, J. (1977) 'Women in Organisations', in S. Clegg and D. Dunkerely (eds), *Critical Issues in Organisations* (London: Routledge & Kegan Paul).

7 Racialized Identity and the Term 'Black'
NADIA JOANNE BRITTON

I subjected myself to an objective examination, I discovered my black-ness, my ethnic characteristics; and I was battered down by tom-toms, cannibalism, intellectual deficiency, fetishism, racial defects, slave-ships, and above all else, above all: 'Sho' good eatin'.

(Fanon, 1968)

In commonsense everyday language the term 'black'[1] is infused with negative connotations. Indeed, to have a black mark against one's name, to be in a black mood or to be the black sheep of the family is synonymous with having undesirable qualities which prompt others to adopt strategies of exclusion and avoidance. It hardly seems necessary to include a reminder here that the meaning of the term 'white'[2] indi-cates its socially constructed opposition to black by generally signify-ing purity and innocence. Thus, to be whiter than white or to tell a white lie is analogous with having no malicious intent. This chapter examines the contemporary use of the term black to represent a col-lective racialized[3] identity. It is concerned with its meaning in the specific politicized context of a black voluntary organization. The chapter begins by tracing briefly the history of the term in order to provide the background to its current usage. An historical overview is helpful in that it indicates how and why black has been systematically negatively racialized as well as revealing how it has been appropriated as a means of collective resistance.

The purpose of this chapter is to explain how a group of volunteers drawn from various black racialized groups understood their identity to be racialized in the context of the black voluntary organization and more widely. In doing so it engages with the contemporary politicized debate over the most appropriate use of the term black, particularly with reference to the contentious inclusion of Asians[4]. This debate is also summarized below. My primary aim is to suggest a way of achiev-ing a sociological understanding of collective racialized identities which does not unquestioningly prioritize the signifier of skin colour.

134

THE TERM BLACK: AN HISTORICAL PERSPECTIVE

It must be stressed that having a black skin does not necessarily indicate that an individual is an object of racism. Although there is a tendency to assume otherwise, there is nothing about processes of racialization which means that only black people can experience racism. In fact, the meaning of a black skin has not always been the same. What is important is that, over time, skin colour has been attributed with meaning in such a way that blackness has almost invariably been replete with negative connotations. Crucially, the skin colour signifier has contributed to the persistence of processes of racialization which have negative implications for those classified as non-white[5] (see Miles, 1989: 70–1).

For example, in the case of Britain, the reign of Elizabeth I is widely referred to as a particularly revealing period in this respect (e.g, Walvin, 1973; Fryer, 1984). During the sixteenth century an increase in foreign travel resulted in greater contact with people from the African continent. Printed accounts of such expeditions facilitated a growing curiosity about the wider world and its inhabitants. At the same time the symbolic significance of whiteness increased due to the much-admired fairness of the queen's skin, which was likened to the apparent purity of her government. The combining of these two factors encouraged the positing of black and white as opposites with much literary and dramatic potential. The work of Shakespeare is frequently cited as significant in confirming the demonizing of black skin, and thus of black people, in the popular imagination of the day (e.g, Walvin, 1974: 24–8; Fryer, 1984: 139). This occurred during a period in which black slaves were sought after as exotic status symbols of the wealthy.

It is also argued that skin colour signification played an important part in justifying the wider enslavement of black people. For example, in the eighteenth century the philosopher John Locke created a model which counted skin colour as an essential feature of human beings. The model showed blacks as being naturally inferior to whites (Fryer, 1988: 67). Similarly, at the height of the British Empire, from the mid-nineteenth century onwards, the classificatory systems engendered by scientific racism involved considering the accuracy of skin colour as an indicator in determining the quality of 'racial stock' (see Malik, 1996, for a detailed account of scientific racism).

There is plenty of evidence of sustained resistance to these systems of classification and the racialized regimes they have supported, but perhaps one of the best-known forms of collective politicized action in post-war history is the black power movement in the USA. During the 1960s African-Americans inverted racialized conceptions of blackness and adopted 'black is beautiful' as a key rallying slogan (Martin, 1991: 83–6). It was, in essence, a radical response to the limitations of the more liberal civil rights movement in an attempt to achieve justice.

Therefore, the use of the term black cannot be understood without considering the historical, cultural and political context within which a black skin colour is imbued with specific meaning and classified accordingly. Examining the use of the term black goes hand-in-hand with determining for what purpose skin colour is signified in a particular way.

THE CURRENT USES OF THE TERM BLACK

In Britain, and indeed elsewhere, the term black is the focus of considerable debate among theorists of race[6] and ethnicity due to its often contradictory and imprecise meanings (Spickard, 1996). First, it is argued that the term is detrimental to the identity of British Asians because it amounts to an endorsement of the way in which they are primarily defined in terms of colour by Britain's race relations establishment. Tariq Modood has written extensively on this subject with particular reference to Muslims of Asian origin (1988, 1990, 1992, 1994). He has argued:

> The root problem is that contemporary anti-racism defines people in terms of their colour; Muslims – suffering all the problems that anti-racists identify – hardly ever think of themselves in terms of their colour. And so, in terms of their own being, Muslims feel most acutely those problems that the anti-racists are blind to; and respond weakly to those challenges that the anti-racists want to meet with most force.
>
> (1990: 157)

Thus, according to this argument, Asian Muslims are unlikely to be involved in a politicized collective response which organizes around the term black.

Second, and in relation to the above argument, by prioritizing differences based on skin colour, rather than cultural or religious differences, the interests of Asians can be seen as subordinated to those of the African-Caribbean population which is more commonly defined as black. However, it follows that the interests of African-Caribbeans can be thought to be similarly demeaned by using the term in a way which disguises their African heritage and the specificity of their racialized experiences. As a result, it might be suggested that the term black is of limited utility and is ultimately detrimental to the interests of both Asians and African-Caribbeans.

Third, a distinctively more liberal, and extremely controversial, definition of the term incorporates any minority ethnic group in Britain, and is likely to include, for example, the Irish and Jewish populations. Considering this usage is timely due to the documented increase in the number of asylum seekers and refugees from Eastern Europe. During the 1990s this diverse group gradually became the focus of processes of racialization even though it was not defined by skin colour (Miles, 1993; Cohen, 1994). This definition is wholly rejected by those who favour the use of the term black to refer to people of African origin exclusively. For example, Stephen Small has argued that non-blacks must be excluded from black organizations because they do not understand what it means to be black (Small, 1994).

Having outlined these arguments, it is clear that an inclusive use of the term black by a black voluntary organization was worthy of investigation because of its implications for the likelihood of unified collective action. In short, how could the organization mobilize successfully around this inclusive use when it seemed probable that those participating would reject, or at least question, the definition adopted? Before exploring the related understanding of the volunteers, it is pertinent to consider the research context within which the use of the term black was explored. What follows is an overview of both the voluntary organization and the main research questions.

THE BLACK VOLUNTARY ORGANIZATION

The organization which provided the site for my research was formally established in 1991 by a Home Office grant and has subsequently been funded mainly by a regional probation service. It is accurately marketed as the only one of its kind of black voluntary organization in Britain. Its broad objective is to offer practical advice to local black people about any aspect of the criminal justice process. The main part of its work involves operating a Help On Arrest Scheme. With the agreement of the local police, trained volunteers are available to go to any police station in the city where the organization is based, on the request of an arrested black person, in order to offer practical help and assistance. A telephone rota system ensures that a volunteer may be contacted 24 hours a day, seven days a week. Since its inception the organization has successfully attracted and maintained a body of around 60 volunteers from various minority ethnic groups.

In principle, the organization aims to serve all the minority ethnic groups in the city where it is based. However, during the course of the research there was a working agreement within the organization that non-white groups represent the focus of its work. Thus, although the organization has attracted volunteers from, for example, the Irish population, and would respond to a request for help from an Irish person, it is not actively promoted as an organization serving local Irish people. As a result the organization has not pursued the needs and interests of minority ethnic groups which are usually classified as white and, instead, conforms to the more common definition of the term black as meaning non-white. The organization therefore focuses on both the local African-Caribbean and Asian population.

Two-thirds of the operational volunteers participating in the organization were interviewed. Table 7.1 is a summary of their self-defined minority ethnic origin and their gender. From interviews with these volunteers it was evident that the propensity to volunteer for the organization increases according to three main criteria: being a graduate or undergraduate, having a broadly middle-class socioeconomic status and being, or aiming to be, employed in an area of work which reflects the organization's aims and objectives. Within these categories the volunteers were still extremely diverse in terms of their social characteristics and therefore it must be stressed that the organization

Table 7.1   *Ethnic groups and genders*

	Female	*Male*	*Total*	*Percentage*
African-Caribbean	8	7	15	50
Pakistani	0	8	8	27
Irish	1	1	2	7
White British	1	1	2	7
Indian	1	0	1	3
Chinese	0	1	1	3
Persian	0	1	1	3
Total	11	19	30	100

does not straightforwardly attract a particular type of politicized volunteer. It can, however, be confidently asserted that local people are less likely to volunteer if they are not university educated, if they are unemployed or in unskilled employment and if they have no employment-related interest in the organization's work. Thus, those experiencing the hard edge of processes of racialized exclusion were not represented among the politicized volunteers within the organization. Whether their absence from the organization signifies their comprehensive exclusion from the political process more generally is another issue beyond the scope of this chapter.

The volunteers were interviewed in order to address the three aims of the research. The first aim was to produce much-needed empirical evidence about how volunteers understand the meaning and role of race as they participate in a black voluntary organization. Second, the research was designed to examine how the organization's volunteers understood their identity to be racialized in relation to other black and white people both within the organization and beyond. The third aim was to analyse the nature of the relationship between black people and the police by focusing on how the relevant individuals involved interpret and negotiate the relationship during everyday social encounters. Each of these aims provided the opportunity to explore the question of how far, and why, the volunteers accepted the organization's use of the term black.

RACIALIZED IDENTITY: A SOCIOLOGICAL INTERPRETATION

I would like to suggest that studies of ethnicity within social anthropology have much to offer a sociological investigation of how racialized identities are practised (Barth, 1969; Cornell, 1996; Jenkins, 1994). By adapting the theories advanced in these studies my argument is that, for each dimension of racialized sameness and difference, a symbolic boundary exists to signify who is included and who is excluded according to the criteria used to define the racialized group in question. In fact, each boundary necessarily implies a simultaneous process of group identification and categorizing others (Jenkins, 1994: 23). The distinction between a core and peripheral identity is also crucial to the argument I develop. The former is based on group identification whereas the latter results from being categorized. Thus, I demonstrate below how the term black was understood by the volunteers to represent an optional community of interest, and is valid as the basis for an inclusive, collective resistance to seemingly comparable experiences of racialized exclusion. It is inevitably a peripheral racialized identity and is a weak yet pragmatic form of group identification specifically because it is based solely on politicized, rather than cultural or social, affiliations.

In summary, I suggest that a comprehensive sociological understanding of racialized identity is possible only if its formation is seen as a dynamic process whereby similarities and differences are taken to be of equal importance. The postmodernist preoccupation with difference therefore occurs at the expense of considering the unquestionable importance of constructed similarities (for accounts of the postmodernist politics of identity see, e.g., Turner, 1990; hooks, 1992). The empirical evidence presented reveals the usefulness of studying how racialized identities are practised at both the individual and organizational level. This is a useful corrective to the tendency within the sociological study of race and identity to focus mainly on processes of racialized identity formation and practice at the structural level (e.g. Gilroy, 1987; Small, 1994).

WITHIN A BLACK RACIALIZED GROUP

According to Stephen Cornell, collective identity varies continuously along three dimensions: shared culture, shared institutions and shared interests (Cornell, 1996: 265–9). The first two of these three dimensions are acutely evident with reference to the volunteers' understanding of the similarities which unite members of a particular black racialized group. I will explore them in turn in order to demonstrate how each significantly contributed to the volunteers' understanding of what they share with other members of their specific racialized group.

The volunteers primarily defined their particular racialized group with reference to a shared community of culture. By this, it is meant that members participate in a symbolic system of norms and values based on a shared cultural heritage which can include language, religion, country of origin, music and food. Membership of a community of culture is not calculated or planned. Instead, it is purely a matter of life and lifestyle circumstances. This does not mean that there is a total absence of choice in belonging to the group. Rather, it means that the racialized boundary separating one group from others is relatively fixed and, as a result, movement into and out of the group is very limited. The volunteers were asked if they understood themselves to belong to a particular community and, if so, what brings this community together.

> Probably the language. The fact that we speak the same language or we're all from the same country. That in itself brings us together, and religion.
>
> (Lata)

> I think that Pakistani communities in particular, you know our culture and that, we're more closer really I think.
>
> (Anwar)

The importance of country of origin was articulated effectively by the following two volunteers who used the now infamous measure of the cricket test to explain their predominant affiliation with Pakistan and Jamaica respectively.

> Now, if say there's cricket and England are playing Pakistan, then I'll support Pakistan because that's where I come from but if England are playing New Zealand then I'll support England 'cause its the country I have the most ties with.
>
> (Jabir)

> If the West Indies are touring, I'm shouting for the West Indies. I don't apologise for that, that is the situation. But, if other UK matches are going on, I'm rooting for England. ... I do consider meself British yeah, but, at the end of the day right, because of my Jamaican heritage, and the African heritage as well, and the sort of upbringing I got from my parents as well right, I look first towards Jamaica.
>
> (David)

Interestingly, when describing what brings members of their racialized group together, none of the Asian volunteers referred to the same aspects of culture as the African-Caribbean volunteers. Therefore, the following quote is representative of those volunteers of African-Caribbean origin only.

> I, for example, am deeply into reggae music yeah, and I like me soul as well, but I don't have anywhere to go in Sheffield, as in night-clubs, to hear that sort of music. So, I tend to either come here (African-Caribbean community centre) on a Saturday night or sometimes I go to the blues. We tend to like the same things ...
>
> (David)

As a result, a community of culture was understood to bind members of a particular racialized group together by providing the common ground of a shared identity. For the volunteers this group identification was achieved through the recognition of diverse, shared symbols ranging from musical styles and food types, in the case of African-Caribbeans, to familiar symbols of national affiliation and pride, in the case of Asians.

Next, the idea of an institutional community featured regularly in the volunteers' description of their racialized group. This type of community comprises a more or less exclusive set of institutions which members use in an attempt to solve life problems (Cornell, 1996: 270). These institutions can be both formal and informal organizational mechanisms. In fact, it is arguably preferable to refer to an institutional community as a community of support because it provides a practical strategy for coping in a social world where particular racialized groups encounter specific problems and difficulties. The volunteers' understanding suggests that it is often a response, and thus a challenge, to the racialized conditions created by others. The volunteers described it as both a formal and an informal network. The following volunteers were asked what brings their community together.

> Well, we all have the same problems, social problems, welfare problems, money problems, you know. The thing that's getting us altogether is discussing our problems and, you know, we can see the chance where we can help each other.
>
> (Veronica)

> It's mainly around the struggle, that's one of the words that comes to mind. One is sharing the similar problems and so we find we sort of link together as a mutual support set-up. ... I went on a black access course, quite a few us went on it, and we sort of keep that support straight through to university.
>
> (David)

For those volunteers of Pakistani origin, a community of support also included the idea of a spatially distinct community in which kinship networks are of considerable importance.

> It's a community where they've always lived together, they stay close together, they don't believe in separation, you know. Your son could get married and he might want to go and live in his own house but his parents would love him to stay at home with his wife ... they believe in sticking together and, you'll find that in a lot of areas, a

lot of Asian people who live close by, they're all related. There's cases where there's a street full on both sides of just relations.

(Ali)

Thus, an institutional community complements a community of culture in that it provides further common ground of a shared identity. This is based on group problem-sharing and problem-solving, and reflects a spirit of mutual support.

It must be stressed that volunteers were keen to highlight differences which they understood to divide members of the same racialized group. The most frequently mentioned were those based on social class, age and lifestyle factors. However, none of these was seen to affect the racialized boundary which denotes who is included in and excluded from a particular black racialized group; thus they were not seen to result in movement across boundaries. Importantly, these differences do not, therefore, affect my argument that similarities based on cultural heritage and mutual institutional support characterize racialized group identification.

On the basis of the volunteers' understanding of what constitutes their particular racialized group, it would appear that the organization's inclusive use of the term black is problematic: it does not denote either a community of culture or a community of institutions, in the terms in which the volunteers spoke of either. This would suggest that the term cannot straightforwardly represent the foundation of a politicized racialized identity. However, the following section reveals that a different picture emerges from the volunteers' understanding of what unites volunteers from different black racialized groups.

BETWEEN DIFFERENT BLACK RACIALIZED GROUPS

The volunteers were unanimous in agreeing that, whilst fulfilling their voluntary duties, they regarded themselves as serving members of all of the black racialized groups represented in the local population. Their views indicate a perceived identification with members of black racialized groups other than their own.

No, I'm not protecting the interests of other West Indians, I'm protecting the interests of any, well, non-white person that needs help. It doesn't matter what race they are.

(Pam)

Yeah. I represent all. I'm not just representing black Afro-Caribbeans. I'm representing black people overall. ... I wouldn't just discriminate against someone because, although they might be black, they're a different ethnic minority group to myself.

(Anne)

The key to explaining the volunteers' understanding lies again with the distinction between group identification and group categorization. The latter is perceived to be defined externally by others. This means that individuals who belong to a racialized category do not choose to be members because, instead, membership is delineated for them, without their consent. In fact, the volunteers understood a crucial racialized category to exist at the level of the binary opposition black–white. Black was primarily thought to be meaningful in describing a common collective experience of being categorized as not white in a social world where whiteness is constructed as the norm, and thus has a privileged status.

For me, black is anybody who isn't white and we all have a common experience in our oppression. It comes in different forms, you know.

(Richard)

That all boils down to them not being white. At the end of the day, that's where the similarity comes into it and it's got to be a big similarity because Britain, the way Britain sees anybody that's not white.

(Alison)

Whiteness was also understood to assume a privileged status because it is commonly regarded as being synonymous with Britishness. Individuals who are not classified as white cannot therefore be classified as British.

I'm sure they [the different black groups] have things in common. That's almost guaranteed because essentially, whether they're born here or not, they're treated essentially as being as not from this country.

(Diana)

I think, if you're white and British, then people look at you and say you're British. If you're black and British, people say you're black and you're living in Britain and I think that's the difference.

(Gary)

In defining black as a form of social categorization, the volunteers prioritized the racialized signifier of skin colour. This, in turn, indicated another, seemingly impermeable, racialized boundary separating all white people from those racialized groups who cannot be described phenotypically as white. The problematic nature of this perceived boundary is explored below but, for now, it is adequate to acknowledge its significance in explaining the legitimacy of the inclusive term black within the organization.

This use of the term is satisfactorily explained as denoting a community of interest (Cornell, 1996). Members who belong to this type of community are united predominantly on the basis of a set of perceived positional interests rather than a shared cultural heritage or institutional support network. As the volunteers explained, external racialized conditions rather than internal characteristics provide the impetus for unity. Consequently, shared membership of either a community of culture or an institutional community is unnecessary. Unlike these forms of community, a community of interest, based on an inclusive use of the term black, is a calculated, formal, politicized response to the negative conditions to which non-white people are subjected. It is inherently conditional and is always crucially dependent on the nature of racialized relations in the wider social world.

The volunteers therefore argued that members of both African-Caribbean and Asian racialized groups can create a politicized form of unity purely as a result of their shared experiences of not being white. Essentially, unity represents a means through which they can address the unequal relations of power that were understood to benefit the white majority at the expense of the black minority. In the specific context of the black voluntary organization, it was thought to be helpful in challenging processes of racialization present within the various, predominately white, criminal justice agencies.

It's simply because when you do actually go on visiting you don't see it as it's going to be a Pakistani or Asian or say Jamaican or even Somalian. You say black. It's more like black people against the, helping black people against the police. It's just the way it is, it's like a pure white organisation.

(Khalid)

Sometimes it makes you quite mad because you think, well, it would be easier to put them together to get the white people out and that, you know.

(Alison)

The inclusive term black therefore denotes a specific dimension of racialized identity. This dimension is based solely on a perceived difference between black and white people regardless of their membership of particular racialized groups. It does not suggest that all non-white groups have anything in common beyond their experiences of racialized exclusion from the privileged white majority. It simply reflects a pragmatic response to one set of racialized circumstances. Thus, the racialized groups subsumed under the inclusive term black are high on shared interests and low on shared culture and institutions. It is a peripheral aspect of racialized identity specifically because it indicates a politicized position only. Thus, the racialized boundary incorporating a community of interest is highly permeable, and there is potentially a great deal of movement across it, and membership of a community of interest is less fixed than that of a community of culture or a community of support.

This dimension of racialized difference is distinguishable from core aspects of racialized identity which include a cultural and social position as well. The volunteers clearly stated key differences between the different racialized groups subsumed under the inclusive term black. For example, the following volunteers identified cultural differences as a source of division.

> We're separate for the simple reason: Muslim is Muslim. Like, I don't think I could go in a mosque, they wouldn't let me for a start. And things what we do they wouldn't do it. Like, they don't go dancing. I go dancing, I ain't no Jesus, yeah? I go dancing and I drink me beer and I have me time, you know what I mean? But that's where we come different like.
>
> (Lewis)

> I think, in one sense, it's a lot harder for them because of the linguistic differences. That makes them stick together more and the religion. You know, Asian people, like a lot of Asian people's religion is a way of life, such as Muslims, whereas a lot of black people it's Christianity. You know, that kind of thing.
>
> (Alison)

In terms of the volunteers' understanding, the voluntary organization's legitimate use of the term black is restricted to reflect exclusively the significance of colour discrimination as a particular dimension of racialized discrimination more generally. The following quotes are representative of the volunteers' understanding.

The [name of black voluntary organization] is black in the political sense that its non-European, non-English. So, everyone belongs to the organization that isn't English.

(Lata)

I think black's OK as a political term as in anybody who's not white.

(Marie)

Importantly, although they accepted the broader term black in a politicized sense, the volunteers in no way endorsed its conflation as an analytical or theoretical category. Instead, they questioned the legitimacy of adopting the term to describe any racialized group accurately.

There's no black language, there's no black religion, there's no black culture, there's no black land. It doesn't exist. For me it's just another tactic to detach us even further from our roots.

(Richard)

Someone's either gonna say to me Paki or black Paki to me. They're not gonna say brown or anything but saying that, I don't know, I've never seen myself to be black, it's just the way I think.

(Anwar)

This meant that black was thought to be acceptable only if and when they choose to define themselves as such. It is useful as a means of engendering a collective politicized response but it is reprehensible if it is used to reinforce the racialized *status quo*. Paradoxically, processes of racialization were thought to be challenged by adopting a term which represents an important source of racialized inequality. The black–white binary opposition is acknowledged and mobilized politically in an effort to overcome it effectively.

Significantly, the volunteers' understanding demonstrates that racialized identity is always negotiable and open to transformation. However, the extent to which individuals are able to choose their racialized identity is inevitably restricted due to the unavoidable interplay between group identification and social categorization. In short, even if individuals wholly reject the term black, it does not follow that they will no longer be categorized as such.

In terms of its use by the black voluntary organization, the inclusive definition of the term black was therefore understood to be the basis for a form of collective resistance to the racialized categorization imposed by others. It was thought to be a politicized response to the unequal power relations whereby any individual who cannot be classified as white is subjected to apparently similar processes of racialized exclusion. However, it was noticeable from the volunteers' responses that this use of the term implicitly discounts the interests of negatively racialized groups usually categorized as being white. This omission is explored next.

BETWEEN BLACK RACIALIZED GROUPS AND WHITE, NEGATIVELY RACIALIZED GROUPS

As has already been stressed, the negative consequences of processes of racialization are not experienced exclusively by black people. Although space does not permit the inclusion of a comparison with the positively racialized white majority, the following summarizes the volunteers' understanding of white negatively racialized groups in relation to their black counterparts.

Within the context of the black voluntary organization, the position of white negatively racialized groups was explored with specific reference to the Irish. This group was chosen because the organization explicitly claimed to incorporate the interests of the local Irish population even though it had a working agreement that the interests of black racialized groups represented its focus. The volunteers' responses revealed a general recognition that the Irish cannot be categorized straightforwardly as part of the positively racialized white majority. They acknowledged that the Irish experience specific forms of racialized discrimination and stereotyping which were, nevertheless, thought to be distinguishable from those based on skin colour. The volunteers were asked if it is acceptable to include the Irish in the organization. The following comments are representative of almost three-quarters of the volunteers who argued that it was acceptable.

> As far as the Irish are concerned, they've been facing segregation and discrimination for as long as I can remember, so it's not as if they aren't discriminated against ... now the Irish are discriminated because of their race. They don't come into the definition of colour but they do come in the definition of the race.
>
> (Lata)

> I don't know whether this is one of the official aims but I see that the aims of the [name of organization] are to help those who have

been in certain instances stereotyped by institutions, and the Irish are no less stereotyped than Afro-Caribbeans.

(Diana)

For those volunteers who rejected the inclusion of the Irish, the racial- ized signifier of skin colour was again prioritized. The following volun- teers described the significance of this symbol in contributing to their experiences as members of a black racialized group.

It's like, I grew up in Heathside and there aren't any black people there, you know. So, if you're walking in the street or, say, when I walked into a classroom, they'd all look round 'cause I was the only black face.

(Pam)

It's a visual thing and, the only way I can say it is if you, if a group of black people were to walk into a room, then they are immediately discriminated against because of the visual thing. If a group of Irish people walked into a room, before you've opened your mouth or done anything, they are still not black people.

(Caroline)

Despite disagreeing on whether the Irish should be included, the related issues of choice and visibility linked the understanding of both groups of volunteers. The volunteers argued that they have no choice but to be categorized as black because they are unable to change their skin colour. The Irish, however, were understood to have the option of disguising their membership of a negatively racialized group. In short, they can arguably hide their racialized origin and, in doing so, avoid discrimination and stereotyping.

Whereas a black person, you're just black aren't you? You can't change the colour of your skin and say I'm not black ... Some people will tolerate Irish people just because they've got white skin, won't they? But they won't tolerate a black person.

(Marie)

An Irish person, they can hide their culture, if they haven't got a strong Irish accent. Whereas a black person can't. You know, they just can't [*laughs and points to herself*].

(Anne)

As the latter comment suggests, the volunteers recognized the poten- tial contribution of other racialized signifiers, such as accent, but insisted that skin colour is a more potent signifier specifically because it is not negotiable.

The volunteers explained how the Irish can exercise their dubious option of invisibilizing their racialized origin. For example, the following volunteer argued that they have the perhaps unrealistic option of not speaking or changing their accent.

> We have to live with it more than you would because at least some Irish people, if they don't open their mouth, will get away with it as white people. But black people, it doesn't matter where you are, if you're in the European countries, you are straight away stigmatized and labelled as a black person.
>
> (Salim)

The likelihood of cross-generational racialized disadvantage among the Irish was also rejected by those volunteers who referred to it.

> I know they suffer from racism but it's difficult because with their offspring, you wouldn't even know, would you, unless they say it? But they are Irish so they can be Irish when it suits them politically and not Irish when it suits them, to their advantage.
>
> (Marie)

This understanding incorporated the view that second-generation white racialized groups are not highly visible. As a result they can choose whether to acknowlege their Irish heritage and, thus, whether to adopt an Irish identity.

For these reasons the volunteers considered the interests of white negatively racialized groups, such as the Irish, to be secondary to those of black racialized groups. Unlike the Irish, black racialized groups were considered to be, unavoidably, highly visible and were thus deemed unable to exercise the same degree of choice in determining their racialized identity.

Regardless of the extent to which the volunteers acknowledged the racialized experiences of the Irish, their understandings tended to see racialized discrimination primarily as colour discrimination. Yet I would argue that individuals are not racialized solely according to skin colour. The examples given by the volunteers to emphasize the specificity of their experiences provide a partial account which ignores many of the ways in which individuals experience processes of racialization. In fact, members of black and white, negatively racialized groups are racialized as a result of a variety of easily distinguishable features including name, address, religion, dress, country of origin and language. Thus, visibility is not determined solely by skin colour. The following comment, from a police officer interviewed as part of the research, demonstrates how the Irish, and their descendants, are easily identifiable by their names alone.

> You know, if you go through the names on the list of officers what are working here, it looks like there's a good fifty per cent of Irish descent.
>
> (Sgt Samways)

The following volunteer argued that a person's voice is indicative of their racialized origin.

> I went for a job and when I phoned this guy up he said 'come down for an interview'. And, when I got there, he just didn't want to know because I was black. And I had a go and said 'why've you wasted my time, you can pay my bus fare' because he must have known on the phone. I mean, I can tell a black voice, I can always tell if it's a black person I'm speaking to.
>
> (Clive)

Furthermore, the volunteers implied that there is a clear, unambiguous racialized boundary separating black and white people. Yet incidents recalled by both the volunteers and police officers interviewed suggest that this is not the case. For example, the following officer described his mistake in offering the services of the voluntary organization's Help On Arrest Scheme to a woman who he thought was of mixed parentage.[7]

> I experienced it with a girl I thought was mixed race and she wasn't, and she was quite upset about it. She looked it. She had got a dark complexion, plus the fact that she'd recently been on holiday in Greece, and she looked of mixed race, you know.
>
> (Insp. Williams)

One of the volunteers described a man she met regularly at her place of work whom she argued, despite his insistence to the contrary, was white.

> There's a guy there who honestly thinks he's black, and it's true [*laughs*]. And, when he comes into the office, he says 'these Caucasians don't understand us blacks do they?' Then they think what is this guy on? But, honestly, he really believes he's black. I find it very sad. I don't know, I've tried to ask him.
>
> (Veronica)

It is unclear in each of these cases which party presented the most accurate racialized identification. However, the cases are significant in highlighting the negotiated nature of racialized identity. Both black and white individuals are able to exercise some degree of choice in determining their racialized identity. They also indicate that it is far from simple to categorize individuals straightforwardly as black or white. Again, this demonstrates the difficulty of prioritizing skin colour as a dominant indicator of racialized discrimination.

Prioritizing the black–white binary opposition, in the way that the volunteers tended to do, may be to the detriment of both white negatively racialized groups and black racialized groups. For example, it discounts the possible ways in which Irish people still experience specific processes of racialization in Britain, and it also detracts attention from the wide variety of processes which operate to racialize groups usually defined as black.

CONCLUSION

It has been argued in this chapter that racialized group identification is primarily based on similarities within a particular racialized group arising from a community of culture and a community of institutions or support. It is a core identification which has an immediate, everyday and enduring influence on an individual's social life. In contrast, the inclusive term black represents an inherently optional community of politicized positional interests. It is derived from racialized categorization but is thought to be relevant as a basis for engendering a collective response to processes of racialization. The term is, however, a peripheral identification which is of much less significance to an individual's racialized identity.

As has been suggested, having a non-white skin colour does not indicate a related uniform experience specifically because, first, skin colour accounts partially for processes of racialization and, second, defining oneself and being defined as black is always, to a certain extent, negotiable. Further, this suggests that the racialization of identity does not eliminate choice for any party. As a result the racialized social world is open to challenge and is, thus, by no means inevitable.

Examples included in the chapter also highlighted how the constructed racialized boundary which apparently separates all white people from all black people in fact disguises the heterogeneous nature of both groups. The common-sense prioritizing of skin colour as the key to explaining the racialized social world tends to disguise the complexity of processes of racialization. Significantly, it detracts attention from the specific experiences of negatively racialized groups usually defined as white. In terms of the black voluntary organization, this meant that it could only secure a successful politicized response by relegating the experiences of these groups to a position of secondary importance.

It is anticipated that this chapter has demonstrated the usefulness of studying how both racialized similarities and differences are understood and practised. In order to achieve a satisfactory sociological understanding of racialized identities, the chapter has also demonstrated the usefulness of investigating empirically how such identities are practised at both the individual and organizational level. By studying further how racialized identities are adopted, negotiated and transformed in everyday social life, a more comprehensive understanding of racialized power and resistance can be established.

NOTES

1. The term black is sometimes enclosed in inverted commas to denote its socially constructed, disputed usage. I have chosen not to do so here as this point is an explicit theme of the chapter.
2. The term white is also a social construct and its use is increasingly the subject of debate. Again, due to the subject of the chapter, I have decided that it is unnecessary to enclose it in inverted commas.
3. The theory of racialization was first advanced by Robert Miles who conceptualised it as follows.

   If 'races' are not naturally occurring populations, the reasons and conditions for the social process whereby the discourse of 'race' is employed in an attempt to label, constitute and exclude social collectivities should be the focus of attention rather than be assumed to be a natural and universal process.   (1989: 73).

4. I use the term Asian to mean people from the Indian subcontinent. They can also be referred to as Southern Asians. Both terms are arguably vague and therefore inadequate.
5. Non-white refers to any racialized group that does not fit the socially constructed norm of whiteness.
6. Like the terms black and white, the word race is often written in inverted commas to emphasize that races are social constructs.
7. Mixed parentage usually refers to people who have one black and one white parent. This interbreeding of apparent races is known as miscegenation. Historically, people of mixed parentage have been known,

among other terms, as half-caste and mixed race and, as a result, have been subjected to specific negative processes of racialisation (for an example see Small, 1991).

REFERENCES

Barth, F. (1969) 'Introduction', in F. Barth (ed.), *Ethnic Groups and Boundaries: The Social Organisation of Culture Difference* (Oslo: Universitetsforlaget).

Cohen, R. (1994) *Frontiers of Identity: The British and the Others* (Harlow: Longman Group).

Cornell, S. (1996) 'The Variable Ties that Bind: Content and Circumstance in Ethnic Processes', *Ethnic and Racial Studies*, 19, pp. 265–89.

Fanon, F. (1968) *Black Skins, White Masks* (London: Grafton).

Fryer, P. (1988) *Black People in the British Empire: An Introduction* (London: Pluto Press).

Fryer, P. (1984) *Staying Power: The History of Black People in Britain* (London: Pluto Press).

Gilroy, P. (1987) *There Ain't No Black in the Union Jack: The Cultural Politics of Race and Nation* (London: Unwin Hyman).

hooks, b. (1992) *Black Looks: Race and Representation* (London: South End).

Jenkins, R. (1994) 'Rethinking Ethnicity: Identity, Categorization and Power', *Ethnic and Racial Studies*, 17, pp. 197–223.

Malik, K. (1996) *The Meaning of Race: Race, History and Culture in Western Society* (Basingstoke: Macmillan).

Martin, B. L. (1991) 'From Negro to Black to African–American: the Power of Names and Naming', *Political Science Quarterly*, 106, pp. 83–107.

Miles, R. (1989) *Racism* (London: Routledge).

Miles, R. (1993) *Racism after 'Race Relations'* (London: Routledge).

Modood, T. (1988) 'Black, Racial Equality and Asian Identity', *New Community*, 14, pp. 397–404.

Modood, T. (1990) 'British Asian Muslims and the Rushdie Affair', *Political Quarterly*, 61, pp. 143–60.

Modood, T. (1992) *Not Easy Being British: Colour, Culture and Citizenship* (Stoke-on-Trent: Trentham Books).

Modood, T. (1994) 'Political Blackness and British Asians', *Sociology*, 28, pp. 859–76.

Small, S. (1991) 'Racialised Relations in Liverpool: Contemporary Anomaly', *New Community*, 17, pp. 511–37.

Small, S. (1994) *Racialised Barriers: The Black Experience in the United States and England in the 1980s* (London: Routledge).

Spickard, P. R. (1996) 'Mapping Race: Multiracial People and Racial Category Construction in the United States and Britain', *Immigrants and Minorities*, 15, pp. 107–119.

Turner, B. S. (1990) *Theories of Modernity and Post-Modernity* (London: Sage).

Walvin, J. (1973), *Black and White: The Negro and English Society, 1555–1945* (London: Allen Lane, Penguin Press).

8 Caribbean Nurses: Racisms, Resistances and Healing Narratives

LORRAINE CULLEY, SIMON DYSON, SILVIA HAM-YING and WENDY YOUNG

INTRODUCTION

In this chapter we examine some of the processes by which Caribbean-born nurses working in the National Health Service (NHS) construct their identities. We begin with a history of recent Caribbean migration to Britain and the occupational history of minority ethnic nurses in the NHS. We then consider sociological theories of ethnic identity formation, and introduce the source of our empirical material, that is in-depth interviews with 14 Caribbean nurses, describing their life histories of migration to Britain, their occupational careers in health services, and their experiences of civic society. Finally, we consider the role of narrative in identity formation and refer to empirical material from the interviews to illustrate our argument that identities are constructed in the context of potentially damaging life experiences, but may be 'healed' through the construction of preferred narratives.

CARIBBEAN MIGRATION AND NURSING IN THE NHS

The period of postwar immigration between the 1948 British Nationality Act and the 1962 Immigration Act expanded rather than created the presence of black people in the UK since they have a long history of settlement in Britain (Fryer, 1984; Ramdin, 1987; Small, 1994). During the Second World War Britain actively recruited labour from the Caribbean to help with the war effort (Fryer, 1984) and many from the Caribbean also fought in the armed services (Gilroy,

1987). Indeed half of those on the *Empire Windrush*, the famous ship bringing Caribbean migrants to Britain in 1948, had served in the forces or munitions factories during the war and were returning to Britain having been dissatisfied with the situation in Jamaica upon their return (Harris, 1993).

The 1948 British Nationality Act gave citizens of Commonwealth countries special immigration status, with the right to freely enter, work and settle with their families. The Act may be seen as a product of a desire to tap sources of labour and a continuing romantic attachment to the idea of empire as a family of people sharing common rights (Mason, 1995). Thus postwar migration to Britain from the West Indies started in 1947–8, peaked in the early 1960s and was effectively over by 1973, by which time the Caribbean-born population of Britain was about 550,000 (Peach, 1986). The Commonwealth Immigration Act of 1962 established legal controls over the entry of Commonwealth citizens for the first time and this restriction on primary immigration was extended by both Conservative and Labour governments in 1968 and 1971. The 1971 Act effectively put an end to all new primary immigration from the so-called 'New Commonwealth' (Mason, 1995).

Shortages of labour power existed in the newly formed NHS at all levels, with an estimated shortfall of 54,000 nurses in 1949 (Harris, 1993). White British workers were, on the whole, reluctant to work the long hours and shifts for low pay. Previously hospitals had relied on Irish workers to make up shortfalls in staffing levels. However, postwar there was a noticeable reduction in Irish immigration. Overseas nurses, and indeed doctors, played a significant role in filling the gaps in the delivery of the service. Substantial numbers of Caribbean-born men and women entered the NHS from the early 1950s (Doyal *et al.*, 1980; Baxter, 1987). Although it was important in shaping the movement, direct recruitment by British agencies was not numerically dominant and mainly affected Barbados, where just under a quarter of the emigrants in 1960 left on sponsorship schemes. Two of our 14 respondents were directly recruited to the NHS from Barbados in 1955 and 1957. Both underwent a selection process in Barbados and were transferred directly to their respective hospitals on arrival in the UK.

The absence of comprehensive ethnic monitoring makes any estimate of the extent of the contribution of Caribbean-born workers difficult, but available evidence suggests a substantial concentration of black migrants in ancillary work such as domestic, catering, cleaning and maintenance jobs. Nevertheless, many Caribbean migrants also entered nursing. By 1971 it was estimated that there were over 15,000 'overseas nurses' in the NHS. Thomas and Morton-Williams (1972) found that 9 per cent of hospital nurses were born overseas and that 'immigrants' were 20 per cent of pupil nurses, 15 per cent of midwives and 14 per cent of student nurses. Of the 9 per cent, half were from the West Indies, 25 per cent from Africa and 25 per cent from Asia. This early study identified an under-representation of overseas nurses in senior grades and found that overseas nurses were more likely to be found in the less popular and less prestigious specialities such as geriatric and mental health nursing. The number of Caribbean recruits declined from 1970 and by the mid-1980s recruitment had virtually ceased.

A review of the evidence on the experiences of ethnic minority nurses (Akinsanya, 1988) made the point that, despite the presence of a large proportion of ethnic minority nurses, there was little research or data on their fate within the service. It was not until after the 1976 Race Relations Act that the issue of possible racial discrimination in the NHS was directly addressed. Moreover, it was not until 1992 that a large-scale national study of the careers of ethnic minority nurses was carried out by the Policy Studies Institute on behalf of the Department of Health (Beishon *et al.*, 1995). Evidence from the early years is fragmentary, yet suggests that many nurses suffered racial discrimination (Gish, 1971; Thomas and Morton-Williams, 1972; Hicks, 1982). Several small-scale qualitative studies paint a very bleak picture, highlighting difficulties that these nurses face at all stages of their careers (Baxter, 1988; Lee-Cunin, 1989).

Many of those who migrated to Britain and who have worked in the NHS during this period are now at or approaching retirement age. In the intervening years black people have suffered racism in society at large (Fryer, 1984; Ramdin, 1987), in citizenship legislation (Rushdie, 1982), and in general employment (Brown, 1984; Ohri and Faruqi, 1988). They have been discriminated against in terms of both health service provision as clients (Pearson, 1986; Mares *et al.*, 1987; McNaught, 1987; NAHAT, 1989; Ahmad, 1993; Smaje, 1995) and in terms of employment in the health service as workers (Baxter, 1987; Ward, 1993). Indeed recent evidence has suggested that in a period of increased difficulty in recruitment to the health services (George, 1994) people of Caribbean descent are less likely to enter the health-care professions. Whilst there are calls for racism to be addressed in health service provision (NAHAT, 1989), in recruitment as health service workers (King's Fund, 1990), and in the working environment of nurses (Beishon *et al.*, 1995), there has been little research into the experiences of those of Caribbean descent, some of whom have contributed their entire working lives to the NHS.

RACIALIZED IDENTITIES

In this respect it is necessary to consider how experiences of visible minority ethnic groups impact on the formation of their identities. For example, Sivanandan (1982) and Ramdin (1987) are amongst those who use 'black' as a political term to signal the shared class interests of those of Caribbean and South Asian descent. Such formulations tend to cast black middle-class peoples in the role of traitor to a political cause, but as Hall (1992) and Boneham (1994) have argued, ethnicity is only one of a number of forms of self-identity, and for particular people in certain circumstances and at given times may not be the most decisive.

Another problem with what Modood (1994) has called 'political blackness' is its essentialism. Ethnic identities are socially constructed by social processes of boundary formation rather than being pre-given, fixed essences inherent in an individual. Furthermore the factors defining boundaries are varied and may be symbolic or real (Barth, 1969). Okamura (1981) has developed this further in the concept 'situational ethnicity' in which multiple and contingent identities are possible according to context and according to the creativity of the social actor, and Gillborn (1995) has referred to 'plastic ethnicity' in an attempt to capture the active as well as the constraining dimensions of ethnic identity. Thus even within the dimension of ethnicity itself, Modood *et al.* (1994) have suggested that new forms of ethnic identity are currently being forged both drawing upon ethnicities of religion, language, family customs and also in opposition to different forms of racisms.

With specific regard to migrants from the Caribbean, James (1993) notes that a Pan-Caribbean identity is formed in Britain, and does not exist in the Caribbean itself between disparate islands hundreds of miles apart from one another. He further argues that Caribbean migrants to Britain would have been shocked to discover the racism meted out irrespective of their place in a 'pigmentocracy', a situation he claims pertained in the Caribbean where lighter-skinned peoples are accorded greater cultural status. The shock of the new racisms may constitute what Giddens (1991) describes as 'fateful moments', full of new sets of risks and possibilities. The possibilities involve forms of 'reskilling', or empowerment, in which the challenge of how individuals are to live their lives in their changed circumstances is intimately bound up with the ongoing construction of their self-identities.

Gilroy (1987) emphasizes the contingent and partial belonging of black people in Britain, their ambiguous assimilation, and the emergence of new global structures of cultural exchange, particularly in younger people of Caribbean descent. He refers to an African diasporic consciousness formed counter to the constrictions of nation-states, and argues that contemporary black identities are identities forged out of passions and challenges to colonialism and the postcolonial world. Whilst this may hold true for younger people of African-Caribbean descent born in the UK, we need to distinguish the identities of our respondents in several respects. Firstly, being a migrant may have instilled a sense of identity as 'guest'. Secondly, if a quick return to the Caribbean was initially envisaged, a short-term perspective in which adversities could be tolerated in anticipation of a return home may have influenced the formation of identities. And thirdly, Caribbean-born nurses may be of Indian (as was one of our respondents) or Chinese, as well as African, descent.

THE RESPONDENTS

This chapter draws on interviews with eight female and six male respondents, all of whom were first-level nurses or midwives with several initial and post-basic nursing qualifications (see Table 8.1). The distinction is now not embedded in nurse education, but, until the 1980s, first-level nurses had a longer period of training and undertook a wider range of responsibilities than second-level nurses who worked under their guidance (The Nurses, Midwives and Health Visitors Rules, 1983). Many Caribbean nurses were channelled into the second level, state-enrolled nursing. They were also heavily over-represented in the less prestigious specialties of psychiatric and 'mental handicap' nursing. All six of the men and three of the women are qualified and have worked as mental health nurses. (Of these, four of the men and one of the women were also dual qualified in general nursing.) The remaining five female respondents trained as general nurses and subsequently three specialized in midwifery and had registered midwife qualifications. Six of the fourteen (four men and two women) had achieved fairly high-level positions within nursing, as Nursing Officer,

Table 8.1   *Profile of the respondents*

Respondent	Position	Age at interview	Arrival in UK	NHS service (years)	Total service (years)
A	Home manager	72	1957	18	34
B	Nurse manager	64	1955	34	34
C	Midwife	70	1958	31	31
D	Nurse manager	52	1962	31	31
E	Midwife	61	1959	35	35
F	Nursing officer	64	1954	39	39
G	Manager	60	1957	35	40
H	Senior nurse	56	1960	34	37
I	Nursing officer	59	1959	34	34
J	Senior sister	59	1956	39	39
K	Senior nurse	51	1966	27	32
L	Home manager	52	1966	20	32
M	Staff nurse	62	1960	25	30
N	Nursing sister	54	1963	12	28
		Mean = 59.7		Mean = 29.6	Mean = 34.0

Nurse Manager or Senior Clinical Nurse, before retirement. This level of occupational achievement marks our interviewees out as different from the respondents in Fenton (1988) and Lee-Cunin (1989) and may explain why their reported experiences are complex rather than overwhelmingly negative.

The respondents were aged between 51 and 72 years, with a mean age of 59.7 years, and have all worked in the health service for a substantial number of years. The sample of 14 have 414 years of service in the NHS between them, and 476 years if one counts further years of employment in Social Services and/or the private nursing sector, and in one case five years work abroad. The actual number of years service in the NHS ranges from 12 to 39 years. The number of years service worked in health/social care more broadly defined ranges from 28 to 40 years.

The respondents migrated to Britain in their early adulthood, having all their formal schooling therefore in their islands of origin. The youngest migrant was 17 on arrival and the eldest 34 years old. Five respondents came from Barbados in 1954, 1955, 1957 (two) and 1959. Four originated in Antigua, entering Britain in 1956, 1958 and 1959 and 1960. Three respondents came from Trinidad in 1960, 1963 and 1966. One came from Montserrat in 1962 and one from Jamaica in 1966.

The majority describe their Caribbean backgrounds as materially secure though not affluent, with parents/carers working as school teachers (two), a carpenter, a plumber, small businessmen (two), a member of the armed forces, religious workers (two), a nurse, landowners (two), and civil servants (two). All come from a background of Christian religious belief. Eleven of the 14 describe themselves as regular church attenders and the remainder have also until more recently had close connections with the church. For most of the sample, this religious background has been of some significance in their working and community lives.

Evidence from several early studies of West Indian migrants (Glass, 1960; Patterson, 1965; Daniel, 1968; Lawrence, 1974) indicates that few had intentions to settle permanently in Britain, and this was the case with the majority of our respondents. The fact that their original intentions had not been carried through seemed to be viewed with a certain amount of resignation and of humour rather than regret. The prospect of better opportunities in the 'Mother Country', coupled with a lack of good employment prospects at home, had been a major impetus for migration. Ten of the 14 had relatives or close friends who had migrated earlier, but two of the men had no contacts at all on arrival, other than the people they had met on the long boat journey to Britain. These respondents had been directly recruited to mental health nursing in Barbados by a selection team who had gone to the Caribbean specifically to recruit to nursing. Neither of these men had been particularly attracted to nursing as a career before their contact with the recruitment teams, but had seen nurse training as an opportunity to go to England and obtain a qualification which would provide a good basis for work at home or elsewhere. A third male respondent had no specific intention to enter nursing when he left the Caribbean, but was sent to a local hospital by the Labour Exchange shortly after arrival to stay with friends. This was also the experience of one of the women, who approached a local hospital 12 days after arriving in Britain and was immediately accepted for nurse training. One of the women had hoped to teach, but had 'settled for' nursing, and another had hoped to go into nursing when she left the Caribbean but had not been recruited before arrival. This woman also recalls being readily accepted for nurse training. These accounts demonstrate that this group of migrants had a remarkably easy entry to nurse training at this time of labour shortage. Several were taken on almost immediately and worked on the wards until they were able to join a cohort of entrants to begin formal training.

Nine of the respondents indicated that they intend to stay in Britain now that they have retired. One has returned to the Caribbean, two hoped to commute between homes in Britain and the Caribbean and two were undecided. Return migration to the Caribbean has always been significant (Peach, 1991). However, the majority of our respondents saw no real permanent place for themselves in their islands of origin and/or feel tied by strong relationships with family (especially children) and friends. Most have been fortunate in being able to return to visit the Caribbean on a very regular basis over the years and this contact is valued.

THE IMPORTANCE OF NARRATIVE

It was Rogers (1945) who first identified the resonances between in-depth research interviews and the therapeutic counselling interview. Whilst accepting the caveat of Bellaby (1991), who cautions against the assumption that reminiscences will automatically be either thera-peutic or damaging, attention has previously been drawn to the importance of narrative and 'stories' in accessing the worlds of respondents on their own terms (Graham, 1984; Plummer, 1995; Weeks, 1996). Such narrative structures have important features including the capacity to order (or indeed to disorder) experiences; to set experiences into spatial and temporal context; to establish the parameters of a teller, an audience and a point of view; and to suspend conversational turn-taking in favour of ceding to the teller the capacity to signal the end of the tale.

Hiles (1994) has contended that the narrative format dominates counselling sessions and moreover that narrative itself should be regarded as a cognitive process. Furthermore, he suggests that the structure of narratives may contain within them potential for healing qualities. Bass *et al.* (1991) have similarly suggested that one orientation of a primary care physician might conceivably be to regard a patient in general practice as effectively saying 'My story is broken, can you help me fix it?' Our intention in conducting in-depth interviews with the respondents was to enable them to relate their experiences through narrative accounts within their own frames of meaning.

Radley and Billig (1996) have questioned the notion of distinct public and private accounts raised by Cornwell (1984). Whilst we do not believe that, as a research team with varied ethnic backgrounds, we have been given a sanitized 'public' account which cleans up the worst dimensions of racisms experienced and therefore differs fundamentally from a 'private' account latent within our respondents (see Rhodes, 1994), neither do we believe we have uncovered phenomenologically pure, albeit complex, accounts. The accounts given to us have clearly also been influenced by our own identities (a team mixed ethnically, professionally, and in terms of the extent and nature of contact with Caribbean communities in the UK). One relevant aspect of the research context we have created is the shared professional or former professional status of respondents and interviewers.

In the same way that the compilation of a curriculum vitae in applications for employment involves the construction of a positive career pattern, so the element of 'career retrospective' which we have introduced by the contents of our interview checklist may be a key in the mutual construction of narratives here. Coleman (1991) suggests that where a life lived has been regarded on the whole as relatively successful, then reminiscence is a positive experience in which negative experiences are healed in the process of recounting. What we are suggesting is that the respondents' conceptions of self as successful, coupled with the shared professional status of interviewees and research team, may create a powerful impetus to situate negative experiences within a particular narrative which mitigates against the damaging dimension of reminiscence.

Freedman and Coombs (1996) have developed a theory within counselling in which the damaging dominant storyline which the counsellee presents, laden with problems, contains individual components of resistance and success, which the counsellor can help amplify in order to validate a different narrative. Whilst this different narrative remains true to the constituent elements (for unrealistic flights of fancy would not be therapeutic), it has a different, and crucially, a healing trajectory. It is something akin to this process which we believe to be occurring here. Furthermore the related counselling work of White and Epston (1990), who draw attention to the healing potential of community databases composed of the experiences of survivors of challenging circumstances, suggests that documenting and circulating such stories can have a beneficial effect.

In the case of the Caribbean nurses we interviewed, the narratives within which episodes potentially attributable to racism were recounted tended to place such episodes in a different storyline, which the interviewee found helpful in validating her/his moral career. There were three main 'narrative strategies' used by our respondents. In some instances the storyline 'deconstructed racism', by situating the experience within narratives in which age, status or gender were relatively more important. In other instances the narrative involved a retrospective, though still tentative, construction of the experiences lived through as indeed constituting racism. In yet others the story was one of moral resistance to racism, unambiguously regarded as such. In the latter, the narratives may be held to contain the potential for healing in that racisms could be named and faced in retrospect precisely because the subject had developed a narrative in which she or he was not a passive, damaged victim.

More precisely, it may be argued that it is the extent to which the respondent formulated a viable alternative narrative that allowed her or him to name experiences as racism without this account being further damaging. This may explain why 11 of our respondents named some experiences as racism, and some experiences as potentially attributable to racism, but three respondents explicitly stated that they had little or no experience of racism. Whilst this is a salutary reminder of the complexities and variabilities of individual experiences and perceptions of those experiences, it does seem improbable that different respondents should have either extensive experience of racisms or virtually none. This perhaps means that those who let experiences wash over them were not so easily able to reminisce about named racism without it causing further distress. In other words, where the storyline was one of affability and an ability of self to get on with a wide range of others, a predisposition was engendered whereby ambiguous experiences were 'given the benefit of the doubt' for they would otherwise disturb the equilibrium of the 'friendly-self' storyline.

Before we turn to a more detailed account of the three narrative strategies, it is worth listing negative experiences recounted by our interviewees, as these provide the context within which their narrative strategies should be understood. Taken as a whole, the interviewees were subjected to the following: physical violence; discriminations – in promotion, in having to take additional entrance tests, in disproportionately not receiving official rewards, in being refused choices in work patterns afforded to others; name-calling; public humiliations – brutal references to alleged sub-human qualities of black peoples (monkey noises in Outpatients; references to recent emergence from the jungle; enquiries about living in mud huts), inviting our respondents to share in the running down of other groups of black people; patients refusing their attempts to care for them, colleagues refusing to sit next to black staff or to work under black staff, white colleagues refusing to return everyday pleasantries; petty vindictiveness – white workers taking credit for the work of black people, being thought of as a thief until proved otherwise; and racial stereotyping – always happy-go-lucky, magical powers of healing, knowledgable about tropical diseases.

DECONSTRUCTING RACISM

The narrative strategy of deconstructing racism involved not reifying racism, not using it as a taken-for-granted starting point in constructing experiences and identities. Structurally, our interviewees were at the intersection of many complex and contradictory forces, and it is at least possible that awareness of this position of ambiguity heightened the astuteness of their observations.

Our respondents were nurses and midwives, not doctors and psychiatrists. As Davies (1995) argues, as nurses they were the means by which doctors and psychiatrists achieve professional status and they hold a somewhat ambivalent position in the articulation of disciplinary power. Their status as visible ethnic minorities in a racialized division of labour further added to the indeterminacies of their status.

> ... it didn't occur to me to think in terms of being a doctor. Because in those days you just thought of doctors being male, and in our country anyway they were all sort of white males anyway.
>
> (Respondent H)

The health service contained contradictions for our interviewees. On the one hand it was, as we shall see, the location of racisms of white staff and white patients. On the other hand the institutional setting provided a refuge from certain wider societal racisms.

> The other thing that cushioned people like me who came to work in the hospital service ... there were such things as nursing homes ... so we didn't have the trauma of having to look for accommodation and being rebuked and rebuffed and discarded.
>
> (Respondent G)

Moreover, in an increasingly creditialist profession (Witz, 1992), many Caribbean nurses had credentials at least comparable to those of white nurses, having experienced a traditional British curriculum through the colonial education system. Thus the importance of qualifications within the structures of the profession and the health service was potentially experienced both as oppressive to the extent that Caribbean nurses had to prove themselves from scratch, or as the underpinning of their own professional status.

Taken together with a reticence to make irreversible and presumptuous judgements about a country in which they thought of themselves as guests, these ambiguities appeared to foster an element of reflexivity in which negative experiences were carefully weighed and thought equally likely to originate in relations of age, status or gender as in racism.

> Do you know the charge nurses ... they all sat ... over there. They never said a word to you and this would go on for six weeks. All new students were ignored by charge nurses for six weeks. They are the laws you know. And the girls used to say the same, that the matron was a Jesus Christ! I suppose it was our breeding that made us like that, but we did see the English fellahs subdued too in those days [*laughs*], very subdued. And we were so surprised that six weeks gone now and the charge nurse pat me on the shoulder and said 'How you going on me old duck?' My friend was there and we walked down the corridor together and we had a very small charge nurse who would tell us almost everything and said, 'How you getting on on the ward?' and we said, 'Fine', and he said, 'Such and such your charge nurse, is he talking to you now?' And I said, 'Yes, what do you mean?' and he said, 'Six weeks pass. Charge nurses don't talk to students under six weeks.' In truth, and that was true, six weeks to the day that we were patted on the shoulder and offered cigarettes and things like that. And before that nothing. Funny world we live in. Very strange, very strange.
>
> (Respondent A).

In this extract negative experiences which could conceivably have been attributed to racist attitudes have apparently been interpreted as a function of a hierarchical division of labour which applied irrespective of ethnicity and as a 'rites-of-passage' occupational socialization, in which acceptance comes only when the transition from student status has been made.

> I was asked to come and hold this patient while he get the pre-anaesthetic injection for ECT that you had to give them minutes before, so they work and the last injection seconds, and then the

ECT. Now he was a black patient and I was a black nurse. Now I wasn't called because I was a black nurse, I was called because I was *A Nurse* ... on the ward. In those days they used to put tall, they thought, strong fellahs, that's what they thought.

(Respondent A)

In this instance, too, the respondent suggests a line of analysis which we might call ethnic matching, in which the treatment is best given by someone from the same ethnic group as the patient. However, this is rejected in favour of an analysis which emphasizes his masculinity/ strength, because physical restraint of patients was a common feature of earlier mental health nursing (Fretwell, 1985). However, this might be read as racial stereotyping in that black men are stereotyped as strong and athletic, and our respondent was a weightlifting champion in his youth.

Yes, she was a white girl that got the sister's post. And I learned after this, because of the inter-relationship with one of the senior managers, the usual thing [laughs]. I did not know this at the time [laughing].

(Respondent D)

Here, thwarted prospects for promotion are attributed to sexual relations between a white man and a white woman, and although this is acknowledged as corrupt and as an exemplar of generalized gender power relations, it is presented as an individualized piece of bad luck and timing, and initial suspicions of racism are implied to have been mistaken in retrospect.

Some of them [patients] still, especially the older type and they still say 'Oh, I don't want you to lift me up; you know and like everything ... I said, 'OK, I'll get somebody else to lift them if they ask me to do it. But again that was over a period of time they sort of came round, they see your face and recognize that I was a nurse. I think this is something that people don't always realize that older peoples always recognize a young lady or a woman as a nurse, they never recognize a guy um even now even in this day and age.

(Respondent F)

The nature of the discrimination here is felt by the speaker to be one of a generation gap in understanding that a man could be a nurse, though one could argue for racism in any case by virtue of a systematic lack of understanding that a black person could be qualified (because

if they were not a nurse, then in the eyes of the older patient they presumably could only be an unqualified auxiliary, assuming they would
not have objected to a doctor lifting them).

> The funny thing about living in nursing homes in those days is that
> you actually develop something like on board ship, camaraderie,
> you're all in it together. We were all low paid, we all had to do the
> same mucky old jobs and so, I mean people, we weren't singled out
> for those ... if you did the worst job it was according to how junior
> you were as opposed to where you came from. So I have to say I
> didn't meet much neg. There was the odd negative ... my first inter-
> action with patients there were the odd negative situations. But I
> think really, as you mature, or are maturing, I think you learn to,
> not so much ignore that, but cope with it and don't see it as a threat.
>   (Respondent G)

The negative experiences of racism are acknowledged in this extract
but downplayed because (i) there was a camaraderie (presumably with
white colleagues) in working together in adversity; (ii) negative experiences were from patients not colleagues; and (iii) following on from
(ii), the professionalism of occupation is also adopted in personal
development terms.

> ... I'm looking back now and trying to find a kindly sister and I
> don't think I can find one. I think they're all fairly sort of ... brutal
> really and very hierarchical and do-as-you're-told and so on. So I
> think if there is racism being sort of dished out to me then it was all
> part and parcel of a very, a fairly harsh regime really.
>   (Respondent H)

Racism is (unusually) directly named here, and is perhaps allowed to
remain as a possible explanation, though the account is indeterminate
since it is not clear whether the line taken is that what was experienced was oppression of occupational hierarchy alone or whether the
weight of oppression was such that whether or not it was racism hardly
mattered.

> It wasn't the going that bothers me, it was the manner in which I
> was forced to go, out. I did get a letter ... thanking me for my
> loyalty, but that's not the point. I don't want to do anything, in fact
> I'm happy that I don't have to go to work. I'm just peeved about the
> way that I was expected to end it. But I can't say that people were,

that I have, that people have been, it may be because I'm black, I don't know. But I can't say this happened to me because I'm black, because it happened to others as well that weren't black. I mean maybe I could say it happened to me because of my age.

(Respondent I)

This respondent reflects somewhat bitterly on early retirement. There is a clear recognition that this is happening to white colleagues of the same age in the multiple NHS reorganizations, and is cause enough for legitimate bitterness at an occupational contribution belittled. Whether there was racial discrimination at work is felt to be impossible to judge from an individual perspective, and the implication is that one would have to examine the patterns to make such a case. The poor quality of ethnic monitoring in the NHS suggests these patterns may remain hidden. Though there may be a social world of Caribbean-born nurses to receive and validate such a story, this very interpretive world is marginalized (see Plummer, 1996) by enforced occupational retirement. The resignation in the account of the respondent suggests that the nurses themselves are resigned to such patterns never being discovered.

The point we wish to make about these narratives is that they contain within them the potential for being re-told as unambiguous illustrations of racism, and in different contexts (a disillusioned return to the Caribbean, perhaps or a blocked career as a second-level nurse) might have been. The accounts given by our respondents are therefore not congruent with the overwhelmingly negative experiences of nurses reported by Baxter (1987) or Lee-Cunin (1989), not the sadness, disappointment and anger in the reflections of Caribbean migrants interviewed by Fenton (1988).

TENTATIVELY CONSTRUCTING RACISMS

The second narrative strategy used by our interviewees involved a gradual and tentative grasping towards an understanding of racism in the complex raw material of their experiences as nurses. It appears that racism was not widely named in the interpretation of experiences, at least in the early years of migration. These workers had to search more contextually for the meaning of adverse experiences, with the result that, even in retrospect, not all oppressions were expressed as racism.

> Their [white workers'] response was very sugar coated. We were very loving and whatever on the ward, but we were given the saintly higher jobs. The dirty jobs, and we didn't realize that at the time. We didn't realize that the dirty jobs would be our jobs, like the cleaning of the toilets. We didn't have a lot of ... erm ... domestics then. We would have to clean the toilets, mop the floors and count the linen. Count the dirty ... um ... clothes, vests and underpants and these sorts of things and pack them in the skip and send them to the laundry. We had all sorts of dirty jobs to do. The charge nurses would get the clean things. ... the dust and all that we had to shake from the sheets. We had to line up all the beds like a dormitory and had a string which stretch from one bed to the other, and where this top sheet come over, has to be in line, and the legs has to be in line with the crease of the floor. So that when the officer comes in he looks like that [demonstrates person looking down a line studying it].
>
> (Respondent A)

This account suggests a gradual realization of racism at work. Yet within this account other possible explanations are not entirely ruled out, including the shortage of domestic staff leading to any junior nurse being required to do the dirty work; the hierarchy which presupposed that in any case junior nurses would be required to do the dirty work and the charge nurses the clean work, and the hierarchy which required both junior and charge nurses to be subordinated to the nursing officer.

It is also be vital to bear in mind the research of Lawrence (1974: 52), who found that discrimination in employment was relatively covert compared to the open and personal hostility faced by black people in other areas of public life.

> Because when I qualified, when I got my general, I recall going to see the chief male nurse. I told him, I want to discuss the future, what my situation would be like if I stayed on, and he said, 'You come to ask me for advice, I will say to you get out', he said, 'there's nothing here for you.' Well I didn't run off and say his views are racist. I just took his advice and I decided, well, I'm going and try elsewhere.
>
> (Respondent B)

This type of situation is echoed in other accounts, not cited here, by respondents D and G. And still it retains some ambiguity as to whether the experience evidenced racism in promotion, or whether the advice was a realistic appraisal of a racist society, or whether the ostensibly realistic appraisal of a racist society was actually a more sophisticated and self-protecting racism in operation.

MORAL RESISTANCE TO RACISMS

The third narrative strategy employed by the respondents we have termed 'moral resistance'. If, as Foucault claims, power is not centralized but diffuse (Lupton, 1997), then the exercise of racisms must operate through myriad micro-encounters, specifically relations with co-workers and patients. But if the operation of power is indeed localized, local resistances are both possible and meaningful in the sense of representing an immediate amelioration in the life of the worker, notwithstanding the relatively insignificant impact of this resistance in altering the wider articulations of racisms. Such resistances are also key in the formulation of personal identities. As Modood *et al.* (1994) have argued, unwelcome statuses ascribed on the basis of racism are not passively accepted, but may be challenged, modified, or otherwise used in more positive ways in the creation of identities. This can be seen in the strategy of moral resistance, through which some of our interviewees were able to resolve their complex and contradictory experiences by means of a 'healing narrative'.

These healing narratives tended to unfold in three stages. Firstly, there would be the confrontation with the undesirable qualities in others. Secondly, a contrast would be drawn with the cultured image of white people they had carried with them from the Caribbean. And thirdly, emerging from this contrast, there would be the construction of a sense of their own moral worth.

Even as they confronted hostile and discriminatory behaviour, and unlike those effecting such discrimination, the respondents often specifically referred to 'keeping an open mind', not making pre-judgements of others, not judging a whole group on the basis of the behaviour of some and so on. This is all the more creditable in the face of the second stage, the contrast between colonial images of white people and the realities of some white behaviours and cultures.

... you know when you see an English person in the West Indies with bright coloured clothing looking clean and erm, well-shaved and rather arrogant and full of themselves, and you almost begin to believe that they're better than yourself. Well when I arrive[d] at Southampton myself I saw rather drab looking men in long gaberdine coats, um, smoking Woodbines and looking er, half starved almost, you know. ... I met some chappies from very good backgrounds in Barbados, walking the streets of Birmingham in tears 'cos they were being, 'cos they were seeing you know, accommodation advertised and then they would go along and the minute they saw they were black they would say, oh sorry its gone ... we really believe[d] that thing about, you know, fairness in Britain and erm, and that we were really part of this thing called the Empire and the Commonwealth and that, and that we would be welcome. Because we thought, why would people come and invite you to come to their place, if they didn't want to treat you well.

(Respondent G)

Some white people were discovered to be uneducated, inarticulate, unhygienic, dirty, lacking in interpersonal respect, disrespectful of teachers, two-faced, lazy, sadistic, cowardly when confronted individually, aggressive in groups, unfriendly, violent, drunkards, mentally cruel to others and much more besides. Some of these qualities were regrettably found in white 'friends' they had come to trust. Against this backdrop, it is easier to see how the basis for resistance to racisms could take the form of strong moral frameworks in which the storyline became one of a stoic pilgrimage through many trials and tribulations, and of self-consciously behaving well in the face of others behaving badly. Two aspects of this storyline are cited here. The tolerance shown others is conceived as maturity, with the black person as responsible adult and the white person as immature child:

I remember once going for an interview and this chappie read it [the reference] out and he said, they thought that you're a leader, but generally in the wrong direction. You're a bit of a rebel. ... If the person who wrote that reference meant that if I felt something was unjust that I was just going to sit on my hands and say nothing about it. Well, I said, that's, that's immature I said, that's childlike. That's like being, you know, you know.

(Respondent G).

INTERVIEWER: So what advice would you have for a young black person in dealing with the type of negative experiences you have received?

RESPONDENT A: The advice I would give to them, the one I had, the one I have inside, that is don't get high, don't get up high about little things, don't be annoyed about little things, don't let your path be blocked by little things, being called black. You are black. I know it's an insult but every insult is not too bad. Think of your family, and if you can, if you can, can say well I'll let that go by. Cos if you are little, you had a baby, literally a little child in your arms and it trying to get you hard and it hit you in the face and it break your glasses and a piece cut your face, you're not going to slap that little child. I don't tell you if, that someone outside did it, that you're going to knock their head off, but if you can just bear it, the little words, then that shouldn't so badly. Just don't take it on board. Find some sort of thing inside of *you*, to repel it and live long, live ha' more contented and everything there is open to you.

(Respondent A)

Another strand of the 'moral resistance' strategy involved emphasizing the importance of treating others as you would be treated yourself. One respondent used the metaphor of a mirror, of being a mirror-in-the-world, with oneself judged by one's own actions.

And the world see you as a mirror … because you are wondering how they are going to react to you. At the same time they too are wondering, wonder how that person's going to feel coming into our environment, coming into our home. And it what, what you reflect in that mirror, is what you are going to get out of it. And I try to teach my children in that way. And the same for every young people, if you want something, go out for it. Don't think that because you are of a different origin or a different skin colour that's going to prevent you. Yes, not everybody's going to open their door to you, but don't let it be a put off. Try another area. And I think that that's the advice I would be to any young people. If you have an ability and you know that there are certain demands that are required of you; certain expectations to be properly educated to meet the changing situation today.

(Respondent D).

The sustenance for this moral framework seems to derive from a variety of sources, including the Christian church, family values taught in the Caribbean, external bureaucratic validation of achievement (exams, qualifications), personal character, island philosophy, professional code of conduct (not hitting back at a patient who spits in your face) and the behaviour of, according to different individual accounts, either the majority or a minority of white people encountered.

The resolution of the pilgrimage appeared not to be in ostensible rewards but in learning to recognize the rewards which are worth having. Respondent A valued succeeding in persuading elderly residents to eat who had stopped eating, upset at his transfer from their particular home. Respondent B recalled reconciling father and daughter hours before the father's death and, as a valedictory microcosm of applying skills learned over a long career, valued his disarming a man high on drink and drugs who had been threatening to use a knife on himself and others. This achievement was accomplished without violence and in the spirit of helping the man with his illness. Respondent H valued her widening circle of white and Asian friends as validating her ability to get on with a wide range of people.

However, neither is the journey a triumphalist procession. Most of the respondents felt that they could and should have achieved more. Their lives were a success, but a qualified (in both senses of that term) success, and the nature of that qualification will continue to shame postwar Britain until this passage of history is more widely known and recognized.

> I believe I could have gone further, but being black kept me down
>
> (Respondent A)

> I just have this ache because I can't understand why people find it so difficult, when black people say they've had a hard time.
>
> (Respondent H)

In summary, the third narrative strategy was one of moral resistance which involved developing a healing narrative. This strategy itself had three components: confronting racisms, contrasting the experienced brutalities of some white people with the urbane image of white people they had carried with them from the Caribbean, and finally constructing healing moral accounts of the type we have described.

CONCLUSION

Our respondents came from financially relatively secure origins in the Caribbean, and certainly by the end of their careers had been upwardly mobile within the professional middle classes. As such, they did not fit neatly into the race and class analysis suggested by Sivanandan (1982) and Ramdin (1987). On the other hand they had experienced at least some overt racism and some aspects of their identity had been formed in opposition to that. In particular, and in support of the thesis of James (1993), a Pan-Caribbean (or 'West Indian' in the preferred terminology of the respondents) identity is formed only in the sharing of circumstances of migration to Britain, beginning, as some of our respondents themselves remarked, on the boat bringing migrants across the Atlantic. Moreover, the cultural shock of the brutality of white people, especially the white working class, is, as Gilroy (1987) argues, a process of identity formation provoked by a challenge, by the creation of a passion. But our respondents are not the protagonists of street youth culture, and the passion which arises is to draw on spiritual, moral values to guide behaviour in the face of adversity, and to learn to view values, not material things, as sacred.

Our contention is that this group of Caribbean nurses developed three different narrative strategies in the creation of their self-identities. Firstly, some refused to take racism for granted; they deconstructed it so that it was not assumed that all negative experiences could be attributable to racism. As Hall (1992) suggests these respondents had other identities to draw upon, which included student nurse status, age, gender and professional nurse status which cut across their experiences of racism and the processes of ethnic identity formation, and which provided alternative narrative structures within which to situate their experiences. Secondly, some also gradually learnt, perhaps partially as a shared language for naming racism became available, to construct certain experiences as racisms, though this was done tentatively, and did not exclude other possible explanations. And finally, some experiences were construed both then and now as racisms, and a sense of moral worth was constructed by our respondents through which they were able to transcend their negative experiences. In developing these healing narratives they were able to create robust identities which underpinned considerable occupational and civic contributions to British society, in the face of adversities whose damage they have not only resisted, but also borne the responsibility themselves to heal.

ACKNOWLEDGEMENTS

We record not only our usual thanks to our respondents for their time generously given in conducting the interviews, but also our enormous respect and gratitude for their contributions to the NHS in the face of adversity. The research was funded by the Faculty of Health and Community Studies at De Montfort University.

REFERENCES

Ahmad, W. I. U. (ed.) (1993) *'Race' and Health in Contemporary Britain* (Buckingham: Open University Press).

Akinsanya, J. A. (1988) 'Ethnic Minority Nurses, Midwives and Health Visitors: What Role for them in the National Health Service?', *New Community*, 14(3), pp. 444–50.

Barth, F. (1969) 'Introduction', in F. Barth (ed.), *Ethnic Groups and Boundaries* (Bergen, Oslo: Universitets Forlaget) pp. 7–38.

Bass, M. J., Brody, H., Helman, C. G., Howie, J. G. R., Lamberts, H., Norton, P. G. and Starfield, B. (1991) 'What Does the Primary Care Physician Do in Patient Care that Makes a Difference? Five Approaches to One Question', in P. G. Norton, M. Stewart, F. Tudiver, M. J. Bass and E. V. Dunn (eds), *Primary Care Research: Traditional and Innovative Approaches* (London: Sage), pp. 209–20.

Baxter, C. (1987) *The Black Nurse: An Endangered Species – A Case for Equal Opportunities in Nursing* (London: National Extension College).

Bellaby, P. (1991) 'Histories of Sickness: Making Use of Multiple Accounts of the Same Process', in S. Dex (ed.), *Life and Work History Analyses* (London: Routledge), pp. 20–42.

Beishon, S., Virdee, S. and Hagell, A. (1995) *Nursing in a Multi-Ethnic NHS* (London: Policy Studies Institute).

Blakemore, K. and Boneham, M. (1994) *Age, Race and Ethnicity* (Buckingham: Open University Press).

Brown, C. (1984) *Black and White Britain: The Third PSI Survey* (London: Heinemann).

Coleman, P. G. (1991) 'Ageing and Life History: the Meaning of Reminiscence in Later Life', in S. Dex (ed.), *Life and Work History Analyses* (London: Routledge), pp. 120–42.

Cornwell, J. (1984) *Hard Earned Lives: Accounts of Health and Illness from East London* (London: Tavistock).

Daniel, W. W. (1968) *Racial Discrimination in England* (Harmondsworth: Penguin).

Davies, C. (1995) *Gender and the Professional Predicament in Nursing* (Buckingham: Open University Press).

Doyal, L., Hunt, G. and Meller, J. (1980) *Migrant Workers in the National Health Service: A Report to the Social Science Research Council* (London: Department of Sociology, Polytechnic of North London).

Fenton, S. (1988) 'Health Work and Growing Old: the Afro-Caribbean Experience', *New Community*, 14(3), pp. 426–43.

Freedman, J. and Coombs, G. (1996) *Narrative Therapy: The Social Construction of Preferred Realities* (New York: W. W. Norton).

Fretwell, J. (1985) *Freedom to Change* (London: Royal College of Nursing).

Fox, N. (1997) 'Is There Life after Foucault?', in A. Petersen and R. Bunton (eds), *Foucault: Health and Medicine* (London: Routledge), pp. 31–50.

Fryer, P. (1984) *Staying Power: The History of Black People in Britain* (London: Pluto Press).

George, M. (1994) 'Racism in Nursing', *Nursing Standard*, 8(18).

Giddens, A. (1991) *Modernity and Self Identity* (Cambridge: Polity).

Gillborn, D. (1995) 'Racism, Identity and Modernity: Pluralism, Moral, Antiracism and Plastic Ethnicity', *International Studies in the Sociology of Education*, 5(1), 3–23.

Gilroy, P. (1987) *There Ain't No Black in the Union Jack* (London: Hutchinson).

Gish, O. (1971) 'Doctor Migration and World Health: the Impact of the International Demand for Doctors on Health Services in Developing Countries', in *Nursing Migration: A Study of Overseas Midwives in the UK*, Occasional Papers on Social Administration (43), Appendix 2.

Glass, R. (1960) *The Newcomers* (London: Allen & Unwin).

Graham, H. (1984) 'Surveying through Stories', in C. Bell and H. Roberts (1984) (eds), *Social Researching: Politics, Problems, Practice* (London: Routledge & Kegan Paul).

Hall, S. (1992) 'The Question of Cultural Identity', in S. Hall, D. Held and T. McGrew (eds), *Modernity and its Futures* (Cambridge: Polity Press)

Harris, C. (1993) 'Post-war Migration and the Industrial Reserve Army', in W. James and C. Harris (eds), *Inside Babylon: The Caribbean Diaspora in Britain* (London: Verso), pp. 9–54.

Hicks, C. (1982) 'Racism in Nursing', *Nursing Times*, 5 and 12 May.

Hiles, D. R. (1994) 'Narrative as a Sequence of Motivated Signs', *Proceedings of the International Association for Semiotic Studies, Berkeley, California*, 12–18 June , 1994.

James, W. (1993) 'Migration, Racism and Identity Formation: the Caribbean Experience in Britain', in W. James and C. Harris (eds), *Inside Babylon: The Caribbean Diaspora in Britain* (London: Verso), pp. 231–87.

King's Fund (1990) *Racial Equality: The Nursing Profession* (London: King's Fund Equal Opportunities Task Force).

Lawrence, D. (1974) *Black Migrants, White Natives* (London: Cambridge University Press).

Lee-Cunin, M. (1989) *Daughters of Seacole: A Study of Black Nurses in West Yorkshire* (Batley: West Yorkshire Low Pay Unit).

Lupton, D. (1997) 'Foucault and the Medicalization Critique', in A. Petersen and R. Bunton (eds), *Foucault: Health and Medicine* (London: Routledge), pp. 94–110.

Mares, P., Baxter, C. and Henley, A. (1987) *Training in Multi-racial Health Care* (Cambridge: National Extension College).

Mason, D. (1995) *Race and Ethnicity in Modern Britain* (Oxford: Oxford University Press).

McNaught, A. (1987) *Health Action and Ethnic Minorities* (London: Bedford Square Press).

Modood, T., Beishon, S. and Virdee, S. (1994) *Changing Ethnic Identities* (London: Policy Studies Institute).

Modood, T. (1994) 'Political Blackness and British Asians', *Sociology*, 28(4), pp. 859–76.

National Association of Health Authorities and Trusts (NAHAT) (1989) *Action Not Words* (Birmingham: NAHAT).

Ohri, S. and Faruqi, S. (1988) 'Racism, Employment and Unemployment', in A. Bhat, R. Carr-Hill and S. Ohri (eds), *Britain's Black Population*, 2nd edn (Aldershot: Gower), pp. 61–100.

Okamura, J. Y. (1981) 'Situational Ethnicity', *Ethnic and Racial Studies*, 5(4), pp. 394–420.

Patterson, S. (1965) *Dark Strangers: A Study of West Indians in London* (Harmondsworth: Penguin).

Peach, C. (1986) *West Indian Migration to Britain* (Oxford: Oxford University Press).

Peach, C. (1991) 'The Caribbean in Europe: Contrasting Patterns of Migration and Settlement in Britain, France and the Netherlands'. Research Paper in Ethnic Relations No. 15 (Coventry: Centre for Research in Ethnic Relations, University of Warwick).

Pearson, M. (1986) 'Racist Notions of Ethnicity and Culture in Health Education', in S. Rodmell and A. Watt (eds), *The Politics of Health Education* (London: Routledge and Kegan Paul).

Plummer, K. (1995) *Telling Sexual Stories: Power, Change and Social Worlds* (London: Routledge).

Plummer, K. (1996) 'Intimate Citizenship and the Culture of Sexual Storytelling', in J. Weeks and J. Holland (eds), *Sexual Cultures: Communities, Values and Intimacies* (Basingstoke: Macmillan), pp. 34–52.

Radley, A. and Billig, M. (1996) 'Accounts of Health and Illness: Dilemmas and Representations', *Sociology of Health and Illness*, 18(2), pp. 220–40.

Ramdin, R. (1987) *The Making of the Black Working Class in Britain* (Aldershot: Gower).

Rhodes, P. (1994) 'Race-of-interviewer Effects: a Brief Comment', *Sociology*, 28(2), pp. 547–58.

Rogers, C. (1945) 'The Nondirective Method as a Technique for Social Research', *American Journal of Sociology*, 50, pp. 279–83.

Rushdie, S. (1982) 'The New Empire within Britain', *New Society*, 62, pp. 417–21.

Sivanandan, A. (1982) *A Different Hunger: Writings on Black Resistance* (London: Pluto Press).

Smaje, C. (1995) *Health, 'Race' and Ethnicity: Making Sense of the Evidence* (London: King's Fund).

Small, S. (1994) 'Black People in Britain', *Sociology Review*, 3(4), pp. 2–4.

The Nurses, Midwives and Health Visitors Rules Approval Order 1983, *Statutory Instrument No. 873* (London: HMSO).

Thomas, M. and Morton-Williams, J. M. (1972) 'Overseas Nurses in Britain: PEP Survey for the UK', Council Broadsheet no. 539, Political and Economic Planning (now Policy Studies Institute).

Ward, L. (1993) 'Race Equality and Employment in the National Health Service', in W. I. U. Ahmad (ed.), *'Race' and Health in Contemporary Britain* (Buckingham: Open University Press).

Weeks, J. (1996) 'Review Article: Telling Stories about Men', *Sociological Review*, 44(4), pp. 746–56.

White, M. and Epston, D. (1990) *Narrative Means to Therapeutic Ends* (New York: W. W. Norton).

Witz, A. (1992) *Professions and Patriarchy* (London: Routledge).

9 Orientalism and Resistance to Orientalism: Muslim Identities in Contemporary Western Europe
MALCOLM D. BROWN

INTRODUCTION

This chapter is about Orientalism and Muslim identities in Western Europe, particularly insofar as the production and reproduction of Muslim identities constitute a response to Orientalism. One's identity consists only partly of how one sees oneself; it also consists of how one is seen by others. As such, while this chapter is clearly about religious identities, it can be situated within the sociological debates about racism and ethnic identities which have taken place since the mid-1980s. Muslims are often defined in the West in racialized terms. By racialization we mean 'those instances where social relations between people have been structured by the signification of human biological characteristics in such a way as to define and construct differentiated social collectivities', and 'a process of categorisation, a representational process of defining an Other (usually, but not exclusively) somatically' (Miles, 1989: 75). In contemporary Britain and France, Muslims are often stereotyped as 'Pakistani' or *'maghrébin'*, terms which may connote an irreconcilable 'racial' difference based on a perception of somatic features, such as skin colour.

The way in which Muslim identities are produced can be seen as similar to the way in which ethnic or 'racial' identities are produced. This chapter provides an analysis of Orientalism (in this context, Western representations of Islam and of Muslims), and examines how this plays a role in the production of Muslim identities. This approach reflects, to some extent, Robert Miles's analysis, in which racialization precedes racism: racism is 'a particular form of (evaluative) represen-tation which is a specific instance of a wider (descriptive) process of racialisation' (Miles, 1989: 84). The existence of Pierre-André Taguieff's 'auto-racialization', or of Michael Banton's ethnic or racial consciousness, is further down the line (see Taguieff, 1988: 348–54; Banton, 1997: *passim*).

I begin with an explication of Edward Said's analysis of Orientalism, and of how Orientalism has developed and changed over time and in reaction to changing circumstances. This chapter then applies this analysis to representations of Muslim communities in Western Europe, and looks at what options exist for resisting, or at least addressing, these representations. Within this context I look at how Muslim communities in Western Europe actually respond to Orientalist representations, whether this be through a separatist Muslim identity, an assimilated Western identity, or a combined Muslim–Western identity. In order to address and empirically ground these issues, I refer to fieldwork undertaken in the north of France in 1996 and 1997. This was part of a continuing PhD project, based at the University of Glasgow, examining the construction of Muslim identi-ties in Britain and France.[1] I also draw on empirical research which has been done by other researchers in Britain. Finally, I examine the significance which Orientalism and resistance to Orientalism have for sociological praxis.

EDWARD SAID'S ANALYSIS OF ORIENTALISM

The basic thesis of Said's *Orientalism* (1995; first edition, 1978) is that the Orient was a Western conception, a Western creation, and a tool of Eurocentrism. He argues that a dualism of Orient and Occident has been created through Western literature, politics and popular dis-course since at least the eleventh century, with roots stretching back to the Greco-Roman period, and reaching its apogee in the colonial period. He identifies three types of Orientalism: a comprehensive Western discourse (literary, journalistic and academic); an academic discipline; and a system of colonial institutions. What they had in common was that they presented the Orient as fundamentally different from, and essentially inferior to, the Occident, and as homogeneous and unchanging. While they were often articulated separately, they were also interconnected, and legitimated each other.

The dynamic of Orientalism as a comprehensive discourse is that the West considers the Orient to be fundamentally different from itself, and therefore produces an image of the Orient which does not need to be validated outside its own system. One example was Marx and Engels's notion of the Asiatic mode of production, according to which all history was the history of class struggle, so the absence of evidence of class struggle in India led to the conclusion that 'Indian society has no history at all, at least no known history' (Marx and Engels, 1968: 81; see also Said, 1995: 153–7). Another example could be Max Weber's contrast between the asceticism of the Protestant ethic and the sensuality of Islam (see Turner, 1994: 98f.).

At an innocent level, Orientalism as an academic discipline is merely the academic study of the Orient. Many universities, for example, have departments of Oriental studies. However, since the Orient has been defined into existence by the West, and perceived as inferior, homogeneous and unchanging, it is this perception which has been studied by academic Orientalism, not the 'real' Orient (which does not exist in itself). Indeed, academic Orientalism has contributed to the perpetuation of this perception. As Said writes:

> Orientalism overrode the Orient. As a system of thought about the Orient, it always rose from the specifically human detail to the general transhuman one; an observation about a tenth-century Arab poet multiplied itself into a policy towards (and about) the Oriental mentality in Egypt, Iraq, or Arabia. Similarly a verse from the Koran would be considered the best evidence of an ineradicable Muslim sensuality.
>
> (Said, 1995: 96)

As is implied here, this kind of academic discourse provided a legitimation for colonialism, which is how the perception of an unchanging Orient was perpetuated. So another type of Orientalism is defined by Said as 'the corporate institution for dealing with the Orient – dealing with it by making statements about it, authorizing views of it, describing it, by teaching it, settling it, ruling over it: in short, Orientalism as a Western style for dominating, restructuring, and having authority over the Orient' (Said, 1995: 3). Said expounds the logic of a speech by Arthur J. Balfour in the House of Commons in 1910, about 'the problems with which we have to deal in Egypt', as follows. Because of the history of ancient Egyptian civilization, 'England knows Egypt'. Then:

> Egypt is what England knows; England knows that Egypt cannot have self-government; England confirms that by occupying Egypt; for the Egyptians, Egypt is what England has occupied and now governs; foreign occupation therefore becomes 'the very basis' of contemporary Egyptian civilization; Egypt requires, indeed insists upon, British occupation.

(Said, 1995: 34)

Said clearly considered the nineteenth century to be the 'great age' of Orientalism, so one criticism of his thesis has been that it underestimates the impact of historical change and heterogeneity within Orientalist discourse itself (see Turner, 1994: 5–7). However, Said does identify a number of historical events and processes which brought about a paradigm shift in Orientalism. The nineteenth-century perception of the Orient was of a world of harems, belly dancers, snake charmers – in short, a kind of 'bad' sensuality, which was contrasted with the privatized, sometimes repressed, sexuality of Victorian Europe. Today, we rarely hear about the sensual Orient, but we do hear about the danger of Islamic fundamentalism. This is a term which is commonly used, even by some Muslims, and which constitutes an important part of the way in which Islam and Muslims are perceived in the West. I would avoid using the term in sociological analysis, but Aziz Al-Azmeh takes a slightly different approach. He notes the Protestant origin of the term 'fundamentalism', but gives it a working definition which enables it to be applied to all religions: 'I define fundamentalism as that moment in all religions which gives primitivism and primevalism precedence over history, which seeks to eliminate history and regards it as, at best, an illegitimate accretion onto the pristine beginning, and as such regards the present condition and its immediate precedents as corrupt, or at best as corruptions of an abiding beginning' (Al-Azmeh, 1996: 135). Al-Azmeh argues that the homogeneous, essentialist stereotype of Islam is propagated both by Western Orientalism and by 'neo-Afghanism', a strand in contemporary Islam which is implicitly linked with 'Muslim fundamentalism'.

The paradigm shift from an Orientalism which concentrated on the sensual Orient to a discourse of Muslim fanaticism was at least partly due to certain historical events. After the building of the Suez Canal the distance to the Orient was, in a sense, reduced, and its *exoticism* was destroyed. In addition, twentieth-century anticolonial movements and the emergence of new nation states destroyed any idea that the Orient was homogeneous and unchanging. The formation of the state of Israel, the oil crisis of the 1970s, the Iranian revolution, and the emerging possibilities of globalism in communication and travel, all have contributed to this paradigm shift. The oil crisis and the Iranian revolution endangered the supply of 'our' oil, and the fanatical stereotype of the Orient legitimated this discourse. Images of Muslim extremists who cut off the hands of suspected criminals, force women to wear opaque veils, and carry out acts of terrorism reinforce a neo-Orientalist perception that 'we' are intellectually more advanced than 'them', so 'we' have to make 'their' decisions (economic, political, and so on) for 'them'.[2]

'INTERNAL ORIENTALISM'

The end of classic colonialism marked the beginning of large-scale migration from the former colonies to the West, and it can be argued that this migration was part of a process by which the West maintained its power over those who had been classified 'Oriental'. We could refer to this as an expression of 'internal Orientalism'. Michael Hechter (1975), and, in a different way, Jurgen Habermas (1987), have demonstrated that colonialism can be practised internally, so the same can be said of Orientalism, which is basically a colonial discourse. Said (1993: 8) argues that imperialism is a general cultural phenomenon as well as a specific political, ideological, economic or social practice. Orientalism has effectively privileged 'Western' culture, so, even though 'other' cultures and practices exist in the West, they are seen as Oriental, alien, exotic or, in the case of contemporary Islam, threatening.

There has been a Muslim presence in Western Europe since the seventh or eighth century, notably in Spain between 710 and 1492, and colonial links led to the building of a number of mosques in the late nineteenth and early twentieth centuries (for example Berlin in 1866, Woking in 1889, Paris in 1926). However, it was the demand for labour migration as part of the postwar reconstruction of Western Europe which led to the movement, and eventually settlement, of significant Muslim communities in Western Europe. At a rough estimate there are now about 4 million Muslims in France, over 2 million in Germany, 1.5 million in Britain, and another million or so elsewhere within the European Union.[3] There is a diversity of countries of origin – principally North Africa, Turkey, the Middle East, the Indian subcontinent and Indonesia – though we could estimate that about 50 per cent have been born in Western Europe. The number of Western European converts to Islam is likely to be approximately 100,000. While Muslims are predominantly working class, and the level of unemployment is higher than for Western Europe as a whole, a Muslim middle class has begun to emerge, some of whom are professionals or members of the political elite.

To put it systematically, internal Orientalism has the following characteristics. Firstly, it exists in a postcolonial frame, in which colonial control has been prolonged through the process of postwar labour migration to Western Europe. Secondly, the quasi-autonomy which the Orient once had by virtue of its distance, despite being a Western creation or simulacrum, has been destroyed. Thirdly, rather than distant territories being colonized, the lifeworld of the 'Orient', or of the 'migrant communities' is colonized (compare Habermas, 1987: 318 *et passim*). Fourthly, the form of this colonization centres on cultural practices and symbols, where there is an alleged incompatibility between Western values and the values of the Other within. Concomitantly, internal Orientalism may involve an element of differentialist racism, asserting or supposing that ethnically defined groups are naturally different and unable to mix with each other (see Taguieff, 1988: 348–54).

Examples of internal Orientalism in practice include some Western reactions to the Rushdie affair and the *affaire du foulard* in France. In the former case the publication of Salman Rushdie's novel, *The Satanic Verses*, led to protests about its alleged blasphemy and deliberate offence to Muslims, leading to its burning in the streets of Bradford, and Khomeini's infamous *fatwa* which called for Rushdie's death.[4] In the latter case the suspension of teenage Muslim girls from state schools in France for wearing the *hijab* (a form of Islamic headscarf) has led to a debate in which one side has accused the other of religious intolerance, which has been reciprocated with an accusation of undermining the values of the secular republic.

Said implies that the Rushdie affair can be analysed as an expression of internal Orientalism, looking at it as an example of his contention that the West has been capable of knowing Islam only in a demeaning way:

> The space between the bashing of other religions or cultures and deeply conservative self-praise has not been filled with edifying

analysis or discussion. In the reams of print about Salman Rushdie's *The Satanic Verses*, only a tiny proportion discussed the book *itself*.

(Said, 1993: 397)

Michael Keith and Steve Pile's account is a part of this tiny (but growing) proportion – they show that the genesis and progression of the Rushdie affair reflected the novel itself, as the characters' search for their roots in London (Ellowen Deeowen, geographically far from their roots, but full of metaphors, or reminders, of those roots) reflected Muslims' search for spatial identity in Britain and 'the West' (Keith and Pile, 1993: 22–3). Central to what became known as the Rushdie affair was an imagined (though not imaginary) polarization between the West and Islam:

> Symbolically at the heart of global power, 'the West' is a linguistic condensation of the globally powerful. It is in this context that, in both orientalist imagining and in counter memories of resistance, Islam is placed in literal and symbolic opposition to this force. Such positioning by no means exhausts a description or analysis of contemporary Islam but it is constitutive of it. Such positioning also has literal and symbolic dimensions and it was into such configurations of power that *The Satanic Verses* was thrown; in Rushdie's own terms, a political event that was used in the cultural politics of Indian sectarianism and then reimported, tragically signified in the homologous binaries of Islam against anti-Islam, faith against faithlessness, powerless against powerful, Good against Evil.
>
> (Keith and Pile, 1993: 22–3)

These 'homologous binaries' seem very like the Orientalist dualism of Orient and Occident, except that the Islam which is still the Other is no longer perceived as being at a safe distance. Perhaps inevitably, the question of how the West should respond to this perceived danger has arisen. The Rushdie affair and the *affaire du foulard* in France have highlighted the possibility that this response may not always display the tolerant credentials on which the West has prided itself. It is true that intolerance was displayed on both sides, but criticism of some Muslims (which soon became criticism of all Muslims) for burning copies of *The Satanic Verses* implied that the act of book burning had a single, homogeneous, universal cultural significance. However, the significance which is attributed to book burning in Western Europe is strongly informed by European history, notably Nazi Germany and the Inquisition. This meaning is not universal, and its application to other cultures constitutes an act of imposing meanings on other cultures. In other words, it is an act of cultural and symbolic colonization, which is one characteristic of internal Orientalism.

Jørgen Nielsen (1995: 158) draws some parallels between the two 'affairs', focusing on the perceived incompatibilities between Islamic values and Western secularism, and between the rights of parents to determine the education of their children according to their own cultural or religious values and the principle of education into a national culture. Another parallel is the way in which media (and academic) discourses about 'Islam', and sometimes the threat of the Muslim 'enemy within', have partially replaced discourses about 'immigration', 'ethnic minorities', 'race relations' and 'integration'. If one were to look through the issues of many British social scientific journals from before 1989, one would find articles about 'the Pakistani community' in Britain, processes of immigration, the experiences of the 'second generation', but few about British Muslims. After 1989, one would find articles about British Muslims to be comparatively plentiful.

In the French case, much discourse about the *affaire du foulard* has also been premised on a homogenizing view of *Islam* and of *Muslims*, and this has replaced some of the self-congratulatory material about *intégration à la française*, which has focused on culture and democratic values. John Crowley (1992: 165) refers to this as an 'apparently complacent adherence, even among social scientists, to the virtues of the traditional French model of integration'. Some of the newer discourse, as expressed, for example, by Guy Coq (1995, 1996), an editor of the French journal *Esprit*, and Camille Lacoste-Dujardin (1995), an important French writer on ceremonies, festivals and gender roles in Arab–Muslim societies, has associated the *hijab* with contemporary Islamist ideology. While Lacoste-Dujardin's argument in particular is sophisticated, based on an analysis of Arabic language and culture, Coq's polemic sometimes seems to imply that behind every schoolgirl wearing a *hijab* is a fanatical warrior bent on terrorizing France into becoming an Islamic Republic. He denounces:

> … l'hypocrisie consistant à refuser, au nom du prétexte de la liberté religieuse, le sexisme inhérent au foulard islamiste et l'aveuglement volontaire quant à la signification du foulard pour les partis islamistes.
>
> (Coq, 1996: 6)[5]

Even the most sophisticated form of this analysis contains a basic error, and that is the homogenizing view of Islam and Muslims to which we have referred. The *affaire du foulard* has not been a simple, two-sided, France-versus-the-Muslims, conflict. Some (non-Muslim) French people have supported the right of schoolgirls to wear the *hijab*, while some Muslims have opposed it. A range of arguments has been used for and against the *hijab*, from Muslims and non-Muslims. Some have argued that it is a symbol of patriarchy or Islamic fundamentalism. Others have seen it is a challenge to the separation of religion from public education in France, and therefore a threat to republican principles, including religious liberty. Meanwhile, some Muslim women see the *hijab* as liberating and affirmative of their identity, and struggle to wear it, while others see it as oppressive, so wear it with a *rejet intérieure*, or decline to wear it at all. It means different things to different people (see Gaspard and Khosrokhavar, 1995, particularly the biographical examples in chapters 2 and 3). But the reality of internal Orientalism has prevented this heterogeneity from being fully recognized.

OPTIONS FOR RESISTANCE/RESPONSE

What options exist for Muslims in the West to resist, or at least respond to, homogenizing internal Orientalist discourses? Clearly, there are a vast number of options, and it is not for me to pontificate about which option should be taken. To do so would suggest that I could define how Muslims should live in Western society, and this would mean participating in another form of Orientalist control, albeit symbolic. Consequently, I shall limit myself to identifying the available options. Since these options are numerous, it is heuristic to represent them with three ideal types: assimilation; withdrawal; and a combined Muslim–Western (or Western–Muslim, or Muslim/Western) identity. I shall look at each ideal type in turn.

Assimilation

In responding to internal Orientalism, some Muslims may choose to assimilate, reduce their cultural distinctiveness within the context of Western society, practise Islam in a private way, perhaps even become 'non-practising' Muslims, and demonstrate to the West that they are 'normal' people. While this option is relevant to Muslims throughout Western Europe, it is perhaps most obviously significant in France, where the principle of assimilation has been central to state policies on immigration, religion, education and other areas. It must be emphasized that the term 'assimilation' as used here denotes an ideal type, and some of the groups to which I refer are quite opposed to assimilation as the term is used in French political discourse. One formula which I heard frequently when doing fieldwork in France was 'for integration, against assimilation'. Bearing this in mind, we can identify four areas in which the assimilationist approach has been articulated: in the 'established' Islam of the *Mosquée de Paris* (Paris mosque); in the attempts to create a representative body for Islam in France; among French converts to Islam; and among the 'non-practising' Muslims.

The *Mosquée de Paris* represents, or is widely perceived as representing, an articulation of Islam which is very close to the establishment. The link with the French state, a secular republic in an historically Catholic country, is surprisingly strong. It was built by the French government in the 1920s, partly in recognition of the Muslims who had fought for France in the First World War, partly in order to consolidate France's position as a 'Muslim power', that is, as a colonial project. Its Rector was appointed by the French government until 1982, when control passed to the Algerian government. Given this history, it is not surprising that successive French governments have considered the *Mosquée de Paris* to be the legitimate voice of France's Muslims (see Kepel, 1991, 1994a).

Nevertheless, divisions between French Muslims, and the need to negotiate more effectively with the government, led to a number of attempts to create a representative body for Muslims in France. The CORIF (*Conseil de Réflexion sur l'Islam en France*) was the only one constituted according to the establishment principle of the *Mosquée de Paris*, being established by and answerable to the Ministry of the Interior (the minister at the time being Pierre Joxe). Others, such as the FNMF (*Fédération Nationale des Musulmans de France*) and the UOIF (*Union des Organisations Islamiques de France*[6]), had their own agendas, but they were still responding to the state's demand for a unified body to speak on behalf of all French Muslims, and this demand was contingent on a homogeneous perception of Islam.

When we speak of converts to Islam, we must bear in mind that only some can be classified under the assimilation ideal type. Others may display a commitment to Islam as *din wa dunya* (religion and way of life) or *din wa dawla* (religion and state) in such a way as to negate assimilation, and some respondents in France told me that converts had a tendency to be more isolated and 'fundamentalist' than Muslims of North African origin. Those converts who do assimilate may do so for theological reasons, considering that, as Muslims constitute an *ummah* (worldwide community), Islam should be adaptable to different cultures.[7] Other converts may become Muslims for more pragmatic reasons, such as marriage (Telhine, 1991), thus becoming Muslims in a relatively nominal sense, without negating their previous assimilation into French society.

Finally, there are some 'non-practising' Muslims. Again, this is an ideal type, and we must be careful not to categorize individuals too easily. Nevertheless, some see themselves in this way, ranging from '*croyant non-pratiquant*' to those who regard themselves as Muslim solely because their parents are Muslim, or due to their ethnic origins. As a rough estimate, based on my fieldwork in France, I would say that about 15–20 per cent of Muslims in France are fully practising; that is, they perform *salat* (the five-times-daily prayer), *jummah* (for men, attending the mosque for the Friday midday prayer) and *as-sawm* (the fast of Ramadhan). About 20 per cent perform *salat*, slightly more perform *jummah*, and something between 40 and 60 per cent observe *as-sawm*. To take another example from my fieldwork, I found that the 'non-practising' Muslims tended towards assimilation: one interviewee was involved with the creation of a Muslim elite and middle class in France, but insisted on drinking wine whenever he went to a restaurant; another made a point of not following the news from Morocco, where he was born, in order to be more fully integrated into French society.

Withdrawal

The second ideal type for categorizing ways in which Muslims may respond to internal Orientalism is withdrawal. This entails accepting an exclusion from Western society, forming a world-rejecting *Gemeinschaft* (to combine the ideas of Troeltsch, 1931: 993;[8] and Tönnies, 1955: 42–73), and carving out a distinctive identity in the West. The *Tablighi Jama'at*, a movement which originated in Pakistan, and now has a worldwide membership, including in Britain and France, has some characteristics which come close to this ideal type. As a movement it 'addresses itself entirely to Muslims, and makes no attempt to preach to the unconverted', and some members 'who live within the movement rather than in society tend to wear specific dress' (King, 1994: 14, 18). The principles as set down by the founder, Muhammad Ilyas, in 1934, seem to fit well the withdrawal ideal type:

Article of faith;
prayer;
acquisition and dissemination of knowledge;
adoption of Islamic appearance and dress;
adoption of Islamic ceremonies and rejection of non-Islamic ones;
seclusion of women;
performance of *nikah* or marriage ceremony in the Islamic manner;
adherence to Muslim dress by women;
non-deviation from Islamic beliefs and non-acceptance of any other religion;
protection and preservation of mutual rights;
participation of responsible persons in every meeting and convention;
pledge not to impart secular instruction to children before they have had religious learning;
pledge to strive and endeavour for the preaching of religion;
observance of cleanliness;
pledge to protect the dignity and respect of one another.

(Haq, 1972: 110–11)

The *Tabligh* has been particularly concerned to promote harmony between Muslims and non-Muslims in Western society. Although it has shown an unwillingness to participate in interreligious dialogue, it has emphasized that 'Tabligh wants Christians to be good Christians, just as it wants Muslims to be good Muslims. If this ideal is achieved, friction between the adherents of the two faiths will be dissolved.' However, as John King (1994: 23) notes, the *Tabligh* has been perceived by others as a Muslim fundamentalist association, and Gilles Kepel (1994b: 34) has analysed the *Tabligh* as an expression of 're-Islamization from below'. Hervé Terrel (1994: 348) argues that there is a radical difference between the *Tabligh* and Islamist movements which are constituted after the model of the Muslim Brotherhood in Egypt: specifically, the *Tabligh* does not find its *raison d'être* in the political situation of the country of origin. Some Muslims, however, have condemned the *Tablighi Jama'at*, apparently for not being 'fundamentalist' enough:

... the movement known as Tablighi Jama'at is being utilised by the enemies of Islam as an effective instrument in their continuing struggle to prevent the emergence of a true Islamic movement in Europe and elsewhere. ... If, quite contrary to being threatened, the *kafir* [unbelieving] authorities positively welcome what is happening, as they clearly do in the case of the Tablighi Jama'at, then it must be that something other than true Islam is being propagated ... We therefore call on the leadership of the Tablighi Jama'at ... to teach their members a correct and complete understanding of the *deen* [religion] of Allah, particularly in respect of the obligation of *jihad* [struggle] against the *kuffar* [unbelievers].

(Bewley, 1992: 6, 27, 37)

Combined Muslim–Western Identity

The third option for responding to internal Orientalism, as an ideal type, is a combined Muslim–Western identity. This may be seen as a midpoint on the assimilation–withdrawal continuum, and may involve transforming Islam into what Kepel calls a *citadelle intérieure* – as one of his interviewees put it:

> ... le fait d'être musulman nous donne une dimension et même une grande dimension de sécurité intérieure qui nous permet d'affronter parfois ... d'être mieux armés contre les agressions extérieures.

(Kepel, 1991: 31–2)[9]

This approach combines elements of assimilation and withdrawal. On the one hand, it is accepted that Muslims in the West live in a non-Muslim society; that is, a society whose norms and values are founded on a set of principles other than Islam. On the other hand, it is affirmed that Muslims in the West will remain Muslims. More obviously, it contains elements of a Muslim identity and a Western identity. The precise shape which this will take depends on a multiplicity of other factors, including the nation state in which a Muslim finds herself or himself. Being Muslim and British is quite different from being Muslim and French because, among other things, the model of the nation is quite different. Since the revolution of 1789, French nation building has consisted largely of an attempt to construct a homogeneous cultural, linguistic and political entity, which partially explains the logic of an assimilationist approach to the 'integration' of 'immigrants', and the difficulty of gaining acceptance for the idea that one can be Muslim and French. The United Kingdom, however, has seen a *de-facto* multiculturalism (English, Scots, Welsh and Irish) and limited religious pluralism (Anglican and Presbyterian), so being Muslim and British seems less contradictory – at least in theory.

It may seem as if the *Mosquée de Paris* and the CORIF should be classified under this ideal type, because they have sought to enable Muslims to lives as Muslims in a non-Muslim society. However, they have had as much to do with attempts by the French state to assimilate Muslims, as with the desire of Muslims to live in French society. The combined identity comes from below, and is more internalized, perhaps even individualist. As an ideal type, neither identity would take prominence (in practice, either identity could take prominence, but it would not necessarily be one or the other), whereas assimilation tends to prioritize the Western identity, and withdrawal clearly prioritizes the Muslim identity.

THE DURABILITY OF ORIENTALISM

Neither of these three options for resistance – assimilation, withdrawal, or a combined identity – represents a final rebuttal of internal Orientalism. Indeed, it can be argued that, whichever option is chosen, Orientalist stereotypes are likely to be reinforced rather than effectively challenged. Where the decision is taken to assimilate, the perception that Western culture and values are superior to their 'Muslim' or 'Oriental' equivalents is reinforced. Those Muslims who are valued by the West are valued according to a perception of what they have in common with the West. From Muslim women who refuse to wear the *hijab* or resist arranged marriages, to Muslim academics who have apparently signed up to the Western scientific worldview (even though this worldview has its roots in Arab–Muslim thought[10]), even Muslim traders who sell 'Western' products – what is valued is that they are perceived as being Western.

On the other hand, those Muslims who decide to withdraw are perceived as negating these Western values, which are equated with civilization itself. Like the *Tablighi Jama'at*, they are seen as fundamentalist, a label which connects the wearing of the *hijab* to Western images of Islam-inspired fanaticism and terrorism. Thus, the perception of Islam as being radically incompatible with Western, 'civilized' values is reinforced. When classical Orientalism alleged an incompatibility between Islam and the West, Muslims were seen as a somewhat exotic people, this perception forming part of the sensual stereotype referred to earlier. But where this view is seen in a context of internal

Orientalism, the perception of Islam changes. As the Runnymede Trust argue in a recent consultation paper:

> In the case of the new coining 'islamophobia', both kinds of dread are implied: the object of fear is both out there, beyond national boundaries, and also here, all too close to home. Precisely because Islam is perceived to have this dual location it is all the more feared and disliked by many non-Muslims. Recurring metaphors to refer to Muslim communities within Europe include fifth column, bridge-head, enclave, trojan horse and enemy within.
>
> (Commission on British Muslims and Islamophobia, 1997: 6)

The intermediate position, a combined Muslim–Western identity, can also be used to reinforce internal Orientalist stereotypes, as it can be seen as contradictory and irrational. The logic of this is clear: Islam and the West have been defined for centuries not only as incompatible, but as opposites. So how can one be Muslim and Western at the same time? Even though all personal and social identities are to some extent contradictory and irrational, it is presupposed that there must be something behind the combined Western–Muslim identity, whether it be a barrier against the West (a negative interpretation of Kepel's *citadelle intérieure*), or an attempt to infiltrate the West. A classic statement of this perception is cited in the Runnymede report:

> You can be British without speaking English or being Christian or being white, but nevertheless Britain is basically English-speaking, Christian and white, and if one starts to think that it might become basically Urdu-speaking and Muslim and brown, one gets frightened and angry. ... Because of our obstinate refusal to have enough babies, Western European civilization will start to die at the point where it could have been revived with new blood. Then the hooded hordes will win, and the Koran will be taught, as Gibbon famously imagined, in the schools of Oxford.
>
> (Moore, 1991; cited in Commission on British Muslims and Islamophobia, 1997: 11)

Even if the internal Orientalist response to a combined Muslim–Western identity is not always as extreme as this, there remains a perception that Muslim and Western values are radically incompatible. This remains the case where 'assimilated' Muslims are perceived as having accepted the superiority of Western culture and values, or where the combined identity is seen as contradictory and irrational (whereas Western identities are consistent and rational). The whole process gives rise to what could be called a negative dialectic of Orientalism and resistance to Orientalism. In other words, Orientalism and resistance to Orientalism are in a situation of mutual antagonism, which makes them increasingly different and polarized. When this polarization occurs, they are constituted in opposition to each other, which means that, increasingly, they reinforce each other. They do this by looking at each other and defining what is essential about their own identities, cultures and practices, and what different-iates them from the Other. As a result they seek new and different forms of expression, which also leads to a fragmentation of their dis-courses. For example, the West is increasingly distinguishing itself from the Islamic world on the basis of state judicial systems and respect for human rights, which is a different stereotype from the fun-damentalist terrorist who works against, rather than through, the state.

CONCLUSION: SOCIOLOGICAL PRAXIS

Such fragmentation may be part of a process of polarization, but it also facilitates the development of pluralism *within* and *against* Orientalist discourses. Said (1985: 25) notes three preconditions for a critique of Orientalism: an awareness of the diversity of the critic's potential subjects and audiences; a praxis which is secular and/or plural, and in opposition to the authoritarian tendencies of main-stream Orientalism; and an openness to all sources of knowledge which are '*against* the grain, deconstructive, utopian'. Said compares the latter principle to Theodor Adorno's negative dialectics which, as we have noted above, constitutes the dynamic of Orientalism and resistance to Orientalism. Adorno (1973: 365) writes: 'If negative dialectics calls for the self-reflection of thinking, the tangible implica-tion is that if thinking is to be true – if it is to be true today, in any case – it must also be a thinking against itself'; and Adorno wrote this as a response to another case of religious and ethnic discrimination, which culminated in systematic mass murder.

What does this mean in practice? Said's first two principles need to be linked into the discussion here, and extended beyond the critique of Orientalism to a general sociological praxis. Had there been an awareness of the diversity of subjects and audiences at the time of the Rushdie affair, much of the misunderstanding could have been avoided. The act of book burning could have been seen in its context, rather than linked automatically with European histories and meanings. At the same time, those who carried out this act might have been aware of the diversity of potential receptions. A praxis which is secular/plural, seen in the context of 'thinking against itself', could have avoided the Islamophobic and cultural supremacist overtones which were present in the defence of French *laïcité* against the *hijab*. In a word, plurality would have been valorized as a universal, while secularism would have been seen in its social and historical context.

The negative dialectic of Orientalism and resistance to Orientalism does not mean that there is an *inevitable* polarization of Muslims and Westerners. Nor does it mean that 'we' have to understand Muslims better if such polarization is to be avoided, for it is precisely the 'us'/'them' distinction which is at the root of the problem. The homogeneous, essentialist stereotype of Islam, which is propagated both by Western Orientalism and by 'neo-Afghanism', demands the most rigorous critique and deconstruction: what must be asserted is that Muslim cultures and values are heterogeneous and plural, as are Western cultures and values. It must also be recognized that Islam and the West are compatible, capable of mutual integration and mutual enrichment. Thus, not only is it desirable to defend a heterogeneous society, and the freedom to be different within a society and within a community, it also becomes possible.

NOTES

1. Thanks are due, and willingly expressed, to Professor Robert Miles and Dr Nicole Bourque for their supervision of this project.
2. Said discusses the media propagation of this phenomenon in *Covering Islam* (Said, 1997; 1st edn, 1981).
3. The history and demography of Muslims in Western Europe are discussed by a number of writers. Nielsen (1995) provides a clear and concise summary, and underlines the fact that demographic figures are inconsistent, not always current, and should be treated with caution. See also Vertovec and Peach (1997: 14), though note that their estimates are generally lower than mine. My estimates are higher to allow for changes since the late 1980s.
4. It should be noted that, contrary to much popular opinion, a *fatwa* is not a death sentence. It is a legal opinion from a suitably qualified Islamic scholar, and the extent to which it confers legal obligations on other Muslims is a matter of debate among experts in Islamic law.

5. '... the hypocrisy which consists in refusing to accept, in the name of a pretext of religious liberty, the sexism inherent in the Islamist [*sic*] headscarf and the voluntary blindness to the meaning of the headscarf for Islamist parties' (my translation).
6. Significantly, the UOIF was originally the *Union des Organisations Islamiques en France*. The *en France* (in France) was later changed to *de France* (of France).
7. It is interesting to note that the Ismaili Muslims also take this view (see Aga Khan, n.d.).
8. According to Troeltsch (1931), some 'sects' 'live apart from the world', some are in active opposition, and others accommodate themselves to the world, becoming transformed into 'denominations' or 'churches'.
9. '... being Muslims gives us a dimension, in fact a large dimension, of internal security which sometimes enables us to confront ... or to be better equipped against external aggression' (my translation; original ellipsis).
10. The influence of Arab–Muslim thought on Western philosophy and science is expounded systematically by Hunke (1987). For a relevant account of the development of Islamic philosophy itself, see Netton (1984).

REFERENCES

Adorno, T. W. (1973) *Negative Dialectics* (London: Routledge and Kegan Paul).

Aga Khan, H. H. Prince, III (n.d.) *Islam: The Religion of my Ancestors* (London: Shia Imami Ismaila Association for the United Kingdom).

Al-Azmeh, A. (1996) *Islams and Modernities* (London: Verso).

Banton, M. (1997) *Ethnic and Racial Consciousness* (London and New York: Longman).

Bewley, H. A. S. A. (1992) *Fatwa on the Tablighi Jama'at: A Clarifying Legal Document* (Granada: Murabitun).

Commission on British Muslims and Islamophobia (1997) *Islamophobia: Its Features and Dangers (A Consultation Paper)* (London: Runnymede Trust).

Coq, G. (1995) *Laïcité et république: le lien nécessaire* (Paris: Editions du Félin).

Coq, G. (1996) 'Foulard islamique: pour un retour à la loi républicaine', *Libération*, 6 October, p. 6.

Crowley, J. (1992) 'Immigration, racisme et intégration: Recent French Writing on Immigration and Race Relations', *New Community*, 19(1), pp. 165–73.

Gaspard, F. and Khosrokhavar, F. (1995) *Le foulard et la République* (Paris: La Découverte).

Habermas, J. (1987) *The Theory of Communicative Action*, vol. 2 (Cambridge: Polity).

Haq, M. A. (1972) *The Faith Movement of Mawlana Muhammad Ilyas* (London: George Allen & Unwin).

Hechter, M. (1975) *Internal Colonialism* (London: Routledge & Kegan Paul).

Hunke, S. (1987) *Le soleil d'Allah brille sur l'Occident* (Paris: Albin Michel).

Keith, M. and Pile, S. (1993) 'Introduction, part 2: the Place of Politics', in M. Keith and S. Pile (eds), *Place and the Politics of Identity* (London: Routledge).

Kepel, G. (1991) *Les banlieues de l'Islam* (Paris: Editions du Seuil).

Kepel, G. (1994a) *A l'Ouest d'Allah* (Paris: Editions du Seuil).

Kepel, G. (1994b) *The Revenge of God: The Resurgence of Islam, Christianity and Judaism in the Modern World* (Cambridge: Polity).

King, J. (1994) *Three Asian Associations in Britain* (Monograph in Ethnic Relations no. 8; Coventry: CRER, University of Warwick).

Lacoste-Dujardin, C. (1995) 'Le *hidjâb* en France: un emblème politique', *Hérodote*, 77, pp. 103–18.

Marx, K. and Engels, F. (1968) *On Colonialism* (London: Lawrence & Wishart).

Miles, R. (1989) *Racism* (London: Routledge).

Moore, C. (1991) 'Time for a More Liberal and "Racist" Immigration Policy', *Spectator*, 19 October.

Netton, I. R. (1994) *Allah Transcendent: Studies in the Structure and Semiotics of Islamic Philosophy, Theology and Cosmology* (Richmond: Curzon Press).

Nielsen, J. S. (1995) *Muslims in Western Europe* (Edinburgh: Edinburgh University Press).

Said, E. W. (1985) 'Orientalism Reconsidered', in F. Barker, P. Hulme, M. Iverson and D. Loxley (eds), *Europe and its Others*, vol. 1 (Colchester: University of Essex).

Said, E. W. (1993) *Culture and Imperialism* (London: Vintage).

Said, E. W. (1995) *Orientalism: Western Conceptions of the Orient* (London: Penguin).

Said, E. W. (1997) *Covering Islam: How the Media and the Experts Determine How We See the Rest of the World* (London: Vintage).

Taguieff, P.-A. (1988) *La force du préjugé* (Paris: La Découverte).

Telhine, M. (1991) 'Les convertis de la Grande Mosquée de Paris', *Hérodote*, 60(1), 209–34.

Terrel, H. (1994) 'L'enclave islamique de la rue Jean-Pierre-Timbaud', in G. Kepel (ed.), *Exils et royaumes: les appartenances au monde arabo-musulman aujourd'hui* (Paris: Presses de la Fondation Nationale des Sciences Politiques).

Tönnies, F. (1955) *Community and Association* (London: Routledge & Kegan Paul).

Troeltsch, E. (1931) *The Social Teaching of the Christian Churches*, vol. 2 (London: George Allen & Unwin).

Turner, B. S. (1994) *Orientalism, Postmodernism and Globalism* (London: Routledge).

Vervotec, S. and Peach, C. (1997) 'Introduction', in S. Vertovec and C. Peach (eds), *Islam in Europe: The Politics of Religion and Community* (Basingstoke: Macmillan).

10 Citizenship and Identity: the Case of Australia
EMMA CLARENCE

INTRODUCTION

National identity plays an important role in identifying who we are as individuals. However, we are not born with a sense of national identity, it has to be inculcated. What it means to belong to a particular nation, to have a sense of that identity, is constructed by a diverse range of forces, including governments, the media and the community lived in. This chapter sets out to explore how the federal government of Australia sought to construct national identity around a particular idea of citizenship in an attempt to construct an identity that recognized and was inclusive of the ethnic and cultural diversity that existed within Australian society.

Australia has undergone significant social change since the end of the Second World War. The Australia of 1945 has been transformed from an overwhelmingly 'white', Anglo-Celtic society to one of significant ethnic and cultural diversity. This change has occurred as a result of immigration policies and programmes implemented abroad by the federal government. Australian citizenship itself was only created by the 1948 Australian Citizenship Act, before which Australian residents were British, with the exception of Aboriginals, who were wards of the federal government, and those residents who were citizens of other states. Recognition of the post-1945 changes wrought on Australian society was slow, and it was not until the mid-1970s that the federal government initiated domestic policies to complement the ethnic and cultural diversity that had been brought into being. That policy was known as 'multiculturalism' and it has had a profound effect on the way in which Australian national identity has been constructed. Multiculturalism survived, in differing guises, two changes of government; whether it will survive a third is open to question. Since the election of the Liberal Party in March 1996 multiculturalism has come under considerable attack

199

and its survival as a formal, funded, government programme is questionable.

The chapter goes on to examine the way in which Australian national identity was constructed during Paul Keating's time as Prime Minister (1991–6), with a particular focus on the use of citizenship as a tool with which to bind multicultural Australia. It will then briefly assess what has occurred since March 1996 during the Liberal Party's time in office. This chapter offers a brief examination of the post-1945 immigration programme and the emergence of government policies which sought to address the changes that had occurred and so provides an overall image of Australian society in the late 1990s.

NATIONAL IDENTITY

An individual's identity is multifaceted and complex. There are many factors that go towards making up our identity and at different stages of life individuals will place varying emphasis upon aspects of their identity (Hobsbawm, 1990). One aspect of identity is 'national identity': the sense of belonging and identification that an individual feels to a particular nation or state. It is important to recognize from the outset that the words 'nation' and 'state' are not interchangeable; they refer to two very distinct entities. The state is a definable territorial/political unit, whilst the nation is a more complex, often intangible entity (Connor, 1978). The commonplace term 'nation-state' presumes that the geographic boundaries of the nation and the state are analogous – a contestable presumption in a world of multinational, multiethnic and multicultural states.[1] In popular assertion national identity can therefore refer to identifying with a nation, identifying with a state and even, in certain circumstances, identifying with both the nation and the state.[2]

The nation is not 'natural'; it is a constructed form of social organization. Accordingly, national identity is a constructed identity, intrinsically linked to how the nation itself is constructed. Broadly it is possible to identify two types of nations – ethnic and political. Ethnic nations use ethnicity as their basis for construction. A key feature of this construction is the presumption that there exists an ethnically homogeneous group of people around which the nation can be identified. Alternatively, political nations are those that use ideas of citizenship and citizen's rights, duties and obligations for their construction with no reference to the ethnic make-up of the nation.

Anthony Smith (1991), in his work *National Identity*, identified five fundamental features of national identity: an historical territory, or homeland; common myths and historical memories; a common, mass public culture; common legal rights and duties for all members; and a common economy with territorial mobility for members. National identity, as presented by Smith, would appear to be based on the perception of the nation as an ethnic-nation, with a passing acknowledgement to political nations.[3] However, there is little space for 'multicultural' nations to construct a sense of national identity within these boundaries. For multiethnic and multicultural nations there is a need to develop an identity that recognizes the differences between people whilst simultaneously constructing something which binds individuals together, regardless of difference.

Understanding how that identity is constructed and maintained is important in understanding the identity that is being established. Michael Billig's work on the 'banal nationalism' of 'the established nations of the west' argues that 'there is a continual "flagging", or reminding, of nationhood', which, whilst not overtly nationalistic, serves to remind people of their place and their nation's place in the world (1995). This reminder involves both 'forgetting' and 'remembering': forgetting the violence that brought the nation/state into existence and the relative shortness of that existence (Billig, 1995), and remembering the events and myths that have been presented as 'defining' to the nation's existence. In small ways individuals are constantly reminded – whether it be by the flag hanging over a national building, or other unobtrusive, 'banal' symbols – of their nation and their identification with it. The language spoken by the government and in the media, the images created and perpetuated all serve as powerful reminders of who belongs – and who does not; thus the idea of a 'true Aussie' or a 'true Brit' implies that there are 'untrue' Australians or Britons. By providing constant reminders of national identity it is possible, in times of need, to convert the 'banal' into a more overt nationalism.

National identity is a flexible form of identity, open to construction and manipulation from a multiplicity of sources. Governments play an important role in developing and articulating a particular version of national identity. The education system, immigration policy, cultural programmes (including funding the arts and broadcasting policy) and other government policies (including foreign affairs, economic and trade programmes) can be used to propagate a government's or political parties' particular vision of national identity. Other areas including the media, political parties and community and cultural organizations also play a role in constructing national identity or indeed challenging a government's interpretation. In the case of Australia the Hawke/Keating federal government of the 1980s and 1990s sought to construct Australian national identity around ideas of multicultural-ism and citizenship.

CITIZENSHIP

Citizenship involves more than simply identifying those who are members of a particular state; it extends beyond this to questions of participation and access, as well to the rights and obligations of the citizens themselves. In his seminal work *Citizenship and Social Class,* T. H. Marshall proposes a tripartite conception of citizenship: civil, political and social citizenship. The first of these consists of the rights to secure individual freedom and justice; the second is the right to participate as an elector or member of bodies which exercise political power; and social citizenship is the right to economic welfare and security, as well as the right to participate and share in the 'social her-itage' and live according to acceptable societal standards of the day (1992: 8).

Whilst Marshall's categories are broadly useful, his work has been criticized on a number of different fronts, including for its concentra-tion on Britain and its lack of universality (Rees, 1996; Mann, 1996), its failure to acknowledge differences of gender and ethnicity (Bottomore, 1992) and its lack of reference to the increase in state power in relation to rights of citizenship. These are important criti-cisms for they point to contemporary desires to expand the concept of citizenship to further include differences of gender, ethnicity and sexual orientation. There is a search for a notion of citizenship that empowers individuals to effectively participate in decisions which impact upon their lives and one that also addresses the economics of access and participation.

Marshall's contribution to the discussions and debates on citizen-ship has been important but, I would suggest, it reflects the ethos of a political past. Rather in the same manner as entitlement theory, it is an interesting lens through which to view contemporary social and economic rights. The particular idea of citizenship propagated by the federal government in Australia in the late 1980s and 1990s as a tool to construct Australian national identity was informed by the same tradition of which Marshall is a part, but it had moved beyond it and drew from some of its criticisms. Indeed a central focus of the citizenship propagated by the federal government was the recognition of ethnic and cultural difference and a demand for equality of the sexes.

FROM ASSIMILATION TO INTEGRATION

One of the first acts passed by the newly formed Federal Parliament in 1901, the Immigration Restriction Act, or 'White Australia Policy', sought to prohibit 'undesirables' from emigrating to Australia. Federation was presented by its proponents who dominated the arenas of politics and the media as the best way of ensuring Australian 'racial purity' (McKenna, 1996). The threat of 'cheap, coloured' labour was used by trade unionists to argue for federation and a strict immigration policy. Even opposition to the 'White Australia Policy' from the British Secretary of State for the Colonies, Joseph Chamberlain, failed to inhibit the vigour with which it was pursued. The Immigration Restriction Act prohibited entry into Australia by a person who could not pass a dictation test in any European language.

At the end of the Second World War it became apparent to the federal government that Australia needed to increase its population quickly and significantly if it was to be militarily secure and economically prosperous (Freeman and Betts, 1992). Slogans such as 'populate or perish' became commonplace. It was with the 'White Australia Policy' apparently entrenched and consensual that the Labor Government began to consider Australia's future population requirements. A figure of 2 per cent was accepted by the newly appointed Minister for Immigration, Arthur Calwell, as the target by which the Australian population ought to be increased each year, approximately 1 per cent by natural growth and the other 1 per cent by independent and assisted immigration (Collins, 1988). In a statement to the House of Representatives Calwell made it clear that Australia was to continue to be an overwhelmingly 'British' society, with one 'foreigner' accepted for every 10 British immigrants. This policy, according to the former Liberal Prime Minister, Sir Robert Menzies, in his autobiography, marked the end of a Labor Party – trade union accord on no 'assisted migration' to Australia (Menzies, 1967).

The immigration programme was never able to meet those criteria, due to the lack of available shipping and an overestimation of the number of people who would wish to immigrate. Instead the

Australian government sought to encourage increasing numbers of people from Europe, other than Britain, to immigrate into Australia. To this end numerous bilateral agreements with European governments were signed outlining the number of immigrants that would be accepted by Australia and the services with which they would be provided. The services included a period of time at a 'training' camp and then direction to work on various projects for two years (Freeman and Jupp, 1992). All immigrants were expected to 'self-assimilate' into Australian society upon their arrival. However, the assimilation policy was deemed a failure in the mid-1960s, with migrants suffering from residential and labour market segregation and low educational attainment (Jakubowicz, 1981; Castles, 1992a). The discourse of the day did not allow for investigation of the proposition that these segregations and ultimately return migration may have been the expressions of a current of resistance to non-negotiated assimilations. Increasing rates of migrant return forced the federal government to reassess the immigration programme and the expectation of assimilation. As a direct consequence of these failings there was a subtle shift away from assimilation towards a policy of integration (Castles 1992b). Although integration had as its basis the belief that immigrants would ultimately assimilate into Australian society and become Australian citizens, it lessened the expectation of immediacy and enabled the government to introduce programmes targeted at assisting immigrants in becoming effective, participating citizens.

THE MULTICULTURAL PROJECT

The decision to allow a limited number of highly skilled Asian immigrants into Australia in 1966[4] (Freeman and Jupp, 1992; Castles, 1992b), and the shift away from assimilation towards integration was a benchmark in an undeclared abandonment of the 'White Australia Policy'. However, it was not until the election of the Whitlam-led Australian Labor Party (ALP) government in 1972 that these two policies were formally brought to an end (Price, 1987; Castles, 1992b). The 'White Australia Policy' was replaced with a racially non-discriminatory immigration policy that ended the privileges that had been extended to British migrants. At the same time, expectations of assimilation and integration were replaced by the adoption of 'multiculturalism' as government policy. Multiculturalism under the ALP was less about a theoretical conception of cultural diversity, and more a practical programme of policies. Whilst the ALP government highlighted the enrichment, both social and economic, that Australian society would experience as a result of cultural and ethnic diversity, at the same time it placed greater emphasis on the provision of welfare services that addressed some of the problems immigrants and their communities faced.

The concept of multiculturalism, as it has existed in government policy in Australia, has not been static. It has been reinterpreted pragmatically by governments as and when deemed necessary according to a range of social, economic and political factors. The sacking of the Whitlam government in 1975, and the subsequent election of the Liberal Party led by Malcolm Fraser, did not end multiculturalism in Australia, rather it produced a re-rendering of it. Neo-liberal economic policies, as pursued by the Liberal Party, precluded the same emphasis on the provision of welfare services as there had been during the ALP government. This prompted a shift in the balance of the government's policy of multiculturalism towards one that focused primarily on cultural pluralism. There was also a move towards enhancing the role and responsibility of ethnic community-based organizations in providing welfare services, away from the expectation of federal government provision (Castles, 1992a). Immigration based on non-discriminatory measures continued as government policy. The immigration programme was substantially increased, and the Liberal government allowed greatly increased numbers of Asian refugees to enter Australia. Malcolm Fraser committed his government to the project of constructing an inclusive national identity for Australia, one that acknowledged the changing social and cultural make-up of Australian society. For that reason a programme of multiculturalism was retained as an important tool in constructing national identity.

The return of the ALP in 1983 began a long period of ALP government in Australia that came to an end only in March 1996. The 13 years the ALP spent in government can be divided into two: Bob Hawke's period as Prime Minister (1983–91), followed by five years with Paul Keating as Prime Minister. During Hawke's period as Prime Minister the type of national identity that was to be constructed by the government was less than clear. Economic difficulties in particular had an impact on government policy towards both immigration and multiculturalism. Indeed the established ethnic communities were required to defend multiculturalism from funding cuts during the early years of the ALP government. The final years of Hawke's leadership saw the government beginning to display a more coherent understanding of what form Australian national identity should take. It was, however, predominantly during Keating's Prime Ministership that there emerged strong government policies and programmes aimed at constructing Australian national identity around ideas of multiculturalism and citizenship.

The increasing proportion of Asian immigrants entering Australia became an important issue in 1984 when Professor Geoffrey Blainey, an eminent conservative historian at the University of Melbourne, attacked Asian immigration. Claiming that Australia's policies were driven by guilt and an attempt to gain broad political support in international fora from the Asian states along with the rest of the 'third world', Blainey began a wide-ranging public debate as to the future direction of Australia's immigration programme (Blainey, 1984). The relationship between immigration and multiculturalism, then as now, is seen to be a close, mutually self-reinforcing one. Accordingly, the attack on immigration was broadened into a more general criticism of both immigration and multiculturalism. In particular the perceived high levels of government expenditure on multicultural service provision and programmes during a time of economic recession and unemployment came in for sharp criticism. Upon taking office in 1983 the ALP government had been confronted by the highest levels of unemployment since the 'Great Depression' of the 1930s. Although the government had initially slashed immigration from over 100,000 in 1982/83 to 62,000 in 1983/84 this had not appeased opponents who continued to associate high unemployment with increased immigration (Collins, 1988).

Continuing economic problems and an apparent loss of support for multiculturalism led the federal government to decrease funding for multicultural programmes in the 1986 budget, including cuts to English-language programmes and the merger of the Special Broadcasting Service with the Australian Broadcasting Corporation. However, the ALP had failed to recognize the importance with which established ethnic minority communities, particularly those who had been prominent in the immediate post-1945 immigration programme, including Italian, Greek and Yugoslav communities, regarded government-funded multicultural programmes. The mobilization of multiculturalism's supporters on the basis of resistance to policy change by budget cuts, particularly in marginal ALP seats, compelled the federal government to reverse many of its funding cuts in 1987. To assure people of the government's commitment to multiculturalism the position of Minister for Immigration, Local Government and Ethnic

Affairs became a senior post within the Cabinet. Furthermore, an Office for Multicultural Affairs was established within the Prime Minister's Office reiterating the importance of multiculturalism and the Prime Minister's own personal concern.

The federal government established the 'Committee to Advise on Australia's Immigration Policies', which later produced the FitzGerald Report, as a result of growing concern within the established ethnic communities as to the direction of Australia's immigration policy. The Committee appeared to accept as a premise that even higher levels of immigration were desirable. It based its conclusions on the assumption that a quota of 150,000 immigrants annually should be introduced from 1988/9 to 1990/1 and then increased further subject to decennial review. Part of this quota was to be met by Asian immigrants, whom the Committee believed would bring with them economic benefits – a result of their personal entrepreneurial skills, as well as their links with the region. The Report also addressed the question of attitudes to multiculturalism, and found that multiculturalism was popularly misunderstood in Australia, and argued that it acted as a divisive element within Australian society by appearing to privilege minority ethnicism (Barnett, 1986). Furthermore, the FitzGerald Report referred to equally popular sentiments concerning the perception that immigration policy had in fact been run for the benefit of ethnic communities, serving their communities' interests, rather than for the benefit of Australia as a whole (FitzGerald, 1988; Birrell, 1988). Such criticism of multiculturalism was as much about presentation as about implementation.

Perhaps the clearest attack by the Committee on multiculturalism, and the role of multiculturalism in Australian society, was related to its attempt to define Australian national identity and its assumption that all immigrants should aspire to that version of Australian identity (Birrell, 1988). The Committee defined Australian identity as 'democratic, individualistic, loyal, egalitarian … relaxed, informal, friendly, full of opportunity … free, spacious and environmentally unique' (FitzGerald, 1988: 27). The Report was challenged by ethnic community organizations and rejected by the federal government, which quickly moved to distance itself from the Report's findings and reaffirmed government support for multiculturalism. However, the federal opposition, the Liberal Party, welcomed the findings of the Report, particularly the negative references to multiculturalism, and argued for a 'one nation' policy for Australia rather than the 'divisive' policy of multiculturalism (Freeman and Betts, 1992).

Economic considerations have played an important role in encouraging greater political and social engagement with Asia. Historically Australia has had a problematic relationship with the region. Australia's perception of itself as a European outpost in Asia, and the fear promulgated during the 1940s, 1950s and 1960s of the Asian menace, Communist or otherwise, served to alienate and isolate Australia from its geographic neighbours (Jupp, 1995). Whilst Australia traded with Asia there was an attempt to remain distant from it politically, but negatively changing economic circumstances, exacerbated by Britain's decision to enter the European Economic Community in 1973, forced Australia to find alternative markets for its products. Asia was an obvious market due to its close physical proximity. A government report commissioned in 1989, entitled *Australia and the Northeast Asian Ascendancy,* highlighted the need for Australia to interact with the region in which it is geographically situated and, as a means of encouraging regional integration, the report noted the importance of Asian immigration to Australia (Garnaut, 1989: 290). Australia's changing relationship with Asia had led to Australia becoming seen as a destination for entrepreneurial and other desirable Asian immigrants which, it was suggested, could only benefit Australia economically. The project of re-siting Australia in an Asian context has not been without its problems, and its opponents, and gained particular attention as a project during Paul Keating's time as Prime Minister.

CITIZENSHIP AS NATIONAL IDENTITY

In September 1988, when Prime Minister Bob Hawke launched the discussion paper of the Advisory Council on Multicultural Affairs, he expressed his perception of Australian identity: 'what makes a person an Australian is nothing more complex or esoteric than a commitment to Australia' (cited in Smolicz, 1991: 50). Whilst this is a somewhat unsophisticated explanation of Australian identity it encapsulates the federal government's attempts to move ideas of national identity away from empirical constructs of cultural and ethnic homogeneity as the basis around which national identity should be constructed. Commitment to Australia is what is important, and it is this construction that has been increasingly formalized through the medium of Australian citizenship and the role given to it by the federal government.

A section of the FitzGerald Report had recommended that Australian citizenship be enhanced, albeit by reducing non-citizens' rights. To this end the Report sought to encourage the government to remove non-survival welfare benefits from non-citizens and to preclude non-citizens from sponsoring immigrants (FitzGerald, 1988: 121).[5] Although the federal government rejected the Report there was a move towards encouraging migrants to take up Australian citizenship. In January 1989 Bob Hawke wrote to households inviting people to become Australian citizens, and a 'Year of Citizenship' was initiated to promote the idea. The publication of *The National Agenda for a Multicultural Australia* by the Office for Multicultural Affairs in the Prime Minister's Office in the same year set out to define clearly what multiculturalism meant in Australia, along with the rights individuals might be expected to enjoy and the duties they might be expected to perform as citizens.

Three features of multiculturalism, and three limitations upon multiculturalism, were identified in *The National Agenda for a Multicultural Australia.* They are important because they establish the framework within which Australian national identity was to be constructed and the idea of citizenship that was to be implemented. The three features of multiculturalism identified were: the right of all people to maintain, share and express their cultural identity; the right of all Australians to equality of opportunity and treatment; and finally, the requirement that all Australians utilize their talents and skills to benefit Australia in its quest for economic efficiency. These features were qualified by the necessity for all people to have a commitment to Australia, one that overrode other loyalties; an acceptance of the basic structures of Australian society, including the Constitution, the rule of law, equality of the sexes and the primacy of English as a national language. Finally there was an obligation to respect and accept other peoples' right to cultural expression (Office of Multicultural Affairs, 1989: vii). Within these features and qualifications are clearly identifiable rights and obligations that have as their overarching theme an individual's commitment to Australia and her/his obligation to do what is deemed to be in the best interest of Australia. They also implicity contain a perception of rights that is conditioned by the primacy of national economic well-being.

Whilst *The National Agenda for a Multicultural Australia* did not advocate the introduction of policies which would punitively discriminate against non-citizens, it was an attempt at formalizing the meaning of Australian citizenship. Part of that construction was to outline and identify the role of multiculturalism in the understanding to be given to citizenship. Constructing Australian national identity has been problematic because cultural similarities and ethnic homogeneity have not been able to be used as a national 'bond'. The FitzGerald Report's attempt to define Australian national identity as it did was nebulous and contradictory, and failed to address the diversity of Australian society. It is no more or less possible to construct national identity around ideas of large open spaces, gum trees and kangaroos, than it is to believe the Report's highly subjective and questionable assertion that Australia is egalitarian. For this reason the ALP government, particularly during Paul Keating's time as Prime Minister (1991–6), sought to focus on the role of citizenship in constructing a cohesive Australian national identity that then takes account of the cultural, ethnic and social diversity that exists in Australia and has been encouraged under the auspices of multiculturalism. Rather than attempting to define what Australia means, the idea of common citizenship has been used to join Australians together by defining a shared sense of what they should do for Australia and what Australia should do for them.

Citizenship continued as the focus of government attempts to construct national identity throughout the 1990s. A new campaign, 'Welcome to our Family', was launched in 1994 to encourage people to take-up Australian citizenship. It is worth noting that the lowest levels of citizenship take up have been amongst English-speaking immigrants, notably British migrants, whilst it is less surprising that the highest rates have been amongst refugees (FitzGerald, 1989: 67–8; Office of Multicultural Affairs, 1989: 10–11).

In 1996 an 'Australian Citizenship Week' was initiated, running from Australia Day (26 January) to the anniversary of the first citizenship ceremonies held in Australia on 3 February. As part of this programme poster competitions, ceremonies and citizenship awards were all used to focus upon the importance of citizenship. In a press release announcing 'Australian Citizenship Week' the Minister for Immigration and Ethnic Affairs and Minister Assisting the Prime Minister for Multicultural Affairs, Senator Nick Bolkus, said:

> In a society as multi-faceted as ours, citizenship is what binds us together. It is central to our national identity, and our development as a fair and inclusive place to be.

> (Bolkus, 1995)

It was planned that the 'Australian Citizenship Week' would be repeated annually until 1999 when it would culminate in a 'Year of Australian Citizenship'. Bolkus explicitly sought to include all Australians in the citizenship programmes and celebrations, noting that:

> it is important not only for migrants who make an active decision to take it up, but for all Australians to think about and celebrate their Australian citizenship.

(Bolkus, 1995)

One of the failings in communicating the sense and meaning of multi-culturalism had been the perception that it was only applicable to ethnic minority communities and had no direct relevance to the majority Anglo-Celtic communities. A belief that Anglo-Celts, the dominant group within Australian society, do not possess an ethnicity, has allowed the idea to develop that multiculturalism is only for migrant communities, ignoring the fact that all Australians, except for the indigenous peoples, have an immigrant heritage. These two concerns, to recognize the importance of citizenship's role in a multi-cultural society and to ensure that all Australians, not simply non-Anglo-Celtic immigrants and other established ethnic communities, recognize their citizenship, articulate the government's attempt to include all Australians in the construction of a cohesive national identity.

REPUBLICANISM

Keating, a staunch republican, used his time as Prime Minister to push for Australia to be a republic by the centenary of federation in 2001. An advisory body, the Republic Advisory Committee, was established in 1993 to examine the options concerning an Australian republic. Arguments in favour of Australia becoming a republic have focused on a number of different areas. For many Australians republicanism is seen as the final move away from Britain, signalling Australia's independence and maturity as a 'nation'. This argument has also been used with reference to Australia's growing relationships within the Asian region. Only when Australia has severed the last remaining formal ties of the colonial legacy will Australia be able to fully participate in Asia, both politically and economically. Supporters of the *status quo* in Australia have argued for the maintenance of the monarch as Australia's Head of State because of the long historical link between Australia and Britain and the stability it provides. However, this argument has been countered by the evident multicultural nature of Australian society, and the meaninglessness of having the British monarch as Head of State to Australians who are not from an Anglo-Celtic heritage. The demand that an Australian should be Australia's Head of State has been a powerful one and one consistent with the view of commitment contained in the construct of citizenship. Whilst Keating was not able to achieve a republic during his time in office, he initiated a debate that continues. Indeed, John Howard, a confirmed monarchist, was obliged to establish a committee to examine the issue as a result of growing public support after the Liberal Party was elected in March 1996. A convention of elected delegates was held in early 1998 which evaluated the options open to Australia, and a referendum on its recommendations is to be held in 1999, the outcome of which may well be a republican Australia.

ABORIGINAL EXCLUSION

Aboriginal Australians remain the most disadvantaged peoples in Australia, not simply in terms of education and employment opportunities, but in the areas of health, life expectancy and living conditions. Aboriginal Australians continue to confront structural and institutionalized racism, as well as racism from within the general community and the perpetuation of negative stereotypes. Although Aboriginals were finally granted Australian citizenship, rather than being wards of the federal government, following a 1967 referendum, the issue of citizenship, its rights and obligations remains a pertinent one for them as for all Australians. As the most marginalized and excluded group within Australian society Aboriginal Australians may legally possess Australian citizenship; however, they are effectively excluded from participating in or enjoying the rights and obligations which that entails. They are also denied a place in the construction of Australian national identity by the failure of the majority of Australians to acknowledge the continuing injustices perpetrated against Aboriginals and the rejection of Aboriginality as a shared part of a common identity.

Exhortations that 'White Australia has a Black history' have failed to encourage white Australians and state and federal governments to address the years of injustice in any significant or meaningful way. The

High Court's *Mabo* decision in 1992 finally ended the legal fiction of *terra nullius* which claimed that Australia was empty land when the British seized it. The decision acknowledged that 'native title' may still exist, but only in such cases where Aboriginal communities could prove continuous traditional links with the land. Previous government policies, including the forcing of Aboriginal communities on to missions, has meant that this decision applied to very few Aboriginals and very little land. However, this did not stop organizations opposed to the recognition of prior Aboriginal title, particularly the mining and pastoral industries, from publicizing and perpetuating myths that the decision, and the subsequent Native Title Act, posed a threat to the 'Australian backyard'. This ensured that sections of the public opposed even the very limited acknowledgement of prior Aboriginal claim to land. The current furore over the *Wik* decision (which allowed for the coexistence of pastoral rights and native title) has only served to further exacerbate tensions.

The 'backyard' metaphor had a sense beyond the intended populist understanding of a threat to lay claim to suburban gardens. The mining lobby also promoted an interpretation suggesting that Aboriginal communities would have rights of veto over exploitation of much of the potentially lucrative interior. This would deprive not only the corporations, but Australia as a nation, of economic benefit. The logical extension of such an argument is that Aboriginals thus motivated would appear to be excluding themselves from citizenship by the apparent withdrawal from one of the three key participatory characteristics of citizenship as identified in *The National Agenda for a Multicultural Australia*: that all Australians strive towards economic efficiency.

In fact the forgone interpretation may not be entirely unrepresentative of Aboriginal activist strategy. Attempts to construct national identity around ideas of citizenship and multiculturalism have met resistance from Australia's indigenous population. While multiculturalism, as government policy, specifically sought to address the reality of an ethnically and culturally diverse society, it did not engage with the long-term structural and social problems encountered by Aboriginals which contribute to the barrier between Aboriginals and other Australians. The link between citizenship and multiculturalism that has been fostered has also precluded the effective inclusion of Aboriginal Australians within a construct of national identity. An all-encompassing Australian national identity might only be constructed when there is formal recognition of white Australia's history and role in the attempt to destroy Aboriginal culture and adequate compensation, reparation or restitution is provided. No government has yet been willing to countenance such a programme.

CODA

The election of the Liberal Party in March 1996 brought to an end the long period of ALP government which had witnessed government policy attempts to construct a cohesive national identity around a citizenship policy. Multiculturalism, at least as government-endorsed, sponsored and nurtured policy, does not appear to have survived. Prior to the election the Leader of the Liberal Party, John Howard, maintained that Australia faced a choice 'between our history and geography' (*Sydney Morning Herald*, 14 December 1995), an attack on attempts by Paul Keating and the ALP government to make Australia into a republic which is engaged economically and politically with Asia. Previous comments by Howard, including the demand for multiculturalism to be replaced with a 'one nation' policy, have ensured that the Liberal Party has been strongly identified with the opposition to multiculturalism, immigration and the 'Aboriginal industry' as Howard has referred to it (*Independent*, 10 October 1996).

Pauline Hanson's election as an Independent Member of the House of Representatives has also had a profound impact upon the multicultural project. Initially selected to be the Liberal Party's candidate for the federal seat of Oxley (Queensland), Hanson was dropped following comments made in the press regarding Aboriginal affairs deemed not to be in line with party policy.[6] Such comments have since been mirrored by those made by John Howard since he became Prime Minister (Four Corners 1997). Hanson won the seat in the 1996 federal election as an independent and went on to establish the political party One Nation. An economic nationalist/isolationist she has argued for greater government intervention to protect Australian jobs, industry and the rural sector, and has proposed a cut in immigration whilst Australicns are unemployed. It is worth noting, however, that Pauline Hanson's economic nationalism and isolationism has led to concern amongst the business and financial communities in Australia as to the effect her statements will have on Australia's trading relationships, particularly with Asian states.

Hanson has also recently become the focus for much of the polemic against multiculturalism, immigration and spending on Aboriginal affairs. Her claim that Australia was 'being swamped with Asians' reignited the long-running polemic against Asian immigration into Australia (*Guardian*, 11 October 1996), and attacks on Aboriginal-specific programmes have fuelled negative perceptions that the Aboriginal communities were being singled out for 'special' treatment. In her maiden speech to the House of Representatives, Hanson claimed that she was 'fed up to the back teeth with the inequalities that are being promoted by the government and paid for by the tax-payer under the assumption that Aboriginals are the most disadvantaged people in Australia', and went on to state that 'abolishing multiculturalism will save billions of dollars and allow those from ethnic backgrounds to join mainstream Australia, paving the way to a strong united country' (Hanson, 1996).[7] In a speech to a meeting in Ulverstone, Tasmania, Hanson reiterated her claims that Aboriginals received 'special' treatment, asking 'Have Aboriginals got a monopoly on being disadvantaged?' (*Sydney Morning Herald*, 12 May 1997).[8]

It is difficult to assess the popularity of Pauline Hanson or her political party 'One Nation'.[9] Regardless of the truth of many of Hanson's statements they have pandered to populist misconceptions and untruths. The decision by three former Labor Prime Ministers, Gough Whitlam, Bob Hawke and Paul Keating, to issue a joint statement condemning 'the bigoted, uninformed, simplistic and subversive nonsense being peddled by Pauline Hanson' and calling for Australians to seek to purge our great country of a malign and angry influence, which, if unchecked, can divide our nation and jeopardize our future economic and social well-being' (Whitlam *et al.*, 1997), indicates the very real belief that Hanson is damaging Australia. Former Liberal Prime Minister Malcolm Fraser has also condemned Pauline Hanson, One Nation and the racist views propagated by them, and noted the 'need to purge ourselves of the "One Nation" policies for reasons of our own self-respect, for our own sense of decency, for our own peace of mind' (Fraser, 1997).

Hostility to multiculturalism in any or all of its facets has spawned 'backlash politics' and violence. The 'backlash politics' that has emerged provides an important indication of the fragility of the Australian national identity as created by the ALP government. The promulgation of multiculturalism since the 1970s, and the concerted effort in the last years of Hawke's period as Prime Minister, followed by Paul Keating, to construct national identity around ideas of multiculturalism and citizenship would appear to have failed to have engendered a strong sense of identity or mass empathy.

It is important to recognize that while government is the main focus of this chapter it is only one of the many actors in constructions of national identity. Other non-state actors, including community organizations, political parties, individuals, the media and cultural groups, have a significant role, particularly in opposing attempts to construct exclusionary models of Australian identity. Already there has been strong resistance to Pauline Hanson, One Nation and John Howard. Howard and Hanson do not represent all Australians, nor have their policies and pronouncements been met with universal support. A multiplicity of organizations and individuals have responded in a multiplicity of ways. The decision by the Queensland Chinese Community Voice to lodge an objection to the registration of Pauline Hanson's political party, One Nation, with the Australian Election Commission was an attempt to operate within the institutional structures that already exist (*The Australian*, 26 April 1997). They were not alone in their protests; over 80 submissions were made to try to stop the registration of One Nation. Rowdy protests have been held outside meetings held by Pauline Hanson across Australia. Artists, writers, curators and historians have established Australian Artists Against Racism, which sought to both 'raise awareness about the impact of racism on contemporary culture' and fight funding cuts to indigenous cultural communities (*The Australian*, 28 April 1997). Other less formal ways of protesting against One Nation have also been used – One Nation was forced to discontinue a toll-free number it provided after it found a message on the internet telling people to call the number, thereby running up their telephone bill (*Sydney Morning Herald*, 14 May 1997). These examples of different attempts to confront and resist the policies and polemics that have sought to divide Australian society are not, however, by themselves enough to ensure multiculturalism a future.

To date, the promotion of multiculturalism has largely been state-sponsored, engendering a sometimes unhealthy symbiosis between the ALP government, its agencies and community and social organizations. A period of adversity for the policy of multiculturalism and a shift of focus to the sphere of civil society was envisaged by former Minister for Immigration and Ethnic Affairs and Minister Assisting the Prime Minister for Multicultural Affairs, Nick Bolkus, in a speech to the Culture and Citizenship Conference held in October 1996. Senator Bolkus stated that, although

> the momentum in this policy area [citizenship] may stall or even regress on a government level, I expect that in the community, at

forums such as this and because of its evolving relevance to many Australians, it will continue as a live, if not a controversial, issue.

(Bolkus, 1996: 1)

The potential and actual problems raised by 'backlash politics' against the policies of the ALP and its attempts to construct a cohesive, inclusive national identity are important ones. They bring into question the ability of any actor, whether it be government, with access to all the resources of the state, or smaller actors such as community-based organizations, to alter almost a century of isolationist, racist and exclusive constructs of identity in a single generation. In particular, 'backlash politics' challenge the ability of multiculturalism to transcend ideas of the centrality of ethnic and cultural homogeneity to societies. During times of crisis 'backlash politics' exacerbate cleavages, real or apparent.

The economic crisis that has gripped Australia, with high levels of long-term unemployment and severe drought affecting rural Australia, plays an important role in the backlash. Indeed Pauline Hanson's economistic and nationalist rhetoric, and her calls to end all immigration, have played on the fears and concerns of many Australians. In the mid-1980s, during a time of high unemployment, the ALP broke the historical relationship between unemployment and immigration; high levels of unemployment usually led to cuts in the number of immigrants entering Australia, and periods of low unemployment allowed for increased levels of immigration. Based on the belief that continuing high levels of immigration would stimulate economic growth and ultimately lower unemployment levels, the ALP maintained immigration levels. The anticipated economic stimuli did not achieve an adequate level and instead there was growing disquiet about immigration levels. Economic problems enabled opponents of immigration and multiculturalism to highlight government spending on their implementation and oppose them on economic grounds. The same lobby also attacked multiculturalism as a self-perpetuating, government-funded 'industry', which they claimed also existed around Aboriginal affairs. By claiming that an 'industry' existed it was possible to argue that the 'industry' was a self-interested one, thus campaigning for the continuation of these policies and programmes rather than for the benefit of Australia as a whole.

Furthermore, opponents of multiculturalism have continued to construct it as a divisive social policy that operates only for the benefit, and in the interests, of the established ethnic minority communities.

A contributing factor to the efficacy of this negative reconstruction of multiculturalism has been the failure of supporters of multiculturalism to convince the dominant Anglo-Celtic communities that they also were a part of the multicultural project in Australia. Instead, multicultural-ism in Australia has been widely perceived to have focused on those people who identified themselves along non-Anglo-Celtic ethnic lines, rather than identifying all people as having some form of ethnicity.

The 'average Australian', or the 'little Aussie Battler' of Australian mythology, has been repeatedly told by some politicians and sections of the media that they are in fact the disadvantaged group within Australian society (Jayasuriya, 1990). 'Backlash politics' is now intent to subsume a previous politics of resentment at the 'special treatment' some sections of society received. The election of John Howard, who in his previous role as Opposition Leader throughout the 1980s had voiced discontent and opposition to multiculturalism and Aboriginal programmes, has helped create conditions for a public backlash. It is alarming to note that in the week following the election of the Liberal Party the media were reporting increases in attacks on Asians. John Howard's failure to condemn Pauline Hanson's racist, xenophobic and bigoted comments, coupled with his own history of opposition to mul-ticulturalism and Asian immigration (Jupp, 1991), implied tacit support, regardless of Howard's protestations that he was not going to deign to respond to her comments. A motion was moved by Howard and seconded by the Leader of the Opposition, Kim Beazley, in October 1996 which reaffirmed the federal parliament's commitment to a non-discriminatory immigration policy, a diverse and tolerant Australian society, a process of reconciliation with the indigenous inhabitants of Australia and denounced racial intolerance (Department of Immigration and Multicultural Affairs, 1997). But this did not end the perception that Howard had not done enough at the right time to counter the impact of Pauline Hanson.

CONCLUSION

The dynamic changes in Australia's ethnic and cultural complexity that have occurred since 1945 have prompted attempts to construct Australian national identity in a way that recognizes these social changes and their impact on Australian society. Successive federal governments between 1972 and 1996 promulgated multiculturalism as government policy in recognition of ethnic and cultural diversity. In the last years of the Hawke government, and particularly during the Keating government, there was a focus upon citizenship as the bond that would unite all Australians, regardless of cultural and ethnic diversity. The concept of citizenship that was promoted by the government was based on the perceived need for Australian society to celebrate multiculturalism and encourage economic efficiency. To that end ideas of equality of opportunity and the utilization of skills were incorporated into citizenship, along with the need for all Australians to respect diversity in all its cultural manifestations.

This policy was relatively enthusiastically embraced by influential sectors of the labour and progressive movements. However, the Labor government's more recent reverses indicate that the policy only carried majority acquiescence in an environment of relative, or potential, economic prosperity. With the failure by successive Labor governments to guarantee economic security to its electorate, disillusionment with Labor's failure to deliver on its economic pledges spread to disillusionment with its policies, including multiculturalism. Multiculturalism then became a prime scapegoat for Australia's economic failings, and specifically for the Labor government's inability to direct resources towards growth, the stemming of unemployment and the restoration of falling standards of living. Global recession, decrease in demand for Australia's agricultural exports and an accompanying negative change in terms of trade were beyond the short to medium term means of government to correct, but were not perceived as the prime cause of Australia's declining standard of living. Instead, the championing of 'the stranger' and 'the other' were identified by Labor's detractors as the prime causes of economic failure and in time-honoured fashion Labor and their policy of constructing national identity based on multiculturalism were demonized and brought to an end by the verdict of the electorate.

NOTES

1. The United Kingdom is one example of a multinational state. It is a state which is the union of the Welsh, Scottish and English nations and the province of Northern Ireland. Iceland is an example of a 'nation-state' where the borders of the nation and state are the same.

2.   Persons identifying themselves as Australian are stating both a national and state identity, However an individual may be, for example, Scottish (a national identity) and British (a state identity).

3.   Anthony Smith's book *The Ethnic Origins of Nations* (1986) develops arguments for an ethnic origin (although not necessarily basis) for nations, and his examination of national identity would appear to derive from that position.

4.   The pre-1966 Asian-derived community had its origins in the 1850s gold rush. In 1854 there were 4000 Chinese in Australia. Attempts to exclude Asian people from entering Australia included the imposition of a £10 levy on ships' captains for every Asian person they brought to Australia (see Manning Clark, 1993: 276–80).

5.   Sponsoring involved Australian residents as private individuals or corporate entities in acting as guarantors to the good behaviour and financial integrity of would-be migrants.

6.   It is worth noting that Pauline Hanson's disendorsement as the Liberal Party's candidate came too late for the Liberal Party to field an alternative candidate. Accordingly, there is some debate about whether or not Pauline Hanson would have actually won the seat if she had been identified as an 'Independent' and opposed by an official Liberal Party candidate.

7.   For a detailed analysis of Pauline Hanson's maiden speech to the House of Representatives on 10 September 1996 see Laura Tingle's report in *The Age* newspaper (internet address: http://www.theage.com.au/special/hanson). This newspaper report not only challenges Hanson's politics *per se* but item by item refutes the factual veracity of her statements.

8.   In a book entitled *The Truth*, ghost written to reflect Pauline Hanson's political views, it was claimed that Aboriginals had practised cannibalism. The furore that developed around the book led her to repudiate the book's contents.

9.   This chapter was written before the Queensland state election of 1998 when One Nation won 11 seats. In stark contrast One Nation failed to win a single seat in the House of Representatives and won only one seat in the Senate in the October 1998 federal election. In addition, Pauline Hanson lost her newly redistributed seat of Blair.

REFERENCES

Barnett, D. (1986) 'How the Bloated Ethnic Industry is Dividing Australia', *The Bulletin,* 18 February, pp. 58–62.

Billig, M. (1995) *Banal Nationalism* (London: Sage).

Birrell, R. (1988) 'The FitzGerald Report on Immigration Policy: Origins and Implication', *Australian Quarterly*, 60(3), pp. 261–74.

Blainey, G. (1984) *All for Australia* (Melbourne: Methuen Haynes).

Bolkus, N. (1995) Press release B111/95 (http://www.immi.gov.au).

Bolkus, N. (1996) Text of speech to the Culture and Citizenship Conference, Brisbane, 2 October.

Bottomore, T. (1992) Commentary, in Marshall and Bottomore (1992).

Castles, S. (1992a) 'The Australian Model of Immigration and Multiculturalism: Is it Applicable to Europe', *International Migration Review*, XXVI(2), pp. 549–67.

Castles, S. (1992b) 'Australian Multiculturalism: Social Policy and Identity in a Changing Society', in G. Freeman and J. Jupp (eds), *Nations of Immigrants: Australia, the United States and International Migration* (Sydney: Oxford University Press).

Clark, C. M. H. (Manning) (1993) *History of Australia* (Sydney: Pimlico).

Collins, J. (1988) *Migrant Hands in a Distant Land: Australia's Post-War Immigration* (Sydney: Pluto Press).

Connor, W. (1978) 'A Nation is a Nation, is a State, is an Ethnic Group, is a ...', *Ethnic and Racial Studies*, 1(4), pp. 377–400.

Department of Immigration and Multicultural Affairs (1997) *Parliamentary Statement on Racial Tolerance* (http://www.immi.gov.au/package/poster.htm).

FitzGerald Report (1988) see *Report of the Committee to Advise on Australia's Immigration Policies*.

Four Corners (1997) 'The New Believers' (weekly current affairs digest), *Australian Broadcasting Commission*, 16 June 1997.

Fraser, M. (1997) 'Why Racial Hatred Hurts Us All'. Lecture given on 21 October and produced in full in *The Age* (http://www.theage.com.au/daily/971022/news/news27.html).

Freeman, G. and Betts, K. (1992) 'The Politics of Interests and Immigration and Policymaking in Australia and the United States', in G. Freeman and J. Jupp (eds), *Nations of Immigrants: Australia, the United States and International Migration* (Sydney: Oxford University Press).

Freeman, G. and Jupp, J. (1992) 'Comparing Immigration Policy in Australia and the United States', in G. Freeman and J. Jupp (eds), *Nations of Immigrants: Australia, the United States and International Migration* (Sydney: Oxford University Press).

Garnaut, R. (1989) *Australia and the Northeast Asian Ascendancy* (Canberra: Australian Government Publishing Service).

Hobsbawm, E. (1990) *Nations and Nationalism since 1780* (Cambridge: Cambridge University Press).

Jakubowicz, A. (1981) 'State and Ethnicity: Multiculturalism as Ideology', *Australian and New Zealand Journal of Sociology*, 17(3), pp. 4–13.

Jayasuriya, L. (1990) 'Rethinking Australian Multiculturalism as Ideology', *Australian Quarterly*, Autumn, pp. 50–63.

Jupp, J. (1995) 'From "White Australia" to "Part of Asia": Recent Shifts in Australian Immigration Policy Towards the Region', *International Migration Review*, XXIX (1), pp. 207–28.

Jupp, J. (1991) 'Multicultural Public Policy', in C. Price (ed.), *Australian National Identity* (Canberra: Academy of the Social Sciences in Australia).

Mann, M. (1996) 'Ruling Class Strategies and Citizenship', in M. Bulmer and A. Rees (eds), *Citizenship Today: The Contemporary Relevance of T. H. Marshall* (London: UCL Press).

Marshall, T. H. and Bottomore, T. (1992) *Citizenship and Social Class* (London: Pluto). [Marshall's essay, 'Citizenship and Social Class', is followed by Bottomore's commentary.]

McKenna, M. (1996) *The Captive Republic: A History of Republicanism in Australia, 1788–1996* (Cambridge: Cambridge University Press).

Menzies, R. (1967) *Afternoon Light: Some Memories of Men and Events* (London: Cassell & Co).

Office of Multicultural Affairs (1989) *The National Agenda for a Multicultural Australia* (Canberra: Australian Government Publishing Service).

Price, C. (1987) 'Australia: Multicultural and Non-Racist', *New Community*, 14 (1/2), pp. 241–4.

Report of the Committee to Advise on Australia's Immigration Policies, (1988) *Immigration: A Commitment to Australia* (Canberra: Australian Government Publishing Service).

Rees, A. (1996) 'T. H. Marshall and the Progress of Citizenship', in M. Bulmer and A. Rees (eds), *Citizenship Today: The Contemporary Relevance of T. H. Marshall* (London: UCL Press).

Smith, A. (1986) *The Ethnic Origin of Nations* (Oxford: Blackwell).

Smith, A. (1991) *National Identity* (London: Penguin).

Smolicz, J. (1991) 'Who is an Australian? Identity, Core Values and the Resilience of Culture', in C. Price (ed.), *Australian National Identity* (Canberra: The Academy of the Social Sciences in Australia), pp. 41–66.

Whitlam, E. G. *et al.* (1997) 'The Hanson Statement', produced in full in *The Age* (http://www.theage.com.au/daily/971107/news/news25.html).

11 Eating into Britishness: Multicultural Imaginaries and the Identity Politics of Food
IAN COOK, PHILIP CRANG and MARK THORPE

INTRODUCTION: MULTICULTURAL IMAGINARIES AND BRITISH CULINARY CULTURE

Lurking behind the simplicity of the aphorism that 'you are what you eat' are much more complex relations between food and identity practice. In this chapter we will be trying to suggest some of that complexity by exploring two aspects of those relations in the British context. First, we will be outlining how everyday practices of commodified food provision and consumption involve the production and consumption not only of foods but of social imaginaries, which position individual dietary practices within wider discursive framings. Second, we will be concentrating on one particular set of such imaginaries: those constituting a multicultural space of different foods, peoples and places. This latter focus is not chosen at random. The postwar internationalization of food provision and consumption within the UK has been widely noted within studies both of the food system and of British diets and tastes (Mennell, 1985; Goodman and Redclift, 1991; Arce and Marsden, 1993; Cook, 1994). It is not only driven by the large retailers' desire to establish global supply chains that counteract the seasonality of production and ensure the cheapest possible sourcing, but also involves a set of promotional commentaries on the global culinary reach of British food providers. Thus the large supermarket chains, responsible for over 70 per cent of food sales in the UK, seek to distinguish themselves from low-cost retailers in terms of food quality and customer care, in part through portraying themselves as

223

providers of a cornucopia of globally sourced produce (for example through the prominent positioning of 'exotic' fruit near store entrances). Food manufacturers and retailers' buyers also look 'abroad' to garner ideas for new, high value-added products, which will display innovation to consumers and commercial competitors. And a common trope in the rhetorics of competitive urban place promotion is the public culture provided by cuisines from all around the world, as epitomized in the editorial of a recent *Time Out* eating and drinking guide for London (on London see also *Time Out*, 1995; on Leeds see Farrar, 1996; on Bombay see Conlon, 1995; on New York see Zukin, 1995):

> London's restaurant scene has changed dramatically over the past few years... . [A]t all levels London is unmatched for quality, variety and spice. Where else is there such diversity of cuisines? In this guide you'll find more than 60 countries and regions represented – from Afghanistan and Azerbaijan, through Georgia, Greece and Gujerat, to Thailand, Tibet, Tunisia and Turkey, on to former Yugoslavia and Zimbabwe.
>
> (Stacey, 1996: 8)

A world of cultural and culinary diversity is currently being served up to British food consumers on their plates, their supermarket shelves and their high streets (Cook and Crang, 1996). This chapter sets out to provide a critical route map through those servings.

At one level, food and notions of cultural diversity have an obvious history of connection. For instance, there are the celebrations and festivals that use food and eating as forms of cultural engagement within wider projects of 'symbolic multiculturalism' (Kobayashi, 1993: 206). These are common enough to require little explanation, but as a trite example, drawn from close to home, University College London's 1997 'Cultural Awareness Week' staged a 'humanity fair' in which one could not only 'celebrate an evening of multicultural expression' but as part of that sample 'an international buffet featuring five exotic cuisines' (quotations from UCL advertisements). The model is replicated in a host of other municipal multiculturalisms. Making the connection in the opposite direction, there are also promotions of food that explicitly appeal to ideologies of multiculturalism. For example, the recently published London food guide, *Food Lovers' London*, presents its review of shops, markets, restaurants and cookbooks under 13 'national cultural' headings (Polish London, Italian London, Greek London and so on), and precedes this information with short descriptions that allow one to 'learn about how multicultural London came into existence with the background history of each community' (Linford, 1997: 1). But culinary constructions of cultural diversity are not limited to these explicit celebrations of multiculturalism. They are played out across culinary talk and practice far more generally, through the provision and consumption of foods and cuisines differentiated culturally and geographically. These can be vague, but still meaningful, differentiations such as the 'exotic' or the 'foreign' (Cook *et al.*, 1999). They can be more specifically located through associations with national and regional cuisines ('Chinese', 'Indian', 'Provencal' and so on). Or they can deploy differentiations somewhere in between, such as in the so-called 'ethnic' food sector (of which a little more later). But no matter what the form of differentiation, food therefore operates as an arena of practice within which understandings of British and global cultural geographies are established, deployed and reworked.

The implications of culinary globalization for understandings of British national identity have unsurprisingly therefore been the subject of a growing number of media commentaries. These are far from univocal, and are complicated by the fact that one of the reasons that food occupies a prominent position within accounts of national identity is that it draws together questions of political regulation (with European Union regulation especially contentious), commercial activity and everyday life. However, one notable characteristic, chiming with broader discussions about the so-called 're-branding of Britain' (Leonard, 1997), has been how these commentaries have increasingly broken from documenting a conservative defence of traditional British fare, instead noting the popularity of 'non-traditional' and 'foreign' foods, and making culinary and cultural diversity a distinguishing characteristic of contemporary Britishness. Key facts – such as the British 'Indian' food sector having a greater turnover than the UK coal, steel and shipbuilding industries combined, or chicken tikka masala being Britain's best-selling ambient ready meal (Leonard, 1997: 57) – are seized upon to highlight the significance of supposedly 'foreign' foods to the productive and consumer lives of British citizens. Therefore, whilst recognizing that constructions of the inedible and the revolting are important aspects of food's relations to identity (Attar, 1985), and that oppositions to 'foreign' foods are a continuing feature of the social landscape of British food tastes (as, for example, in a recent campaign by some Members of Parliament to remove 'foreign, spicy foods' from the menu of the House of Commons canteen), our focus here is on the ways in which a globalized, diverse and outward-looking identity is being constructed through British culinary culture. We are concerned, then, with the ways in which culinary culture acts as an arena through which understandings of British national identity, and especially British multiculture, are constructed and practised.

In critically analysing these understandings our approach will, to borrow Joel Kahn's terminology, be to identify the 'multicultural imaginaries' being constructed through them (Kahn, 1995: 108). In other words, in the spirit of a critical multiculturalism (see Gordon and Newfield, 1996), we want to think about the construction, deployment and use of ideas of multiculture within food practices. In many ways our approach to the identity politics of food is therefore to take a step back from the query Anneke Van Otterloo raised a decade ago in her study of the place of 'Indonesian', 'Italian' and 'Greek' food in Dutch culinary culture, when she asked 'if nationals and foreigners sit down at each other's table [do] the two groups become closer?' (Van Otterloo, 1987: 127). Taking a step back to consider the groups posited here; to think about how they are not pre-established entities meeting through culinary culture but, in part, differentiations produced within it. Taking a step back, then, to think critically about how ideas of culture, multiculturalism and cultural geographies structure the provision and consumption of foods. In summary, our approach is to view culinary culture less as an arena within which pre-existing (culinary) cultures relate to each other, but as a form of identity practice within which cultural differences are constructed and used.

Of course it needs to be noted at the outset that in many respects the multicultural quality of the British diet is nothing new. The history of British culinary culture has long been one of transnational connections and flows (see, for instance, Mintz, 1985 on sugar). The quintessentially 'English' cup of tea, as Stuart Hall has pointed out, embodies an imperial history and a global set of trading networks, 'the outside history that is inside the history of the English' (1991a: 49). Fish and chips, now cast as a domestic fast food competing with the foreign imports of Chinese and Indian take-aways and American burger and pizza franchises, 'conceals a hybrid cultural history ... [being] the result of the ... late nineteenth century ... fusion of French styles of preparing potatoes and an East European Jewish tradition for frying fish' (Back, 1996: 15). To that extent, the recurrent trade and media understandings that portray contemporary trends in the British diet as a radical departure, explainable in terms of postwar immigration – with its impacts on the culinary identities being presented within the restaurant and catering industry – and trends in British tourism – with overseas holidays being cast as crucial in acquainting British palates with both new tastes and an ideology of their desirability – reproduce an unhelpful association of dietary globalization and novelty. Or, to be more precise, they fail to subject this association to the critical scrutiny it requires as an element within multicultural imaginaries. For what is at stake in the identity politics of contemporary British culinary culture is not how to respond to a radical material break with the national past. Rather, it is how to imagine, and practise, an ongoing multicultural national history.

This chapter is therefore structured through a review of different forms of multicultural imaginary within contemporary British culinary culture, each of them eating into Britishness in rather different ways. We identify four such imaginaries, serving up, respectively, a smorgasbord of culinary diversity, an imaginative re-localization of foods through an emphasis on culinary authenticity, the hybridization of cuisines, and circuitous geographies of flow and connection. Our aim in this chapter is primarily to set out these imaginaries and the critical responses they have provoked, but by way of illustration we will draw occasionally on interview materials from a research project we have been undertaking in North London (all interviewees are given pseudonyms in the text). Interpretations of the empirical findings of this work are being more fully written through elsewhere, and a full analysis of them is not our aim here. However, to provide some background, the project has involved work with food consumers – principally interview series work with 12 case study households, selected for variations in household composition, income, age and ethnicity – and with food providers – principally those involved in the supply chains of certain case study foods consumed by all or some of the households. Before turning to any of these materials, though, we want to elaborate a little further on how, throughout, our concern will be with the relationship between identity and practices of cultural differentiation, rather than with the politics of cultural diversity.

EATING CULTURES, EATING PLACES: CULTURAL GEOGRAPHIC DIFFERENTIATION AND IDENTITY PRACTICE

Homi Bhabha makes a distinction between addressing questions of cultural diversity and cultural difference in the following terms:

> cultural diversity is the recognition of pre-given cultural 'contents' and customs, held in a time frame of relativism ... [and] giv[ing] rise

to anodyne liberal notions of multiculturalism, cultural exchange, or the culture of humanity ... [but] cultural difference is a process of signification through which statements of culture or on culture differentiate, discriminate, and authorise the production of fields of force, reference, applicability and capacity.

(Bhabha, 1995: 206)

An example – the trade press coverage of the growth of the so-called 'ethnic food' sector in the UK – may help to illustrate this distinction. The spread of ethnic foods into the mainstream market has been widely noted as exemplary of a new spirit of adventure in British tastes (Hilliam, 1985; Keynote, 1988; Marketing Strategies for Industry Ltd, 1988; Barnard, 1989; Mintel 1989, 1994). What interests us, though, is how this sector is defined in the first place. The dominant trade definition is provided by Mintel, for whom 'ethnic foods ... [are] foods originating from the countries outside Europe' (1994: 1). To demonstrate the conceptual baggage this distinction rests on it is worth quoting at some length from a review of these trade press definitions:

> In the reports cited definition of ethnic foods occurs almost by default. There is an implicit assumption that the reader will know what is meant by the term. It has been argued, tautologically in our view, that the term means foods purchased solely by ethnic minorities (*Grocer* 1983). Market sizes, however, suggest that this is clearly not so.... . An alternative approach to definition suggests that ethnic foods are those foods emanating from outside their countries of consumption and as such the countries of origin become irrelevant. For simplicity, we have decided on the following definition: 'Those foods originating outside the UK but consumed within UK both by members of the indigenous population and by ethnic minority groups.'
>
> At this stage we acknowledge that this has substantial weaknesses since it encompasses many commodities, e.g. fruits, vegetables, grain, not normally considered as 'ethnic' in our sense of the word. An alternative strategy, therefore, is to offer a definition based on consumer perceptions, i.e. 'an ethnic food is what a sample of non-ethnic consumers believe it to be'. Arguably this is too tautologous and to some extent an abdication of responsibility, but it does add dimension to this debate!

(Paulson-Box and Williamson, 1990: 10)

What counts as 'ethnic food' is obviously not a simple matter. It is a complex and confused construction. The grounds for this confusion are clear enough, though. Ethnic foods are 'ethnic' through their association with 'ethnic' people, but this association is not simply a matter of exclusive consumption and so in itself requires an exercise of criteria of significance as to whom foods are actually associated with. In turn, not all people are 'ethnic', it seems. The grounds for assigning ethnicity to people and foods – not a particular ethnicity but ethnicity *per se* – seem to be intuitively felt by those using the distinction but they are not easily explained. In the end, our reviewers are driven to recognizing the constructedness of their ethnic categorization and falling back on to 'consumer perceptions' as the engine of differentiation. Moreover, by giving a particular role to 'non-ethnic' consumers, they highlight how designations of ethnic food are caught up in much wider manoeuvres through which some people (especially some white people) remove themselves from notions of ethnicity, and in the process construct ethnic others (Sollors, 1986). Indeed, what this review ends up recognizing, almost despite itself, is that ethnic food is a construct and one that, like ethnic art or ethnic design, arguably makes sense only through its positioning within broader cultural differentiations (Crang, 1996).

So, in approaching the multicultural imaginaries being deployed in contemporary British culinary cultures we have to go beyond the rubrics of cultural diversity. We have to do more than construct statistics of how many British citizens eat various food types and then interpret these figures in terms of an openness or closedness to multicultural realities. Rather, we have to think about the differentiations being constructed to stage the productions and consumptions of that diversity. Indeed, while we are listing critical requirements, we can go a little further and emphasize again Bhabha's reference to '*process[es]* of signification through which statements of culture or on culture differentiate, discriminate, and authorise'. In other words we can stress the need to treat (multi)culture as part of social practice, and in particular as part of what Jonathan Friedman terms 'the practice of identity' (1994, 1995). In coining this phrase Friedman is attempting to retrieve the culture concept from its overly textualized formulations, casting culture as a process rather than an entity, a series of locally situated performances rather than a set of codes. More particularly, he does this by thinking about culture as the outcome of projects of identity, involving 'the identification of an existential world, the attribution of meaning to the world, to objects, persons and relations' and 'highly motivated practice rooted in the way immediate experience is structured in definite social contexts'

(Friedman, 1995: 86). It is in that spirit that we now turn to the multi-cultural imaginaries being performed in British culinary culture, thinking about the social processes of differentiation through which such diversity is constructed, the forms these differentiations take, and the uses made, or the productivities, of these differentiations.

IMAGINARY ONE: A SMORGASBORD OF DIFFERENCE

Perhaps one of the most common forms of multicultural imaginary constructed within culinary culture is that of a pleasurable and stimulating diversity, one that positions the consumer as an adventurer in search of novelty. For Stuart Hall this is symptomatic of a 'global postmodern' culture, one constantly looking for 'new exotica', and one within which 'to be at the leading edge … is to eat fifteen different cuisines in any one week, not to eat one' (Hall, 1991b: 31). But of course this postmodern ideal is one participated in by consumers well outside any 'foodie' elite. Sometimes it may just be the use of a 'different' food or meal to break out of a perceived boredom in domestic food repertoires. Sometimes it may be a more consistent appreciation of an aura of variety, as in the following comments from one of our interviewees in North London, Kristy:

> I mean, this area is really culturally mixed. Definitely. Just think what's available in terms of restaurants. I mean, you've got your Vietnamese right next door to your Thai. They're very close types of foods, but I'd say, I've never been to Vietnam, but I'd say the cultures are totally different. And you've got the Balti house right next to that and then you've got your fish and chip shop. You've got nearly everything… . I like that feeling. It's variety. I haven't necessarily been there, but you can experience through magazines, just through looking at things and seeing things, you know, you don't have to have been there to experience and see it, you can just say that's really nice, and you've got a feel of it. You know, like Vietnamese in those hats and things, you've got a picture in your mind, whether that picture's right or wrong, you've still got that feel, haven't you?

The cultural politics of this pleasurable 'feel' have already been the subject of a number of critical analyses, which have tended to reconfigure any multicultural claims within such a consumer into rather less benign narratives of consumer cannibalism or culinary neo-imperialism. As bell hooks puts it:

> the message that acknowledgement and exploration of racial differ-
> ence can be pleasurable represents a breakthrough... . [But] [c]ur-
> rently, the commodification of difference promotes paradigms of
> consumption wherein whatever difference the Other inhabits is
> eradicated, via exchange, by a consumer cannibalism that not only
> displaces the Other but denies the significance of that Other's
> history through a process of decontextualization.'
>
> (hooks, 1992: 39 and 31)

Or as one of our interviewees, Terry, put it:

> People don't appreciate ethnic foods for being ethnic, they appreci-
> ate them for being different, and I think that's why it's important
> that you have Chinese and Indian restaurants that serve very good,
> say, Chinese food, ... and present it in a way that it's undeniably
> good food, cooked to the highest standard as opposed to just being
> Chinese food. It's good food, and then it's Chinese food... . I'm not
> saying you should understand Chinese food, and I'm not so sure you
> need a broader cultural understanding, but I think you just have to
> have an intelligent understanding of what you're enjoying. That it is
> food, and in that way it's no different from western food. People
> think it's just a different thing, they don't even see it as food, they
> see it as a fairground ride or something like that ...

A number of concerns rumble through these and other commentaries.
First, and where hooks finishes in the above quotation, there is a
worry about the decontextualization of cultural forms, as they are
removed from their places of birth, nurture and life and transplanted
into alien (and alienating) systems of exchange. Secondly, there is a
highlighting of the self-centred and self-serving logics of plunder governing these decontextualizations of difference. After all, it is argued,
their *raison d'être* is the self-gratification of those who are in a position
to (afford to) appropriate the cultural forms of others. Furthermore,
such consuming passions are the consequence of a desire to explore
otherness whilst maintaining the solidity of 'mainstream positionality'
(hooks, 1992: 23). Indeed, the commodification and consumption of
otherness serves two primary functions: first, it creates foci for the
desires of Western consumers who can, through the commoditized
exposure of non-Western cultures, exercise their fantasies safe in both
the knowledge that their centred positions will not be threatened and

that the reality giving rise to the commodity fetish lies elsewhere; and second, the commodification of cultural otherness depoliticizes cultural differences and reduces all cultural forms to the bland status of the commodity. In so doing, all structures of meaning and biography are stripped away to create a (blank) space for the imprint of Western values and fantasies which give the commodity its momentum in the circuitry of neo-imperial consumption.

Thirdly, this translates into a concern that any engagements with the differentiations produced through such transplants are too spectacularized, too aestheticized, too sealed off from social connections. hooks worries that 'ethnicity becomes just spice, seasoning, that can liven up the dull dish that is mainstream white culture' (hooks, 1992: 21). Mike Featherstone portrays an aestheticized economy of signs and spaces in which consumer culture's already 'fragmented sign-play is made more complex still by the ease of introduction of images, goods and signs extracted from other cultures' (Featherstone, 1995: 82; see also Lash and Urry, 1994). Ethnographers of multiculturalism contrast negatively such 'phantom' connections with the 'more self-conscious forms of attachment [by whites] to black culture in conditions of prolonged contact between … black and white people' (Jones, 1988: xxv). And commentators on multicultural policy decry these aestheticizations as a symbolic multiculturalism that has no mechanism for equal rights but just adds to 'the consumption options of the middle class' (Ley, 1984: 106).

Fourthly, not only are there concerns over the aestheticization of difference, but also over the form these differentiations take, in particular the degree to which they in fact convert difference into sameness through a rather limited differentiating vocabulary (see for example Gottdiener (1997) on the all-too-repetitive tropes of cultural geographical theming). A key issue here is that food providers are keen to package senses of difference and variety in ways that also allow simplicity and legibility. Here, for example, is Justin, a wet sauce buyer for one of the major UK multiple retailers, talking through this need for an order within diversity:

> Wet sauces are a very interesting area… . It was very, very complex, through masses of brands, products, and, umm, the category management thing, through research with consumers, basically threw up … that our fixture was far too complex, and very poorly understood by consumers. The blocking between the different ethnic areas was fairly loose and woolly, and not terribly clear; we didn't do enough to group together products in terms of accompaniments to sauces

and so on. ... And effectively, what we've done now is to streamline the range, and then block better those definitive areas so that the consumer could see them. The next stage is to actually signpost it as such with backboards or whatever. ... If you go into a store, we work on sort of modular blocks, four foot modules, umm, and what had happened in the past was that you know, you'd get Indian running into Oriental, and you know, where's the start of one and the end of the other? Now you can actually see where the Indian stops and the Oriental starts, and so on.

There is, then, a commercial logic to categorizing and stereotyping, to producing exactly the sort of multicultural imaginary Trinh Minh-ha has in her sights when she worries that:

> Multiculturalism does not lead us very far if it remains a question of difference only between one culture and another.... To cut across boundaries and borderlines is to live aloud the malaise of categories and labels; it is to resist simplistic attempts at classifying, to resist the comfort of belonging to a classification, of producing classifiable works.

> (Minh-ha, 1991: 107–8)

A fifth and final strand of the critique of culinary neo-imperialism is the argument that commodified multiculturalisms are all too often underlain by forms of racism that corrupt the seemingly positive evaluations of difference enacted within them. These racisms are constituted both through the binary logics of many commercialized differentiations – the exotic and the mundane/normal, the foreign and the British, and underlying these often the black and the white – and through the criteria deployed in these binary distinctions. For example, in a study of white, middle-class London consumers in Stoke Newington, Jon May identifies a range of racist stereotypes intertwined with their positive evaluations for 'exotic foods', such that they are liked for their naturalness, physicality, hint of danger, and so on (May, 1996).

These critical portraits of consumer cannibalism clearly alert us to the political character of both (culinary) cultural differentiation and the uses to which such differentiations are put. However, partly because of their rhetorical force they have some dangers too. We will briefly raise three. First, in an emphasis on the decontextualization of cultural forms – which, if you remember, is where hooks' quote concluded – they can neglect the recontextualizations facilitated by commodity culture, that is the uses made of foods and their differentiations. These uses cannot simply be read off from a systemic logic. For example, it is a far from simple matter to decide how stereotypes of difference are used (Rapport, 1996), and in particular just how their deployment by consumers in personalized, private imaginative fantasies (Campbell, 1987) might connect into public life and judgements of those others met within it. Accounts of consumer cannibalism often move rather too easily over these usages of differentiations. Second, the emphasis on decontextualization might also (unhelpfully, we feel) be interpreted as a critique of superficial constructions of difference, requiring recontextualization through more knowledgeable differentiations. As we will see shortly, such knowledgeable differentiations have no inherent claim to a less problematic multicultural imaginary. Moreover, as George Lipsitz suggests, albeit in the rather different case of music, decontextualization or the stripping of local meanings is not always disastrous for intercultural communication. Indeed on some occasions it promotes 'creative misunderstandings', in which something of the original feel of a cultural practice is picked up intuitively, rather than knowledgeably, and differently produced in a new context (Lipsitz, 1994). Third, the metaphor of cannibalism can overstate the passivity of people in relation to the cultural differentiations they inhabit. That is, this metaphor allocates the power to differentiate either to the organs of corporate transnational capitalism and/or to consumers of the differentiated 'others'. In many cases, certainly in culinary culture, there is in fact space for a rather more active agency from those to whom differentiations are being applied. For example, 'ethnic' food provision is an important form of economic enterprise for designated ethnic minorities (Keith, 1996) and involves active constructions and sellings of self-identity (Kay, 1985). These constructions are far from unilateral, but they are developed, we would argue, in active negotiations with a range of other actors (consumers, but also competitors, local business and other community groups, media promotionalists and so on) who help constitute the circuits of culinary culture. 'Ethnicities' are not simply projected onto a passive recipient subject.

IMAGINARY TWO: AUTHENTICITY AND AUTHENTICATION

If an emphasis on consumer cannibalism is one way of sharpening a critical edge on multiculinary culture, an equally prominent theme is that of authenticity, or more properly, authentication. This has recently been re-stated by Allison James as she links the rise in the exploration of 'different' foods to a desire to find or re-claim an authentic or traditional mode of eating and living. For James, the key conductors of this endeavour are the 'foodie' media and literati (see also Appadurai, 1988):

> Such claims to authenticity and tradition are common to much contemporary food writing and food journalism.... . The foodie writers seek and find ... the marks of authenticity in diversity, in the small scale and in local artisanal modes of production. Differentiation is celebrated through the quality and authenticity of local food traditions, world-wide.
>
> (James, 1996: 87)

The picture James paints, then, is one in which neo-Romanticism predominates (amongst a specified group of people at least), a culinary *zeitgeist* supported by an expert system which articulates detailed recipes for the appropriation of authenticity and tradition. This appropriation is marked not only by the senses of novelty and adventure apparent in the constructions of culinary cultural diversity reviewed above, but also by ethoses of education and/or scholarship and/or knowledgeability. In turn, it is in the 'local' that authenticity and tradition are to be found. This localism can work through the construction of a range of local cultures and cuisines world-wide. Or, at the same time, there can also be a strong element of nostalgic 'internalized tradition', in the form of culinary icons such as 'traditional' British roasts and game, as well as regional stews, sausages and cheeses. What both these regions and the more 'global locals' share is an antithesis to the logic of contemporary living and consumption in which contamination, in a multitude of guises, proliferates. Of course, as with all such constructions of authenticity, this poses the awkward paradox of how to rationalize the potential contamination of these pure, local traditions as they are 'incorporated' into wider culinary circuits (indeed, as they are actually produced through engagements within those wider circuits). Here, ideals of 'diversion', in which foods and culinary knowledges find their way beyond the local almost 'by accident', are used to smooth over some of these contradictions (Appadurai, 1986).

This ethos of authenticity is not, however, simply limited to certain fractions of the foodie literati. In a more fragmented form it ripples through more 'ordinary' culinary practices. As an example, consider the following exchange between Alexander and Laura, married interviewees in their mid 40s:

> ALEXANDER: 'I was at college with a group of about eight or nine, one of whom was a Palestinian, one was a Pakistani, so we were taught to cook. Habib taught me the middle eastern and Abdul was very demanding of us, he wasn't going to accept standard curry. If we were going to have curry we were jolly well going to do it properly. And it meant there were some spectacularly eclectic Christmas lunches, albeit the curried sprouts left an awful lot to be desired! But that's the tradition with Christmas sprouts, isn't it, regardless. They're meant to be horrible. Anyhow, so we were taught that, and we loved doing it. But for the rest, I wouldn't think of, say, cooking in an Italian style or cooking in a French style, though, come to think of it, our favourite way of roasting chicken is a French style, but we think of it as roast chicken, not in terms of where it comes from.
>
> LAURA: I disagree with you about Italian.
>
> ALEXANDER: Well, we don't think Italy when we're doing a spaghetti.
>
> LAURA: Don't you?
>
> ALEXANDER: It's something favourite that we eat and always you put plenty of tomatoes in it, and what have you…
>
> LAURA: I guess you don't have such high standards if you're just cooking for us, but if I had people around I wouldn't put Italian food together with a Greek salad, I'd do a proper salad.
>
> ALEXANDER: That's certainly true, but in terms of standard cooking, I don't, umm, I don't think 'I'm going to be in a Spanish mood tonight!'.
>
> LAURA: But you said today that you felt like Chinese tonight.
>
> ALEXANDER: Oh, yes. Umm. But I didn't mean it like that. I'm not going to dress up or something.

Here imaginaries of authenticity coexist with other discursive framings (of eclectic diversity, of hybridity), providing one option through which food practices can be organized. In turn, this option is one that seems to be situationally enacted, in this case being part of the proper food served when entertaining (signalling not only knowledge but also effort and attention) but holding a less clear role in everyday or 'standard' cooking.

More generally, there are two rather different ways of critically approaching authenticity as a culinary cultural differentiation. The first is to focus on authentication's reliance on substantial bodies of culinary and cultural knowledge. In contrast to the plundering of commodified difference in cannibalistic multicultural imaginaries, authentication requires consumers, helped by various expert knowledge providers, to not only judge authenticity but also to have the knowledge to provenance it for others. Given the criticisms heaped on cannibalistic consumers for their lack of knowledge about the sources of their differentiated materials, one might think this would be a cause of some celebration. Surely, such knowledgeable consumers construct multicultural culinary worlds with much 'thicker' connections and with much deeper respect for those others being consumed? However, we need to think about the form and purpose of this knowledge quite carefully. Three issues are normally flagged in this regard. First, as Uma Narayan points out, knowledge about the constructed source of a cuisine or food is not the same thing as an understanding of one's own positioning as a consumer within broader culinary circuits (1995). Indeed the ideal of diversion – of authentic foods reaching consumers by accident – actively channels authenticating knowledges away from such concerns. So knowledge of locals does not necessarily impact on the form of relations established with them. Second, knowledgeable constructions of local origins involve a multicultural imaginary in which cultural geographical differences tend to be frozen or reified in time and space. To clarify, then, these localized differences are constructed through imaginations of largely static cultural mosaics, unchanging over time through their adherence to tradition and fixed in space through their territories and borders. Such an imagination is a very particular way to construct cultural geographical differences, in particular leaving little room for cultural affiliations made across diasporic times and spaces (Gilroy, 1993). Third, we have to think about the uses to which knowledge of the local is put. In particular, we can see a connection between knowledgeability and forms of cultural capital, in particular associated with the figure of the cosmopolitan. The cosmopolitan constructs his/her own identity through his/her knowledgeable encounters with one, or more likely a number of, 'locals' (Hannerz, 1996). In part s/he withdraws from the local(s), gazing over it/them from a vantage point elsewhere, but s/he also requires competence in engaging with the local, at staging encounters with it. The cosmopolitan needs the local(s) in order to enact his/her own cosmopolitan status.

One way of thinking about the forms of culinary multiculturalism constructed in processes of authentication is, then, as a set of solidifying knowledges, fixing together peoples, places and foods in constructions of 'locals'. These constructions and knowledges in turn facilitate a self-positioning of the 'cosmopolitan', floating above and occasionally engaging with these local worlds. This is a fairly familiar critical story and it is not one we want simply to jettison. However, we do want to pursue an alternative way into these questions of authenticity, one which concerns itself less with the authenticating knowledges and more with the social processes and performances of authenticity. For if authenticity is a construction, it is not simply an achieved state; it is an ongoing process. And that process is a social and contextual one. One obvious example of this is the presentation of authenticity in restaurants. Drawing on MacCannell's account of staged authenticity in tourist settings (MacCannell, 1973), Shun Lu and Gary Fine have analysed the rhetorics and performances of ethnic authenticity staged in some Chinese restaurants in Athens, Georgia (Lu and Fine, 1995). They emphasize how both ethnicity and authenticity are constructions, 'made real in cultural transactions' (Lu and Fine: 535). Both, then, are judgements or folk ideas made believable through a range of 'rhetorical strategies' (Lu and Fine: 549) and impression managements (see also Crang, 1994). In the case of their Chinese restaurants in America, the rhetorical strategies of the restaurant proprietors were directed at effectively and seamlessly combining two rather different perceived consumer desires: a desire for the authentically 'Chinese', and a desire for something familiar enough to be enjoyable (which restaurateurs framed through notions of 'American' and 'Americanization'). In these restaurants, then, food providers tried to perform an explicit Chinese ethnic authenticity whilst implicitly trying to perform an Americanization of the cuisine and the dining-out experience (for example through the overall construction and ordering of menu items or a greater use of sugar in cooking). These performances were fashioned in relation to understandings of consumer desires, the actual performances of diners (for example, the expressed desire for fast service), and producers' senses of their own cultural and economic well-being.

These socially negotiated performances of ideas such as authenticity or ethnicity are particularly explicit in restaurants. But they are not limited to them. What restaurant performances provide is a rather obvious way into much broader issues about the stagings, displays and enactments of constructed differentiations of foods and the peoples and places associated with them. In other sites of culinary culture the spatialities of these performances may be different. They may be characterized by the marketing departments of food manufacturers, or increasingly likely retailers, setting up a range of performed interactions with product designers, home economists, packaging designers, focus groups of consumers and so on, in order eventually to stage a number of encounters between product and consumer. But whether we are looking at the social spaces of the restaurant or the systems of provision connecting the home into the food system, what we have here is a take on authenticity which raises slightly different questions than the focus on it as a body of knowledge. One that focuses less on pointing out the 'myth of authenticity' (Griffiths, 1994) *per se* and more on how, when and why that myth is adopted by actors coming together (in some form) within the circuits of culinary culture. An approach that recognizes, then, that authenticity is a fabrication, but which does not assume that this is news to anyone. An approach which does not position authenticity as a myth which some believers permanently ascribe to, and which some critics can come along and debunk, but as a negotiated ascription which is used and inhabited by food providers and consumers in particular social times and spaces.

IMAGINARIES THREE AND FOUR: HYBRIDITY AND CIRCUITRY

There are, though, clear signs that the valuation of the authentic within culinary culture is becoming increasingly contested, or at least rivalled by another multicultural figure. This is the hybrid or the creolized. Allison James provides a couple of examples:

> At the side of the main road to Alnwick which runs through the lonely, windswept moorland of north Northumberland a sign catches the eye. Swinging forlornly from its white wooden post it advertises, in the silence of this landscape, the Carib-Northumbria restaurant. These words signify an intriguing pairing, heightened by the painted palm trees which adorn the sign set amongst that so English scene of fields where sheep safely graze. In Northampton, a Midlands town once thriving on the proceeds of the shoe industry, now displaced by warehousing and commuting, an Indian restaurant has been refurbished. Its Taj Mahal-like windows, fabricated from painted plywood placed over plate glass, strike a discordant note among a straggle of plain shop fronts, small businesses from video hire to home brew. Its claim, proudly advertised, is full

air-conditioning. It is as if the heat of an Indian summer can be experienced – literally, rather than just figuratively – inside. Together with the Indian cuisine this contrives to stimulate, for the customer, a momentary taste of India in central England. It is, however, short-lived. The meal's finale brings with it a swift and abrupt relocation: placed on the saucer, alongside the bill, lies a gold-wrapped sweet. Described on its wrapping as an 'After Curry Mint', it mimics – perhaps mocks – the seeming sophistication which the After Eight Mint, in its dark brown envelope, lent to the English suburban dinner party of an earlier era.

(James, 1996: 77)

We might also think of the recent series of Homepride cook-in curry sauce TV advertisements. In these the viewer is taken into the acted-out homes of British–Asian families living in Great Britain. Each of the fictional families featured in the five advertisements is regionally placed – Birmingham, Liverpool, Newcastle, London and Glasgow. Such 'regionality' is signalled by the accentuation of regional accents and caricature local phrases ('Curry and rice; top scran', says the Liverpudlian Naresh). The positioning concept is 'authentic flavours with a local British accent', says the account executive for Howard, Henry, Chaldecott, Lury and Partners, Mark Sands (cited in Kelner, 1995: 49). The aim, then, is to keep some valuation of 'foreign' authenticity and combine it with an explicit marketing of local incorporation. British–Asian caricatures – who signal both their Asianness and their local, regional identity in extreme and unmissable forms – embody this aim.

Such recognitions and displays of cultural mixing deploy a rather different multicultural imaginary than that of the cultural geographic mosaic underlying constructions of authenticity. Notions of discrete cultures and cultural spaces are seemingly disturbed, and preoccupations with placed roots shift into concerns with flows and routes (Hannerz, 1992). Ideas of hybridity have, of course, received wide academic attention and interest within the human sciences. Their presence in popular culinary cultures is therefore intriguing and does, we think, have all sorts of positive possibilities. However, these possibilities need to be judged quite carefully. For a start, we cannot simply assume that the figure of hybridity actually does disturb notions of authenticity and its essentialisms. Ideas of mixing can assume previously unmixed entities which are now being mixed up. In this vein the historian Robert Young has traced out how desirous concerns with racial hybridity and miscegenation in colonial discourse quite happily coexisted with, and indeed depended upon, emergent understandings of clearly defined and separate races (Young, 1995). Incidentally, he also points out how these racist nineteenth-century uses of ideas of hybridity should give us pause for thought in terms of its current application to the realm of culture (Young: 6). More generally, a number of cultural critics have pointed out that citing instances of cultural hybridity can suggest that the rest of the time cultures are not hybrid. On the other hand, if one accepts that 'in fact, all cultures are "hybrid", "syncretic", "creolised", "impure"' (Gillespie, 1995: 4) then 'hybridisation is in effect a tautology, the hybridisation of hybrid cultures' (Pieterse, 1995: 64). There are, then, two rather conflicting ways of thinking about cultural hybridity. The first, identifies 'spectacular' or notable examples of mixing. In culinary culture an example might be Chinese pizza (James, 1996: 78). These jar our usual differentiations of foods, but through their unusualness can reinforce the normality of those differentiations. The second way of thinking about hybridity is to think about all culinary cultures as mixed, but then the fact that some seem more obviously mixed than others remains something requiring explanation (why is it that Chinese pizza jars, when pasta, also a mixture of Italian and Chinese, does not?).

Here for example is Terry, a British–Chinese interviewee in his 30s, giving his response to the Homebred cook-in sauce advertisements mentioned above:

> Yes, now those really annoy me. I was also tempted to write to the Broadcasting Complaints Commission or whatever, because those again, they suggest, you know, that there's something funny about being foreign and having a foreign accent, you know an Indian man with a Geordie accent or three Chinese girls with a Scottish accent, and it's just not funny, they're just ordinary people. I mean, what's the big joke about that?

In a later interview he argues again against the marginalizing of hybridity, making it a cipher for 'ethnicity', but keeping exactly the same marginalizing logic as that running through ascriptions of only some foods and people as ethnic:

> ... the cross-eating thing, I've been thinking about that, and it seemed to be we were talking about it being strange or funny, but it's never struck me as bizarre. The thing is, I think everybody, whether they're English or, umm, say your mother's Scottish and

your father's Welsh, you probably have a strange mixture of things that you'd eat. It's not just a racial difference.

The anthropologist Jonathan Friedman has argued the way to extricate debates over hybridity from such confusions is to re-emphasize that hybridity itself is an actively constructed form of cultural differentiation (Friedman, 1994, 1995). Like authenticity, or themed repertoires of commodity-signs, hybridity is a way of understanding (culinary) culture that is adopted by certain actors in certain situations:

> If the world is understood as creolized today this expresses the identity of the classifier who experiences the transgression of cultural, that is, ethnic, national, boundaries as a global phenomenon... . The problem is that conditions of identification of self and other have changed. Cultures don't flow together and mix with each other. Rather, certain actors, often strategically positioned actors, identify the world in such terms as part of their own self-identification.
>
> (Friedman, 1995: 83–4)

As such, the crucial issue is why and how such forms of differentiation are made, or not:

> The introduction of pasta into the cuisine of the Italian peninsula is a process of globalization, and the final elaboration of a pasta-based Italian cuisine is, in metaphorical terms, a process of cultural syncretism, or perhaps creolization. But such mixture is only interesting in the practice of local identity... . Thus the fact that pasta became Italian, and that its Chinese origin became irrelevant, is the essential culture-producing process in this case. Whether origins are maintained or obliterated is a question of the practice of identity.
>
> (Friedman, 1995: 74)

For Friedman then, and we concur with this, the crucial issue is when, where, how and with what results imaginaries of multicultural hybridity are constructed and used.

He is quite pessimistic about these uses, arguing that they are primarily a reconfiguration in the power claims of the cosmopolitan, now achieved through the tracing out of the separate strands of multiculture rather than through the knowing of authentic, placed, separate, local cultures. We would want to be more open about their potential politics. As we have said, they can, especially if they imply the abnor-

mality of mixture, reinforce differentiations based in ideas of sep-
arateness. No doubt some tastes for the hybrid also amount to little
more than a competing criterion for cultural valuation to the logics of
authentication, mocking its earnestness with a playful aesthetic of pas-
tiche, but equally relying on constructed knowledges of origins for the
'joke' to be got. But there may also be times within discourses of the
hybrid that other possibilities appear, other multicultural imaginaries
that challenge the world showcase of cultures beloved of both the cannibalistic consumer and the aficionado of authenticity. Times when
binary logics of either/or are upset, and when notions of cultural pluralism are supplanted by an attention to the 'polyglot' character of any
cultural space or form (thus multiculturalism becomes less about the
coexistence of different cultures and more about the multicultural
nature of all cultural life) (Back, 1996).

Such possibilities often centre around a moment when the differentiations within British culinary culture become visible as constructions.
An example might be the questioning of ideas of Britishness, and of
foreignness, potentially opened up by an interest in the composition of
the national diet. As a case of this let us take some rather mean-spir-
ited and jaundiced criticism of a recent sociological study of British
eating habits by the journalist Emily Green (1996). The main thrust of
this broadsheet newspaper article was to condemn the project's
concern with questions of cultural politics. Green concludes the piece
by arguing that 'the question worth answering is not what the British
might fancy by way of an exotic meal ... but whether or not the nation
as a whole can afford to eat, and whether or not the food we consume
is safe and nutritious'. Now leaving aside the fact that these are not
entirely separate questions, what intrigues us is how Green attacks the
project's interests precisely by beginning to point out how complex
and contingent cultural differentiations are:

> To start with, 'ethnic' food is a contradiction in terms. Chambers
> English Dictionary defines ethnic thus: 'concerning nations or races;
> pertaining to gentiles or the heathen; pertaining to the customs,
> dress, food, etc. of a particular racial group or cult'. I have yet to en-
> counter a tomato that was one race or another, gentile or heathen,
> or which belonged to a cult. Nor, in common with cattle, turkeys,
> corn and potatoes, is the tomato indigenous to Britain. So ketchup
> is foreign, beloved of the Americans and the Rothschilds, but is it
> ethnic? ... So what is authentically British? ... Chips? No, sorry,
> potatoes were imported. Roast beef? No, a way of eating meat

introduced by the Romans. Eating out? No, sorry. Restaurants came from France. Tea? Indian and Chinese. Mars Bars? No, cocoa from South America, sugar from the Caribbean.

(Green, 1996: not paginated)

So, in a rather garbled form, what one has here is not only the beginnings of a social constructionist account of ethnicity, but also a rather different multicultural imaginary, one we want to draw out through the notion of 'circuitry'.

To speak in terms of circuitry is to emphasize the ways in which any one place can be understood only through its past and present relations with a host of others (Massey, 1991). It is to replace a concern with boundaries, inclusions and exclusions with an interrogation of networks of connection and disconnection. In the context of culinary culture, one way this can be expressed is through a documentation of the commodity systems through which foods are provided for consumers. Ethical consumer organizations make these sorts of links, and in so doing translate the touristic and authenticating concerns with origin of other consumer imaginaries into a rather different politics of connection. Other times it may be more a question of taking apart some neat sense of a consuming 'destination' through a few titbits of historical information (about potatoes and Walter Raleigh, tea and empire, chocolate and cocoa from South America, sugar from the Caribbean). Or indeed it may be to go even further and deconstruct the notion of origin too, as when botanical historians point out that very few foods, in the end, come from anywhere. Rather they come into being through long histories of global circulation.

Culinary culture provides us, then, with an everyday arena within which the hybrid character of Britishness, past and present, lurks just beneath the surface. Whilst food is therefore one arena of everyday life within which notions of cultural mixture are spectacularized, it is also a medium through which a more far-reaching interrogation of the terms of traditional multiculturalisms can be encountered.

CONCLUDING COMMENTS

By way of conclusion, we would like to make two points. First, a summary of what we have said: our argument in this chapter has been that questions of culinary multiculturalism need to be approached through an analysis of the differentiations (the constructions of difference) developed and deployed within culinary culture. That is, to get an understanding of the multicultural character of British culinary culture we cannot simply measure the diversity of participating foods and people nor the popularity (via consumption and provision figures) of these. Such measurements tell us little about how this diversity is understood or the uses to which it is put. Instead, we have argued for an analysis of the differentiations of foods, peoples and places used within culinary culture. We have proposed an analysis that examines their form; how they are produced (or where they are drawn from); and the uses to which they are put. We have argued, then, for a critical multiculturalism which examines how notions of the multicultural are being constructed within culinary culture. This chapter has provided some starting points for that examination, by setting out four different imaginaries of the multicultural, focusing respectively on the commodity-signs of difference, the authentic local, hybrid mixtures, and circuits of connection.

Second, though, we should perhaps finish by signalling what this chapter has left unsaid. If we are going to understand the multicultural politics of culinary culture, not only do we have to identify and analyse the 'multicultural imaginaries' being developed and deployed within it, we also have to contextualize these developments and deployments within everyday practices of identity and representation. We have to see how these imaginaries are performed and used in the identifications of daily life, as well as analysing the subject positions they construct (Hall, 1996). Our on-going empirical research work is using the approach signalled here to begin such an investigation, but more generally it is with the *practice* of identity, by both food consumers and providers, that future research should perhaps be most concerned.

ACKNOWLEDGEMENTS

We thank the Economic and Social Research Council for funding the 'Eating Places' research project of which this chapter is a part (ESRC award no. R000236408).

REFERENCES

Appadurai, A. (1986) 'Introduction: Commodities and the Politics of Value', in A. Appadurai (ed.), *The Social Life of Things: Commodities in Cultural Perspective* (Cambridge: Cambridge University Press), pp. 3–63

Appadurai, A. (1988) 'How to Make a National Cuisine: Cookbooks in Contemporary India', *Comparative Studies in Society and History*, 30(1), pp. 3–24.

Arce, A. and Marsden, T. (1993) 'The Social Construction of International Food: a New Research Agenda', *Economic Geography*, 69(3), pp. 293–311.

Attar, D. (1985) 'Filthy Foreign Food', *Camerawork*, 31, pp. 13–14.

Back, L. (1996) *New Ethnicities and Urban Culture: Racisms and Multiculture in Young Lives* (London: UCL Press).

Barnard, S. (ed.) (1989) 'Focus on Ethnic Foods', *Grocer*, 2 September.

Bhabha, H. (1995; original 1988) 'Cultural Diversity and Cultural Differences', in B. Ashcroft, G. Griffiths and H. Tiffin (eds), *The Post-Colonial Studies Reader* (London: Routledge), pp. 206–9.

Campbell, C. (1987) *The Romantic Ethic and the Spirit of Modern Consumerism* (Oxford: Blackwell).

Conlon, F. (1995) 'Dining out in Bombay', in C. A. Breckenridge (ed.), *Consuming Modernity: Public Culture in a South Asian World* (Minneapolis: University of Minnesota Press), pp. 90–127.

Cook, I. (1994) 'New Fruits and Vanity: Symbolic Production in the Global Food Economy', in A. Bonanno, L. Busch, L. Friedland, L. Gouveia and E. Mingione (eds), *From Columbus to ConAgra: The Globalization of Agriculture and Food* (Lawrence: University Press of Kansas), pp. 232–48.

Cook, I. and Crang, P. (1996). 'The World on a Plate: Culinary Culture, Displacement and Geographical Knowledges', *Journal of Material Culture*, 1(2), pp. 131–53.

Cook, I., Crang, P. and Thorpe, M. (1999) 'The Tropics of Consumption: Columbus, Carmen Miranda and the Golden Age of Shopping in 90s Britain', *Food and Foodways* (forthcoming).

Crang, P. (1994) 'It's Showtime: on the Workplace Geographies of Display in a Restaurant in Southeast England', *Environment and Planning D: Society & Space*, 12, pp. 675–704.

Crang, P. (1996) 'Displacement, Consumption, and Identity', *Environment and Planning A*, 28, pp. 47–67.

Farrar, M. (1996) 'City Cultures: Autonomy and Integration: Thinking about Drinking, Eating and Performing in Leeds', *City*, 5–6, pp. 125–30.

Featherstone, M. (1995) *Undoing Culture: Globalization, Postmodernism and Identity* (London: Sage).

Friedman, J. (1994) *Cultural Identity and Global Process* (London: Sage).

Friedman, J. (1995) 'Global System, Globalization and the Parameters of Modernity', in M. Featherstone, S. Lash and R. Robertson (eds), *Global Modernities* (London: Sage), pp. 69–90.

Gillespie, M. (1995) *Television, Ethnicity and Cultural Change* (London: Routledge).

Gilroy, P. (1993) *The Black Atlantic: Modernity and Double Consciousness* (London: Verso).

Goodman, D. and Redclift, M. (1991) *Refashioning Nature: Food, Ecology and Culture* (London: Routledge).

Gordon, A. and Newfield, C. (eds) (1996) *Mapping Multiculturalism* (Minneapolis: University of Minnesota Press).

Gottdiener, M. (1997) *The Theming of America: Dreams, Visions and Commercial Spaces* (Boulder: Westview).

Green, E. (1996) 'Korma Karma', *The Independent Tabloid*, 12 December.

Griffiths, G. (1994) 'The Myth of Authenticity', in B. Ashcroft, G. Griffiths and H. Tiffin (eds), *The Post-Colonial Studies Reader* (London: Routledge), pp. 237–41.

Grocer (1983) 'Growth in Ethnic Foods', 16 January.

Hall, S. (1991a) 'Old and New Identities, Old and New Ethnicities', in A. King (ed.), *Culture, Globalisation and the World System* (Basingstoke: Macmillan), pp. 41–68

Hall, S. (1991b) 'The Local and the Global: Globalization and Ethnicity', in A. King (ed.), *Culture, Globalisation and the World System* (Basingstoke: Macmillan), pp. 19–40

Hall, S. (1996) 'Introduction: Who Needs Identity?', in S. Hall and P. du Gay (eds), *Questions of Cultural Identity* (London: Sage), pp. 1–17

Hannerz, U. (1992) *Cultural Complexity* (New York: Columbia University Press).

Hannerz, U. (1996) 'Cosmopolitans and Locals in World Culture', in *Transnational Connections: Culture, People, Place* (London: Routledge).

Hilliam, M. (1985) *Ethnic Foods in the UK* (Leatherhead: Leatherhead Food Research Association).

hooks, b. (1992) 'Eating the other', in b. hooks (ed.), *Black Looks: Race and Representation* (London: Turnaround), pp. 21–39

James, A. (1996) 'Cooking the Books: Global or Local Identities in Contemporary British Food Cultures?', in D. Howes (ed.), *Cross-Cultural Consumption: Global Markets, Local Realities* (London: Routledge), pp. 77–83.

Jones, S. (1988) *Black Culture, White Youth* (London: Macmillan).

Kahn, J. S. (1995) *Culture, Multiculture, Postculture* (London: Sage).

Kay, C. Y. (1985) 'At the Palace: Work, Ethnicity and Gender in a Chinese Restaurant', *Studies in Sexual Politics No. 3* (Department of Sociology, University of Manchester).

Keith, M. (1996) 'Ethnic Entrepreneurs and Street Rebels', in S. Pile and N. Thrift (eds), *Mapping the Subject: Geographies of Cultural Transformation* (London: Routledge), pp. 355–70.

Kelner, M. (1996) 'The Curry we all Favour', *Mail on Sunday: Night & Day*, 25 February, pp. 48–51.

Keynote (1988) *Ethnic Foods: An Industry Sector Overview* (London: Keynote Publications).

Kobayashi, A. (1993) 'Multiculturalism: Representing a Canadian Institution', in J. Duncan and D. Ley (eds), *Place/Culture/Representation* (London: Routledge), pp. 205–31.

Lash, S. and Urry, J. (1994) *Economies of Signs and Space* (London: Sage).

Leonard, M. (1997). *Britain^TM: Renewing our Identity* (London: Demos).

Ley, D. (1984) 'Pluralism and the Canadian State', in C. Clarke, D. Ley and C. Peach (eds), *Geography and Ethnic Pluralism* (London: Allen & Unwin), pp. 87–110

Linford, J. (1997) *Food Lovers' London* (London: Metro).

Lipsitz, G. (1994) *Dangerous Crossroads: Popular Music, Postmodernism and the Poetics of Place* (London: Verso), pp. 157–70.

Lu, S. and Fine, G. (1995) 'The Presentation of Ethnic Authenticity: Chinese Food as a Social Accomplishment', *Sociological Quarterly*, 36(3), pp. 535–53.

Marketing Strategies for Industry Ltd (MSI) (1988) *Ethnic Foods* (London: MSI).

MacCannell, D. (1973) 'Staged Authenticity: Arrangements of Social Space in Tourist Settings', *American Journal of Sociology*, 79(3), pp. 589–603.

Massey, D. (1991) 'A Global Sense of Place', *Marxism Today*, 35(6), pp. 24–9.

May, J. (1996) 'A Little Taste of Something More Exotic: or Race, Class and the Imaginative Geographies of Everyday Life', *Geography*, 81(1), pp. 57–64.

Mennell, S. (1985) *All Manners of Food* (Oxford: Blackwell).

Minh-ha, T. T. (1991) *When the Moon Waxes Red* (New York: Routledge).

Mintel (1989) *Ethnic Foods* (London: Mintel).

Mintel (1994) *Ethnic Foods* (London: Mintel).

Mintz, S. (1985) *Sweetness and Power: The Place of Sugar in Modern History* (Harmondsworth: Penguin).

Narayan, U. (1995) 'Eating Cultures: Incorporation, Identity and Indian Food', *Social Identities*, 1(1), pp. 63–86.

Paulson-Box, E. and Williamson, P. (1990) 'The Development of the Ethnic Food Market in the UK', *British Food Journal*, 92(2), pp. 10–15.

Pieterse, J. N. (1995) 'Globalization as Hybridization', in M. Featherstone, S. Lash and R. Robertson (eds), *Global Modernities* (London: Sage).

Rapport, N. (1996) 'Migrant Selves and Stereotypes: Personal Context in a Postmodern World', in S. Pile and N. Thrift (eds), *Mapping the Subject: Geographies of Cultural Transformation* (London: Routledge), pp. 267–82.

Robertson, R. (1995) 'Glocalization: Time–Space and Homogeneity–Heterogeneity', in M. Featherstone, S. Lash and R. Robertson (eds), *Global Modernities* (London: Sage).

Sollors, W. (1986) *Beyond Ethnicity: Consent and Descent in American Culture* (Oxford: Oxford University Press).

Stacey, C. (1996) 'Movers and Shakers', in *Time Out, Eating and Drinking: London's Best Restaurants, Cafés and Bars* (London: Time Out).

Time Out (1995) 'The World on a Plate', 16 August, pp. 31–7.

Van Otterloo, A. (1987) 'Foreign Immigrants and the Dutch at Table, 1945–85: Bridging or Widening the Gap?', *Netherlands Journal of Sociology*, 23(2), pp. 126–43.

Young, R. (1995) *Colonial Desire: Hybridity in Theory, Culture and Race* (London: Routledge).

Zukin, S. (1995) *The Culture of Cities* (Oxford: Blackwell).

Index